ITALY
THE SHELTERED ECONOMY

This publication was made possible through the co-operation of Biblioteca Italia, a Giovanni Agnelli Foundation programme for the diffusion of Italian culture.

ITALY

THE SHELTERED ECONOMY

Structural Problems in the
Italian Economy

FIORELLA PADOA SCHIOPPA KOSTORIS

translated by
John E. Powell

CLARENDON PRESS · OXFORD
1993

Oxford University Press, Walton Street, Oxford OX2 6DP

Oxford New York Toronto
Delhi Bombay Calcutta Madras Karachi
Kuala Lumpur Singapore Hong Kong Tokyo
Nairobi Dar es Salaam Cape Town
Melbourne Auckland Madrid
and associated companies in
Berlin Ibadan

Oxford is a trade mark of Oxford University Press

Published in the United States
by Oxford University Press Inc., New York

British Library Cataloguing in Publication Data
Data available
ISBN 0–19–828748–8

Library of Congress Cataloging in Publication Data
Padoa-Schioppa, Fiorella, 1945–
[Economia sotto tutela. English]
Italy, the sheltered economy : structural problems in the Italian
economy / Fiorella Padoa Schioppa Kostoris ; translated by John E. Powell.
p. cm.
Translation of: L'Economia sotto tutela.
Includes bibliographical references.
1. Italy—Economic policy. 2. Italy—Economic conditions. I. Title.
HC305.P22313 1993 338.945—dc20 93–14905
ISBN 0–19–828748–8

Set by Hope Services (Abingdon) Ltd.
Printed in Great Britain
on acid-free paper by
Biddles Ltd.
Guildford & King's Lynn

To the memory of Professor Livio Pesante,
teacher of Philosophy at the Liceo Petrarca
in Trieste

ACKNOWLEDGEMENTS

THIS work would have been very different without the enthusiastic and intelligent collaboration of Paola Felli and the valuable contribution of Maria Teresa Pandolfi. I also wish to thank those who helped me with the analysis, in particular Alberto Pera and Franco Romani for the first five chapters; Giampaola Galli for Chapters 7 and 8; Alberto Heimler for Chapter 9, Carlo Milana for Chapters 10, 14, and 15; Vincenzo Visco for Chapter 20; Nicola Rossi for Chapters 18 and 21; Martino Ajmone Marsan and Felice Ippolito for various discussions of a general nature; and the leaders of the Operational Units of Sub-project 3 of the National Research Council's First Targeted Project on the Economy, who responded to my invitation to comment on the previous draft of this work, which was circulated at the beginning of 1989. I am equally grateful to Debora Di Gioacchino, Nicoletta Mazzitelli, Francesca Romani, Luca Rizzuto, Sally Anne Dickinson, and Chiara Rossi for their inestimable assistance with research. Finally, I wish to thank the National Research Council (CNR), which provided Sub-project 3 with considerable resources in terms of staff and materials, and the Director of the First Targeted Project on the Economy, Giacomo Vaciago, for his much-appreciated support.

F.P.S.K.

CONTENTS

Contents

Contents

LIST OF FIGURES

LIST OF TABLES

Italian administrative regions

1. Piemonte
2. Valle d'Aosta
3. Lombardia
4. Trentino-Alto Adige
5. Veneto
6. Friuli-Venezia Giulia
7. Liguria
8. Emilia-Romagna
9. Toscana
10. Umbria
11. Marche
12. Lazio
13. Abruzzo
14. Molise
15. Campania
16. Puglia
17. Basilicata
18. Calabria
19. Sicilia
20. Sardegna

Italian partitions according to ISTAT

1. Nord-occidentale (1, 2, 3, 7)
2. Nord-orientale (4, 5, 6, 8)
3. Centrale (9, 10, 11, 12)
4. Meridionale (13, 14, 15, 16, 17, 18)
5. Insulare (19, 20)

Italian geographical areas

1. Nord-Ovest = North-West (1, 2, 3, 7)
2. Nord-Est = North-East (4, 5, 6)
3. Centrale = Centre (8, 9, 10, 11)
4. Lazio = Latium (12)
5. Sud-Est = South-East (13, 14, 16)
6. Sud-Ovest = South-West (15, 17, 18, 19, 20)

Source: Attanasio and Padoa Schioppa (1991)

Introduction

> From truth, liberty; from liberty, truth. It is our most fervent
> desire that someone should want to repeat our research and
> verify the results; we would like especially to encourage young
> people to study closely the various regions of the whole of
> Italy, this unknown land for Italians
>
> (L. Franchetti and S. Sonnino, *La Sicilia nel 1876*, 1876)

This book analyses the structural, and hence endemic rather than
cyclical, problems of Italian economic policy. It represents my view
of the main results of a group of research studies carried out as
part of the Italian National Research Council's (CNR) First
Targeted Project on the Economy. Many dozens of people contributed ideas, producing around 150 articles and books for a sub-
project entitled 'Intervention strategies and techniques', of which I
was academic director for three years from 1985 to 1987.

The authors involved in the Sub-project, including myself, had
complete freedom to tackle the subject as they saw fit and to reach
their own conclusions, within the terms of reference outlined
below. At no stage, from the general definition of the issues to the
overall assessment of the papers produced, did they take part in
collective work, as would have been the case had we been engaged
in group research; the choice of topics, their organization, the syn-
thesis and overall significance of the research presented here are
therefore entirely my responsibility. The repeated references in this
book to 'our research group' or to 'our' studies should therefore be
seen as shorthand for the output of the co-ordinated collection of
people who participated in the Sub-project.

In the original 'feasibility study' defining the area to be covered
in the Sub-project, the National Research Council asked the group
to concentrate on the real side of the Italian economy in a
medium-term perspective, rather than on the monetary, credit, and
financial aspects. In particular, we were asked to focus on the
structural aspects of public-sector intervention in the market

(instruments, objectives, accomplishments), the only exceptions being regional and international economic policy, which were already being examined under the direction of Giorgo Fuà and Alberto Quadrio Curzio respectively.

Within the bounds set by the Council, the leader of the Sub-project was free to make decisions on three points: (1) the issues to be examined in greater detail and the findings to be highlighted; (2) the scientific methods to be preferred; and (3) the interpretation of the individual analyses and their relevance in a wider context.

Taking point 1 first, it was clear that the medium- and long-term real components of Italian economic policy were so numerous, even after excluding the two areas mentioned above, that the field would have to be narrowed further if the ground was to be covered in a three-year project. The selection criterion we adopted therefore gave priority to issues that seemed both highly relevant and little explored. For that reason, this book devotes little space to important but often-visited questions, such as the aggregate multiplier of public expenditure or the indirect crowding-out of private expenditure in Italy, over which dozens of macro-economists[1] have already pored; the few references to these issues are to be found in the chapter on the interrelation between the real and financial aspects of private capital accumulation (Chapter 14). By contrast, greater space is devoted to some related problems that are equally relevant but for which generally accepted solutions have not been found and which need to be investigated urgently; this is the case for questions such as the multiplier in the various regions of Italy, the direct crowding-out relationship between private and collective consumption or the ineffectiveness of macro-economic fiscal measures, to the extent that the Ricardian equivalence proposition is valid and applicable to Italy (Chapter 21), a country where the public debt is felt to be approaching unsustainability, as described in the Concluding Remarks.

Basing the selection of research topics on the criterion of relevance naturally implies focusing attention on hot issues in the Italian economic-policy debate; special emphasis was therefore placed both on the description of these issues and on proposed solutions. However, to ensure that the citizen's impassioned involvement would not overwhelm the rigorous approach of the

---

[1] Including myself, in Padoa Schioppa (1979*b*, 1983).

academic, I made every effort to test the seriousness of the arguments in two ways, as summarized in point 2 described below.

As to methodology, I tried to test all provisional interpretative hypotheses for internal and external consistency, using a wide range of quantitative techniques. Indeed, I believe that at some stage or other any contribution to economic science—however modest, provided it is serious and not rushed—requires the adoption of a theoretical model, preferably a mathematical one, that is capable of explaining the main hypotheses for the behaviour of the various economic agents and their implications for the rest of society, that is apt to be invalidated by observable facts and is susceptible to econometric estimation; the model can then be used to simulate and thus analyse the effects of certain changes, particularly those induced by state intervention in the market.[2] Accordingly, the researchers involved in the Sub-project were asked to adopt an approach that was not only historico-institutional but also logical-deductive and empirical-inductive, attributes that are typical of exact sciences but not the stock-in-trade of the traditional Italian economist. The involvement of predominantly young contributors who had been educated abroad as well as in Italy provided fertile ground for this approach and, hopefully, bore rich fruits.

The book bears no trace of the mathematical and statistical tools that we extensively used, although it contains many quantitative data, which I hope are not too indigestible, as I stress in the Postscript. In fact, formalism is not generally necessary in a wide-ranging debate, and may sometimes even be counterproductive, despite being a better mode of communication in the narrower circles of specialists.

Moreover, and again for methodological reasons, I have tried to make a systematic comparison with other approaches, especially on the more burning and divisive issues. Hence the reader will notice that on some topics on which there now appears to be a considerable degree of agreement, such as industrial and financial restructuring, I have mainly drawn on the work of our research group (Chapters 9 and 10), whereas on other issues, such as the problem of Southern Italy (the Mezzogiorno), on which approaches and opinions differ more widely, I have also quoted from a great many

---

[2] With all due deference to certain proponents of rational-expectation theories, who deny this possibility.

other studies; but I obviously make no pretence of offering even a concise and approximate résumé of all the shades of opinion expressed in the vast body of literature on 'the Southern question'.

Within this framework (as suggested above at point 3), a unifying message emerged clearly from the descriptive and normative assessments of Italian medium- to long-term economic policy set out in this book: to my surprise, and irrespective of the value premisses and ideological convictions of the many participants in the Sub-project, a unanimous awareness emerged that the time has now come in Italy for a shift in the weight assigned to the long hand of the state by comparison with the invisible hand of the market, with the former receding and improving. We seem all to have been persuaded by the formula 'more market and less state, as well as a different kind of state'.

If one accepts the thesis that the presence of the public sector in the Italian economy should be reduced, it follows that the ratio of taxation to GDP can remain broadly unchanged, despite the need to bring the heavy public debt down to sustainable dimensions. State intervention in Italy is not so much out of proportion as self-contradictory, and thus simultaneously excessive and insufficient, for three reasons: (1) because the volume of budgetary resources allocated to (or drawn from) certain activities is too large, while too little is devoted to (or derived from) others; (2) because even within one and the same budget item public measures are excessive in some aspects but inadequate in others; and (3) because some instruments are overworked while others remain underutilized or unused.

As to the first of these aspects, an exhaustive list would be too long. By way of example, the public ownership of natural monopolies in public utilities (Chapters 3 and 4) is not only too widespread but is often harmful, and should therefore be scaled down by means of appropriate liberalization measures where a contestable market probably exists (as in air transport within Europe) or where government failures are greater than the market failures that led to regulation in the first place (as in postal and telephone services). The existence of increasing returns to scale, and scope, which gives rise to natural monopolies, is a necessary but not sufficient condition for public intervention, because the static and dynamic costs of such intervention also need to be measured. If the presence of networks and sunk costs (as in the case of rail transport or electricity distribution) makes the abolition of a legal monopoly inadvisable, the concession-holder—whether a public or regulated private entity—must be prevented from abusing its dominant position by creating forms of 'virtual' competition (self-production, competition *for* the market) or requiring the monopoly to divest itself of services that use the network.

In addition, rescues of companies by government agencies in sectors deemed to be strategic (Chapter 6) but in which there is little real justification for public intervention are too frequent and too costly; one need only think of the 'state *panettone*', a Christmas cake produced by a state-controlled company.

Equally excessive are government transfers to households through the award of pensions over and above accumulated contributions, or sometimes even the payment of salaries to public employees who do not clearly provide an adequate service in return (Chapters 7 and 11). These forms of income-support increase demand, but do not at the same time increase aggregate supply. Transfers to enterprises through financial assistance are excessive, as well as being distorting and unjustified when they encourage financial speculation rather than actual investment or when they lead to sectoral and technological choices with an undesirably high capital/output ratio (Chapters 8 and 15).

As regards tax revenues, personal-income taxation in Italy (Chapter 12) is probably too progressive, leading to a contraction both in the supply of labour and in private-sector employment owing to its tendency to push up salaries, while it is not neutral as far as the propensity to save is concerned, given the liquidity constraints in the market. Finally, honest taxpayers are harassed, particularly if they belong to one of the categories of presumed tax evaders, such as the self-employed (Chapter 19).

On the other hand, the proportion of revenue raised through indirect taxes is abnormally low by international standards. The scale of generalized relief from social-security contributions needs to be reduced as over the long term wages tend to adjust in almost the same proportion; consequently, labour costs decrease only slightly, with the result that the unemployed gain little but those already in work derive considerable benefits and firms modest advantages. The taxation of the various types of investment income is far from uniform, creating opportunities for arbitrage that lead to losses of revenue and distortions in resource allocation and distribution; this book therefore suggests the essential lines for a tax reform that would improve both tax efficiency and horizontal and vertical tax equity (Chapter 20).

On the expenditure side of the budget, the more essential expenditure on pure public goods (such as security, justice, and defence) and on externalities (such as the environment) has been insufficient and declining over the past thirty years in Italy (Chapter 2), while public spending for investment and the maintenance of the capital stock, which directly boosts aggregate supply, though high, is still inadequate (Chapters 1 and 7).

With regard to the second aspect mentioned above, one of the many examples that can be cited is that of the contradiction in Italian economic policy between massive quantitative effort and the disappointingly poor quality of the outcome. While the budget of the public sector in the broad sense, (i.e. the general government plus public enterprises and state-controlled companies) is enormous, equal to far more than half of Italy's gross domestic product, the last few years have seen a fall in the already inadequate standard of public services—both non-marketed services such as state education, social security, and health for which no price is paid (Chapter 17) and those marketed services for which charges are made, such as public utilities (Chapter 5). With regard to the latter, the situation would improve if the operators of public utilities (whether legal monopolies or not) were required to set prices that covered their average costs in accordance with the principle of allocative optimality and were obliged to pay some form of compensation if the service provided fell short of set qualitative standards.

Another example of the contradictions inherent in public intervention in Italy relates to unemployment benefits (Chapter 11). These are insufficient or non-existent for some groups (the very large number of young people seeking their first job receive no state support) but extremely generous for others (benefits from the Wage Supplementation Fund amount to 80 per cent of the worker's gross wage in his previous job, with an automatic adjustment of benefit to wages that has many perverse effects on the level of employment and should therefore be eliminated at the earliest opportunity).

Perhaps the most significant instance in which economic-policy measures within a single budget item can be seen to be simultaneously excessive and inadequate is that of the welfare state

(Chapters 16 and 17). This Janus therefore deserves closer examination. Overall, it absorbs more than half of all general government expenditure, as over one-quarter of public expenditure goes on state education, health, housing, and recreational and cultural services (equal to almost 14 per cent of GDP) and around one-third on social security expenditure for income support (approximately equal to 16 per cent of GDP). Despite this massive commitment of resources, the welfare state provides inadequate coverage for the areas of real need. State old-age, survivors' (i.e. pensions for widow(er)s and orphans), and disability pensions (OSD) for public and private employees are not even equivalent to 40 per cent of the current average wage. The move away from merit-based selection in schools lowers educational standards without providing an effective antidote to class-based selection. The enormous public expenditure on health care has not entirely eliminated private health spending, which is now back at 15 per cent of public expenditure on health, partly owing to the intrinsic ineffectiveness of the state health system (waiting times and low standards).

The cause of this simultaneous expansion and degeneration of the Italian welfare state probably lies in the impossible attempt to achieve general consensus among the population through undiscriminating measures aimed at satisfying everyone but which end up leaving a great many people dissatisfied. The provision of universal health, social-security, and education services is bound to give inadequate support to those who really need it, and the unjustified extension of provision to those who are not in need merely leads to an escalation in the demands placed on the system.

In this way social policy loses sight of its true role, namely to cater efficiently and effectively only for basic and fundamental needs, in respect of which the promises made by Parliament can be honoured at no greater cost than at present. According to the proposals contained in this book, individuals with adequate income should themselves make provision to ensure a flow of income in retirement, suitable levels of education for their children, or health care for their families by selecting the unsubsidized products that satisfy their own requirements from among the services offered by the public or private sectors.

In addition, some aspects of the Italian welfare state are regressive. Take old-age pensions, for example; financing state pensions on a pay-as-you-go basis (rather than by means of a fair insurance scheme) penalizes the fastest growing sections of the population, which record the highest *rate* of growth irrespective of the *level* of economic prosperity, rather than the wealthiest social groups: in other words, the South rather than the Centre–North of Italy, despite the partial relief from contributions the South enjoys (the opposite applies, however, in the case of disability pensions, which the book shows to be disguised forms of unemployment benefit, especially in the Mezzogiorno). The fact that the school selection is not sufficiently merit-based within a system where state education is free both in terms of charges and access (completely free in the case of compulsory education and almost free thereafter up to and including university), and the modest level of grants (as they are not targeted only on 'able and deserving students without resources') perversely accentuate the importance of social origins for professional success, because they deprive the education system of the prestige and ability to be the decisive, formative influence on the life of the individual. Finally, the tax saving that can be achieved with a shrewd mix of private and public consumption of health services always benefits those in higher income brackets.

With regard to the third aspect indicated above relating to the excessive use of some instruments and the insufficiency or absence of others, the example of regulation may be clarifying. Italy has a surfeit of dirigistic regulation aimed at protecting the weak by means of legal and administrative procedures that take no account of market reactions and hence are circumvented or evaded. At the same time, there is a marked lack of regulation by means of incentives able to guide economic agents towards forms of behaviour that are both optimal for themselves and consistent with collective welfare.

Hence, public-utility charges (Chapter 18) are set without reference to any criterion of allocative efficiency, on the assumption—which we show to be false—that in this way they safeguard the purchasing power of the most needy sections of society; on the contrary, it would be possible to improve not only efficiency but also equity if charges were aligned with average costs, thus eliminating the utilities' losses. As another example, in Italy most conditions of employment and wage rates (Chapter 11) are imposed on workers irrespective of their individual productivity, geographic area, sector, age, and sex; the undesirable and unexpected (though totally predictable) result is to increase the cost of employing the very groups one wanted to protect, whereas the imbalances in the labour market could be reduced simply through making the market more flexible by restoring the ability of wages to signal excesses of supply or demand.

By contrast, regulation is rarely based on incentives and rewards. Not that there is any lack of tax concessions or credit subsidies, for example to foster employment or private investment, but in many cases they are ineffective and sometimes produce the opposite effect. This is the case, for instance, when industrial policy's interference with the prices of factors of production actually delays the process of restructuring (Chapters 9 and 10); like dirigistic regulation, incentives too must be judged on their results, not on their aims, for in the words of the proverb, 'the road to hell is paved with good intentions'.

This book therefore proposes the reduction of the existing subsidies—in particular interest subsidies on loans, which often lead to excessive imbalances in the liabilities of companies—and, if anything, comes down in favour of capital grants. Instead, tax benefits should be provided, along the lines of the tax-based incomes policies that are being tried elsewhere (Chapter 13). Progressive tax allowances on profits from actual investment could encourage firms to invest, or reduced progressivity of personal income taxes would lead to a slowdown in wage and price increases for a given average tax rate, with beneficial implications for employment via both the income and substitution effects.

As the economic policy in favour of the Mezzogiorno is the most symbolic example of all three aspects of the contradictory nature of public intervention in Italy, it is appropriate to conclude by describing this in greater detail.

We should preface our remarks by saying that public intervention in the South cannot be considered inadequate by comparison with that undertaken in the rest of Italy, either in per capita terms or in relation to the region's gross domestic-product; indeed, the Mezzogiorno has enjoyed in the last forty years approximately the same high rate of growth as the Centre–North. Yet, as the persistent economic dualism of the country confirms, it falls short as far as overall results are concerned, particularly as regards the still inadequate and unequal provision of infrastructure.

Four main types of intervention in the Southern economy can be distinguished: the most important, in terms of the volume of budgetary funds involved, is state support for households' net disposable incomes; followed by direct public investment and by public transfers to support private investment, mainly through credit subsidies and tax concessions; the latter being part of the more general mechanisms used for market regulation, but dirigistic regulation is prevalent in the Mezzogiornio.

For reasons that will become clear in the text, all these economic measures in the South are open to criticism, although some more than others. It is therefore useful that the description of the problem is followed by proposals, as is the case with all the analyses[3] contained in the book. Four changes in legislation in favour of the South are suggested: modifying the relative weighting of the various budgetary measures; backing up economic policies with other measures aimed at improving internal security in the South, which is instrumental to development; reducing the area of dirigistic regulation; and widening and substantially reshaping the area of incentive-based regulation.

Among the different kinds of public expenditure, priority should be given to those that expand supply, no less than aggregate demand, in the South; public expenditure in the region is bound to have a weaker multiplier effect if it is aimed at increasing households' net disposable incomes without at the same time increasing output, especially as in this case at least part of the marginal demand flows back into the product of the Centre–North or even abroad. Hence it is public investment that should be stepped up, rather than transfers to households or collective consumption.

Public investment in the Mezzogiorno is carried out mainly through a system of procurement, however, giving firms associated with organized crime (Mafia, Camorra, 'Ndrangheta) the opportunity to launder money, even without connivance from political quarters; as these firms are financed cheaply by illegal funds, they do not need to tender prices comparable to those of their competitors, with the result that their submissions always appear attractive.

On the other hand, exchanges of favours between politicians and organized crime probably do go on, as suggested in many recent trials.[4] The presence of organized crime therefore entails an economic cost for the Mezzogiorno, not only on account of unfair

---

[3] The proposals relating to the other structural problems of Italian economic policy are set out mainly in Sections 2.2, 4.2, 6.1, 6.2, 10.3, 13.4, 15.2, 17.1, 18.1, 18.4 and 21.4.

[4] More recent judicial investigations that are taking place while this book is being printed show that the general procurement system for public works has been widely abused in Italy and that illegal procedures were followed in the Centre–North as

competition to the detriment of potential firms but also because of intimidation and racketeering against private firms already operating in the area. More effective action by the state with regard to justice, public order, and internal security in the South is therefore a *sine qua non* for both public and private investment there, and hence for the general development of the area.

Financial assistance to firms in the South in the form of both interest subsidies and capital grants is also a cause of distortions. Given that the bureaucracy is not always qualified or honest, the discretionary procedures for granting assistance lead to an inevitable waste of resources. In order to overcome these handicaps, efforts should be made to improve the qualifications and honesty of public employees and, at the same time, to rely more on automatic mechanisms for granting assistance.

The low effectiveness of financial transfers to firms operating in the Mezzogiorno is also attributable to two other reasons: the fact that it does not always translate into increased productive capacity but may boost firms' liquidity or lead to purely financial speculation rather than factual investment, given that the procedures for releasing funds are not linked to the actual progress of the project; and the further circumstance that, by artificially reducing the cost of capital, it stimulates investment in technologies or sectors with a high capital/output ratio, little spillover, and modest multiplier effects, partly owing to the lack of an adequate network of mutually integrated firms supplying one another in different sectors.

In order to tackle the first problem, new types of transfer to enterprises should be used, aimed not at reducing their costs but at increasing their post-tax profits from actual, observable investments. Adequate tax allowances that increased proportionately with profits (types of regressive tax-based incomes policies, which could also be used to increase the demand for labour by means of marginal employment subsidies) would discourage the use of public funds for purely financial speculation and reward the most efficient firms.

well as in the South. Although no final judgement has yet been issued, it appears that public works were often awarded not to firms offering the most efficient conditions but rather to those willing to share part of their profit by paying kickbacks to high state officials or politicians, obtaining in exchange procurement prices higher than necessary to cover normal costs and profit margins. It appears therefore that in the Italian public work procurement system illegal exchanges do take place between politicians and private firms—not necessarily associated with organized crime—distorting competition and posing a significant burden on society.

To deal with the second problem, the focus of sectoral public intervention in the Mezzogiorno should be changed by directing fewer resources to heavy industry and more to light industry, encouraging labour-intensive technologies rather than capital-intensive ones, improving the quality of support to agriculture and tourism, paying equal attention to services, especially business services, and encouraging the growth rather than the formation of enterprises, especially local ones.

Finally, the problems caused by the fourth type of public intervention in the Mezzogiorno—dirigistic regulation, which creates specific rights and privileges—should be tackled by promoting or allowing the deregulation of wages, prices, and duties in the South. It is clear that the attempt to provide equality of opportunity by means of legal and administrative instruments that pay no heed to market reactions and to protect the weak rather than strengthening them creates a framework of rights that actually become constraints for those they are intended to safeguard.

The fact that this approach rests on a mistaken understanding of equality of opportunity is obvious when one realizes that it is inspired neither by the principle of giving to each according to his needs nor that of giving to each according to his worth. The imposed elimination of regional disparities in nominal base wages, the further narrowing of differentials in nominal net wages via the progressivity of the personal tax system and, in addition, the interference in the price system to favour the Mezzogiorno means that, on average, net real wages rise more rapidly and tend to become higher in the most backward part of the country (the South-West) and lower in the most developed (the North-West). At the same time, uniform real wages across the country are not matched by equal labour productivity, which unfortunately is still significantly lower in the Mezzogiorno, mainly owing to deficiencies in infrastructure that the public sector should rectify as quickly as possible.

In order to restore the flexibility of the labour market in the South and in Italy in general, wages must regain their allocative significance as a signal of scarcity, with differentiation between regions, sexes, age groups, and levels of personal proficiency. The portion of wages linked to individual productivity—which at present is smaller than the parts determined by indexation or by national or local labour agreements—needs to be increased; Italy as a whole, and not just the South, deserves this correction for reasons of both efficiency and equity. It would encourage labour mobility and reduce the excess of labour supply over demand.

Furthermore, it is well to remember that the policy of granting *additional* relief from social-security contributions in the South cannot continue for very much longer; by reducing labour costs per employee, it can provide a modest incentive for employers to move from the Centre–North to the South, but it fails to encourage labour to move in the opposite direction, as net real wages tend to be the same in both areas. Moreover, owing to tax shifting, the policy of granting *generalized* relief from social security contributions primarily benefits those already in work. Since these reductions in contributions are of only limited effectiveness in combating unemployment and impose a cost on the public sector, exacerbating its already large deficit, they should drastically be decreased.

I realize that by presenting here a very stylized and hence provocative summary of the main proposals for economic policy in Italy, I am laying myself open to criticism on two counts: I may appear to adopt an excessively simple *laissez-faire* approach and an equally naïve Enlightenment attitude.

As to the first, I do believe that in general it is legitimate for public intervention to restrict the liberty and free will of individuals only when competing demands cannot be reconciled via market mechanisms, so that economic policy becomes necessary and desirable for the very reasons that motivate individuals to enter into the social contract. In addition, in specific cases that must be weighed up carefully, public intervention in the economy becomes desirable if it is clear that individuals are unable to recognize merit goods or if they exploit privileges in income distribution that modern society judges to be unacceptable.

This Paretian approach, which is discussed in detail in Sections 2.1, 2.2., and 6.1, is typical of 'liberalism' and is not to be confused with *laissez-faire*; accordingly, the reader should not be surprised to find that the book draws inspiration from the best tradition of 'liberal' Italian economists, philosophers or political scientists (among others Croce, D'Azeglio, Einaudi, Gramsci, Nitti, Salvemini, Vico). The quotations prefacing each part, which are drawn from Italian works covering a period of around two centuries from 1744 onwards, are designed to indicate how old are the 'classical' and 'modern' causes of market failures in Italy.

As to the naïve Enlightenment attitude it could be alleged I display, this is supposedly evident in the way in which the structural problems in Italian economic policy are addressed here, where I show that I believe the declarations of intent of the Italian authorities and attribute the discrepancy between the objectives and the results to their incompetence or to mistakes.

It would obviously be conceivable to adopt other standpoints that might appear to be more consistent with the principle of 'what is real is rational'. For example, one could argue, on the criterion that things do not happen by chance, that the public sector does indeed wish to achieve the observed results and that the declared objectives merely pay lip service to the principles held by day-dreamers. Take the obligation—not the right—for pregnant women to stop working two months before their baby is due and to stay at home for three months after the birth, a requirement I judge to be actually unfavourable to women but which was publicly hailed as a milestone in the protection of working women. According to the alternative view, Parliament was aware that by raising the cost of female labour it would reduce female employment (as indeed happened in Italy until 1973) and reinforce the position of women as 'keeper of the hearth'. Similar claims could be made for all situations in which there is evidence of excessive dirigistic public regulation. These are interpreted in this book as instances where good intentions to protect the weak have gone astray, while others take the view that the 'cynical', predetermined objective has been attained, when all along it had been publicly and mendaciously stated that the opposite had been intended.

I reject this approach, because I do not believe in the collective schizophrenia that would allow the politicians to exhibit a systematic bad faith that is not inherent in individuals performing different roles. Like anyone else, the politician is motivated by a mixture of good and bad intentions, but he or she should be judged on achievements, not on motives. In that sense it is difficult for him or her to be successful, for to avoid inertia on the one hand and action for action's sake on the other, the politician must resolutely and skilfully tread the fine dividing line between reality and utopia, a line on which this book also attempts to remain.

This in no way implies that I always share the objective of policy-makers of protecting the 'weak', particularly when there is no attempt to verify such 'weakness' beforehand or when protection is offered indiscriminately to groups rather than to individuals.

For example, in the case of legislation on pregnant women, protection is awarded both to the women who really need medical assistance and to healthy ones, possibly with the commendable aim of avoiding any stigma or with the less commendable aim of acquiring a general consensus from the median voter. What I have discussed so far is the poor selection of instruments and the careless pursuit of goals, for given objectives. In the final pages of this book, which are devoted to an attempt to investigate the Italian 'economic miracle', I shall discuss some of the various contradictory goals pursued by Italian economic policies. I shall also cover the variety of reasons, approaches, and targets of agents in Italian society who are apt to define and achieve, but sometimes also to confuse some of these objectives.

Another approach that one could find more realistic or more grounded in history than mine would be to maintain that the declared objectives are those that policy-makers pursue when setting the rules for the economic system as it should be, while the results obtained represent the goals of society as it is. According to this view, for example, the Minister for the Treasury has been planning to eliminate the budget deficit net of interest payments for the last five years or so, knowing that otherwise the public debt would become unsustainable, with disastrous consequences for the country; however, the budget, both including and excluding interest payments, remains obstinately in the red in Italy—in contrast to most other developed countries—because this is the state of affairs Italians actually prefer.

This argument presupposes that there is little cohesion between citizens and their political representatives. Otherwise, it is impossible to see why the public authorities, who seek to assemble the widest possible consensus among electors, should proclaim objectives they know to be unpopular. It is conceivable that they do not know the market's preferences over the short run, but this seems implausible over the medium term. For similar reasons, it does not seem probable that individuals can for long remain ignorant of the existence and implications of fundamental structural problems, such as those connected with the underlying unsustainability of Italy's public debt.

While some inconsistencies between Italian society and its authorities certainly exist in the short run, I argue in the concluding remarks of this book that policy-makers and the whole of Italian society in the long run both share a set of objectives which are intrinsically inconsistent.[5] A sort of double standard of morality prevails, whereby words are not followed by facts and important general principles are constantly contradicted by actual specific behaviour. This internal inconsistency is all the clearer when contrasting, or at least heterogeneous, social interests are involved and find representation both in Italian society and in its economic policy. Again a mistake of policy-makers emerges to the extent that they are unable to represent the country's general interests. This cannot be due to an imperfect information flow between society and rulers, as in the long run technical information is complete and symmetrical. However, if there are externalities and information that the market does not signal, the individual does not know whether his demands on the community are compatible with those of fellow citizens or with the declared public objective which in the long term he understands and shares. The very existence of free-rider attitudes, externalities, and pure public goods induce citizens faced with market failures to devolve freely to the state the task of achieving the collective will, which is not the sum of the wishes expressed by individuals at any one moment.

In such a situation, the public sector does not violate individual preferences, but it betrays them when it does not responsibly play its proper active role in resolving social inconsistencies by making choices that neither can nor should satisfy the demands of each and every citizen. Policy-makers cannot find and should not search for an impossible and unjustifiable social unanimity.

For all these reasons, therefore, the sometimes dramatic failure to tackle and resolve the structural problems of Italian economic policy is attributed in the pages that follow to incompetence, errors, lack of courage, and sloth, rather than systematic bad faith or systematic ignorance of citizens' true preferences on the part of the authorities or of the true problems of economic policy on the part of citizens.

[5] To a certain extent my viewpoint coincides with the evaluation recently expressed by Lange and Regini (1989: 267) '"Unintended" is perhaps the word that best characterizes the patterns of regulation we have observed in Italy. By this we do not mean that the actors involved in policy-making do not have goals, but that the outcomes do not reflect the intentions of any single actor or coalition. When we look at the regulatory mix in a particular policy area, much less at the mixes across policy areas, we find few signs of design, governing vision, ideology, or even predominant cultural patterning. Instead, there is a crazy quilt of sometimes contradictory, sometimes complementary modes and institutions for regulating the production and allocation of resources and the conflicts among interested parties.'

PART I

The Scale of Public Intervention in the Economy

And what else can economics be, if not mathematics? For as we have seen, its propositions are neither philosophical nor historical, nor even simply naturalistic. It does indeed have a mathematical stamp; not of pure mathematics or arithmetic, or algebra, or calculus—but of applied mathematics, which gives calculus a foundation of concepts drawn from reality, to be considered tangible by comparison with numerical formalism. Economics is simply mathematics applied to the concept of volition or action; it does not enquire into the nature of volition or action, but applies calculus to certain given facts about human actions in order to come to a swift recognition of their necessary configurations and consequences.

(B. Croce, *Filosofia della pratica: I. Economica ed etica*, 1932)

1

Direct and Indirect Action by General Government and Public Corporations

1.1. Direct budgetary intervention

Public-sector intervention in the Italian economy is substantial and increasing, in terms of both the volume and the functional diversity of public involvement. It takes the form of direct action which has an impact on the government's budget, and indirect regulation of the private sector aimed at requiring or encouraging it to adopt certain patterns of behaviour. It is not always easy to distinguish between direct and indirect action, as a glance at the items of income and expenditure in the budget of general government in Italy amply demonstrates (Table 1.1).

Direct intervention can be recognized easily enough whenever the public sector creates value-added[1] by producing or purchasing goods and services (through collective consumption and public investment). It is more difficult to determine which part of public transfers to the private sector corresponds to compensation to a factor of production, the direct provision of a service or purchase of a good (one need only think of composite items such as social-security benefits, interest payments, or investment grants) and which part simply represents income redistribution, perhaps as a result of public regulations requiring individuals to fulfil an obligation or offering them incentives.

Despite these ambiguities, the scale of public expenditure in Italy is evident from the official figures. Table 1.1 shows that in 1988[2]

---

[1] It should be noted that the distinction within public expenditure between items that create value added and those that do not, is arbitrary; by accounting convention, in the absence of a market that can determine the value of public output, the value is equated to the inputs cost. The fact that not all staff expenses lead to the creation of value-added will become clear later, particularly when, with regard to the South, we shall affirm that public spending on personnel is a form of income support or when, with regard to public utilities, we shall show that the standard of service would improve if the workforce were cut.

[2] This is the latest year for which figures are available. Unless explicitly stated otherwise, all budget figures in this book that relate exclusively to the 1980s are drawn from the new national accounts reconstructed by the Central Statistical

TABLE 1.1 Consolidated revenue and expenditure account of general government (in billions of current Lit.)

	1980	1981	1982	1983	1984	1985	1986	1987	1988
Expenditure									
Wages and salaries	42,732	56,135	65,288	76,228	86,421	95,760	104,354	117,244	132,267
Collective consumption	57,013	74,156	87,386	103,568	118,034	133,249	145,120	163,856	185,194
Production subsidies	11,068	13,298	16,898	18,231	22,194	22,545	27,343	25,963	26,754
Social security benefits	54,696	72,805	88,609	109,355	121,556	139,161	154,797	166,897	186,256
Transfers to private social institutions	706	578	663	1,488	2,097	1,645	1,373	1,691	2,129
International aid	367	572	856	951	1,223	1,735	2,500	2,299	3,075
Other transfer payments	1,585	1,538	1,702	2,185	2,160	2,810	3,056	2,948	4,878
Current expenditure net of interest payments	125,521	163,064	196,253	235,949	267,447	301,374	334,430	363,931	408,582
Interest payments	20,479	28,583	38,857	47,320	58,113	65,483	76,411	80,070	88,935
TOTAL CURRENT EXPENDITURE	146,000	191,647	235,110	283,269	325,560	366,857	410,841	444,001	497,517
Gross fixed investment	12,278	16,918	20,335	23,540	26,198	30,577	31,996	34,653	37,229
Net purchases of land	31	44	44	51	70	56	73	49	80
Investment grants	3,638	5,162	7,485	8,219	9,521	12,055	13,996	15,062	16,341
Other transfer payments on capital account	734	170	42	267	454	5,432	757	596	484
TOTAL CAPITAL EXPENDITURE	16,681	22,294	27,906	32,077	36,243	48,120	46,822	50,360	54,134
Total expenditure net of interest payments	142,202	185,358	224,159	268,026	303,690	349,494	381,252	414,291	462,716
TOTAL EXPENDITURE	162,681	213,941	263,016	315,346	361,803	414,977	457,663	494,361	551,651

Revenue

Gross operating surplus	1,263	1,614	1,998	2,437	2,849	3,306	3,972	4,487	5,256
Interest received	2,384	3,249	3,030	3,229	3,765	5,228	6,011	7,169	7,582
Income from land	284	392	550	663	766	826	892	843	985
Indirect taxes	33,522	38,297	46,649	57,987	67,283	72,698	81,680	92,919	109,182
Direct taxes	37,291	50,916	64,534	78,402	91,416	105,489	115,452	130,386	145,074
Actual social-security contributions	44,488	53,130	67,217	79,126	86,955	97,116	111,369	121,816	134,118
Imputed social-security contributions	5,005	6,363	7,391	9,712	11,567	13,006	13,877	14,829	15,782
International aid	143	157	205	227	297	422	408	434	325
Other transfer payments	4,192	5,164	5,004	8,337	8,832	12,636	17,971	15,458	15,348
TOTAL CURRENT REVENUE	128,665	159,390	196,721	240,345	273,961	311,028	352,056	388,770	434,144
Investment grants	232	278	395	442	643	673	647	784	1,006
Capital taxes	317	377	2,905	6,927	2,469	919	787	1,104	1,636
Other transfer payments on capital account	453	884	1,429	441	681	695	908	771	652
TOTAL CAPITAL REVENUE	1,002	1,539	4,729	7,810	3,793	2,287	2,342	2,659	3,294
TOTAL REVENUE	129,667	160,929	201,450	248,155	277,754	313,315	354,398	391,429	437,438
Current balance net of interest payments	3,144	−3,674	468	4,396	6,514	9,654	17,626	24,839	25,562
Saving or dissaving	−17,335	−32,257	−38,389	−42,924	−51,599	−55,829	−58,785	−55,231	−63,373
Overall balance net of interest payments	−12,535	−24,429	−22,709	−19,871	−25,936	−36,179	−26,854	−22,862	−25,268
Deficit (−) or surplus (+)	−33,014	−53,012	−61,566	−67,191	−84,049	−101,662	−103,265	−102,932	−114,213

Sources: Malizia and Pedullà (1988) for data from 1980 to 1987; ISTAT, unpublished data (kindly supplied by Raffaele Malizia of ISTAT) for 1988.

general government expenditure exceeded Lit. 550 trillion, equal to 51.1 per cent of GDP, compared with 41.7 per cent at the beginning of the 1980s (Table 1.2). Even though the general government budget was so large, expenditure on the production of pure public goods (defence, justice, public order, internal security, and other general services) remained between 14 and 16 per cent of the total throughout the 1980s (Table 1.3); the share of this traditional area of public intervention has declined by an average of about 1.3 per cent a year over the last twenty-five years.[3]

More significantly, the scale of public intervention in the market can be seen to be greater if one also includes the expenditure of bodies belonging to the enlarged public sector that are not part of general government[4] because they produce marketed services (e.g. the post office, state telecommunications, railways), gas and water provided by municipal agencies, electricity supplied by the National Electricity Authority ENEL); these bodies which we call public enterprises, accounted for an average of just under 30 per cent of the enlarged public sector's investment spending during the period under examination (Table 1.4), with the proportion tending to increase towards the end of the period. In addition, the figure for public investment would be almost 30 per cent higher if investment by state-controlled companies,[5] which by convention are treated as part of the private sector for national-accounting purposes, were also taken into account.

1.2. *Public corporations*

Although the legal, institutional, and administrative structure of public enterprises (bodies in the enlarged public sector that are not included in general government) differs significantly from that of state-controlled companies, we shall argue that from the point of

Office (ISTAT) for the years from 1980 onwards using the new methods introduced in 1986; by contrast, budget data relating to periods beginning before 1980 are not based on the new national accounts.

[3] This phenomenon is described in Patrizii and Rossi (1986).

[4] The definitions of the enlarged public sector and general government are given in the notes to Table 1.4.

[5] These state-controlled companies are controlled by what used to be state holdings and are now in the process of being transformed into joint stock companies following the law n. 359 of 8 August 1992. The process, which ultimately should lead to various forms of privatization, is far from being completed (see Ministero del Tesoro, 1992).

view of economic analysis it is appropriate to treat them as a relatively homogeneous aggregate labelled public corporations.

At first sight, the theoretical and practical differences in their economic objectives and powers appear to militate against this hypothesis, since grouping them together in this way may negate the very reasons for the genesis of the state-controlled companies. The thinking behind their creation was that the combination of public objectives and private corporate structures would enable these companies to behave in a different way from public enterprises in the narrow sense.

There were two main reasons for this: as commercial objectives were only occasionally overlaid by social objectives, the management of state-controlled companies would have far greater autonomy than their counterparts in traditional public enterprises; moreover, the companies' status as companies limited by shares, possibly involving private partners, would provide much greater incentive than in a traditional public enterprise to strive for efficient resource allocation, inducing management to maximize profits in the same way as private companies. On the other hand, as Romani (1987) recently reaffirmed within our research group, the 'improper costs' to which the public objectives of state-controlled companies give rise would need to be covered by their endowment funds if a private shareholder was to consider it immaterial whether the financial asset he held related to a private firm or a state-controlled company.

According to the original concept, therefore, once political criteria had been built into the decision-making models of state-controlled companies and provision had been made to cover the specific related costs, the firms themselves would have to aim for an optimum that implied the minimizing of all costs, including those due to the political constraints.

If this reasoning, inspired by Saraceno (1976), still portrayed the true situation with regard to state-controlled companies, it would be difficult to equate them to public enterprises in the narrow sense simply on the grounds that they both pursued objectives that are not exclusively market oriented. Nor would we be pursuaded to do so by the argument put forward by Saraceno (1959: 87) that 'the ambiguous category comprising so-called mixed firms should be rejected; in reality, firms in which public and private capital both participate do not constitute a separate category half-way between

Table 1.2. Consolidated revenue and expenditure account of general government (ratio to GDP)

	1980	1981	1982	1983	1984	1985	1986	1987	1988
Expenditure									
Wages and salaries	10.9	12.0	12.0	12.0	11.9	11.7	11.6	11.9	12.2
Collective consumption	14.6	15.8	16.0	16.3	16.2	16.3	16.1	16.7	17.1
Production subsidies	2.8	2.8	3.1	2.9	3.0	2.8	3.0	2.6	2.4
Social security benefits	14.0	15.6	16.3	17.3	16.7	17.1	17.2	17.0	17.2
Transfers to private social institutions	0.2	0.1	0.1	0.2	0.3	0.2	0.2	0.2	0.1
International aid	0.1	0.1	0.2	0.2	0.2	0.2	0.3	0.2	0.2
Other transfer payments	0.4	0.3	0.3	0.3	0.3	0.3	0.3	0.3	0.4
Current expenditure net of interest payments	32.1	34.8	36.0	37.2	36.7	36.9	37.1	37.0	37.8
Interest payments	5.2	6.1	7.1	7.5	8.0	8.0	8.5	8.1	8.2
TOTAL CURRENT EXPENDITURE	37.4	40.9	43.1	44.7	44.7	45.0	45.5	45.2	46.1
Gross fixed investment	3.1	3.6	3.7	3.7	3.6	3.7	3.5	3.5	3.4
Net purchases of land	—	—	—	—	—	—	—	—	—
Investment grants	0.9	1.1	1.4	1.3	1.3	1.5	1.6	1.5	1.5
Other transfer payments on capital account	0.2	—	—	—	0.1	0.7	0.1	0.1	—
TOTAL CAPITAL EXPENDITURE	4.3	4.8	5.1	5.1	5.0	5.9	5.2	5.1	5.0
Total expenditure net of interest payments	36.4	39.6	41.1	42.3	41.7	42.8	42.3	42.2	42.8
TOTAL EXPENDITURE	41.7	45.7	48.2	49.8	49.7	50.9	50.7	50.3	51.1

Revenue

	1980	1981	1982	1983	1984	1985	1986	1987	1988
Gross operating surplus	0.3	0.3	0.4	0.4	0.4	0.4	0.4	0.5	0.5
Interest received	0.6	0.7	0.6	0.5	0.5	0.6	0.7	0.7	0.7
Income from land	0.1	0.1	0.1	0.1	0.1	0.1	0.1	0.1	0.1
Indirect taxes	8.6	8.2	8.6	9.2	9.2	8.9	9.1	9.5	10.1
Direct taxes	9.6	10.9	11.8	12.4	12.6	12.9	12.8	13.3	18.4
Actual social security contributions	11.4	11.4	12.3	12.5	11.9	11.9	12.3	12.4	12.4
Imputed social security contributions	1.3	1.4	1.4	1.5	1.6	1.6	1.5	1.5	1.5
International aid	—	—	—	—	—	0.1	—	—	—
Other transfer payments	1.1	1.1	0.9	1.3	1.2	1.5	2.0	1.6	1.4
TOTAL CURRENT REVENUE	33.0	34.1	36.1	37.9	37.6	38.1	39.0	39.6	40.2
Investment grants	0.1	0.1	0.1	0.1	0.1	0.1	0.1	0.1	0.1
Capital taxes	0.1	0.1	0.5	1.1	0.3	0.1	0.1	0.1	0.1
Other transfer payments on capital account	0.1	0.2	0.3	0.1	0.1	0.1	0.1	0.1	0.1
TOTAL CAPITAL REVENUE	0.3	0.3	0.9	1.2	0.5	0.3	0.3	0.3	0.3
TOTAL REVENUE	33.2	34.4	37.0	39.2	38.2	38.4	39.3	39.5	40.5
Current balance net of interest payments	0.8	−0.8	0.1	0.7	0.9	1.2	2.0	2.5	2.4
Saving or dissaving	−4.4	−6.9	−7.0	−6.8	−7.1	−6.8	−6.5	−5.6	−5.8
Overall balance net of interest payments	−3.2	−5.2	−4.2	−3.1	−3.6	−4.4	−3.0	−2.3	−2.3
Deficit (−) or surplus (+)	−8.5	−11.3	−11.3	−10.6	−11.5	−12.5	−11.4	−10.5	−10.6

Sources: Malizia and Pedullà (1988) for data from 1980 to 1987; authors' calculations based on ISTAT unpublished data (kindly supplied by Raffaele Malizia of ISTAT) for 1988. The figures for GDP are drawn from ISTAT, *Conti economici nazionali*, 1989.

TABLE 1.3. Total general government expenditure by purpose (%age composition)

Purposes	1980	1981	1982	1983	1984	1985	1986	1987	1988
Traditional area	15.4	14.6	13.9	14.1	14.0	15.9	14.9	15.3	15.3
National defence	4.0	3.8	3.7	4.0	4.0	4.0	3.9	4.1	4.1
General services[a]	11.4	10.8	10.2	10.1	10.0	11.9	11.0	11.2	11.2
Welfare state	60.4	59.3	58.1	58.4	56.8	56.5	56.1	56.8	56.9
Education	11.4	11.4	10.9	10.5	10.3	10.0	9.9	10.4	10.3
Health	13.3	11.5	11.3	11.1	10.7	10.6	10.4	10.8	11.3
Housing	3.3	3.3	3.4	3.4	3.3	3.6	3.2	3.2	3.0
Leisure, cultural and religious services	1.0	1.1	1.1	1.1	1.1	1.1	1.0	1.1	1.1
Pensions and other social benefits	31.4	32.0	31.4	32.3	31.4	31.2	31.6	31.3	31.8
Mixed economy	24.2	26.1	28.0	27.5	29.2	27.6	29.0	27.9	27.8
Economic services	15.2	13.9	14.9	14.2	14.3	13.5	13.8	13.2	12.9
Expenditure not specified elsewhere	9.0	12.2	13.1	13.3	14.9	14.1	15.2	14.7	14.9
TOTAL	100.0	100.0	100.0	100.0	100.0	100.0	100.0	100.0	100.0

[a] Including expenditure for public order and internal security.
Sources: Malizia and Pedullà (1988) for data from 1980 to 1987; authors' calculations based on ISTAT, unpublished data (kindly supplied by Raffaele Malizia of ISTAT) for 1988.

TABLE 1.4. Public investment (billions of current Lit.) and typical investment ratios

Public investments	Years						Typical ratios
	1984	1985	1986	1987	1988	1984-8	Five year average 1984-8
General government investment[a]	26,268	30,352	31,973	34,408	37,309	160,310	General government investment/ Enlarged public-sector investment 0.705
Other investment by the enlarged public sector, excluding that by general government (Investment by public enterprises)[b]	10,710	11,349	13,876	15,085	15,972	66,992	Public enterprises' investment/ Enlarged public-sector investment 0.295 State-controlled companies' investment/ Enlarged public-sector investment 0.283
Investment by the enlarged public sector	36,978	41,701	45,849	49,493	53,281	227,302	Public corporations' investment/ Investment of the enlarged public sector + state-controlled companies 0.450
Investment by state-controlled companies[c]	10,193	12,009	13,163	14,098	14,811	64,274	
Investment by public corporations (Public enterprises + state-controlled companies)	20,903	23,358	27,039	29,183	30,783	131,266	

[a] General government comprises: State, Mezzogiorno Development Agency, two autonomous government agencies (National Road Agency (ANAS), State Forests), other general government bodies, regions, provinces and municipalities, hospitals and local health authorities, other local-authority bodies, social-security agencies.

[b] Public enterprises are defined as those bodies included in the enlarged public sector but not in general government. These are: other autonomous agencies (fiscal monopolies, telecommunications, state postal and telephone services), State Railways, Deposits and Loans Fund, municipal agencies (water, gas, municipal transport and electricity, sanitation, milk depots) and the National Electricity Authority.

[c] State-controlled companies are the enterprises controlled by what used to be state holdings, i.e. IRI, ENI, EFIM, and Ente Gestione per le Aziende Cinematografiche.

Sources: Senato della Repubblica (1988) for data on 1984, and (1989) for data on 1985–8.

a public enterprise and a private one. They are private firms if the *controlling capital* is in private hands and public enterprises if it is not.'

Public enterprises and state-controlled companies both seem to us to be public corporations, not because in both cases the controlling capital is public or because their objectives cannot be described entirely in terms of profit maximization, but because their economic behaviour is not dissimilar, in that the path the state-controlled companies have actually followed suggests that they have lost their way.

Indeed, if we trace the development of state-controlled companies through the analysis provided for us by Marzano (1992) and Marzano and Marzovilla (1988: 56–9), we find that

the initial phase, in which the state took a controlling interest in limited companies subject to private commercial law in order to stimulate and strengthen growth in the Italian industrial sector, was followed by a phase of a very different character. When the spread of what has been called the 'crisis mentality' caused priority to be given to requests for assistance at the expense of innovative strategic choices, the growing predominance of socio-political considerations over objectives of efficiency altered the delicate balance between public objectives and commercial needs, with the latter being subordinated to the former. . . .

In reality, the proliferation of objectives assigned to public enterprises and their relative incompatibility increasingly blurred the problem of managing such enterprises, by on the one hand widening the scope for managerial discretion and on the other increasing management's dependence on political directives. As to the first aspect, there is a growing conviction that one of the main problems hampering the establishment of objective criteria for measuring the efficiency of state-controlled companies lies in the multitude of goals they are being given, without a precise priority order. In these circumstances, the management could be excused for washing their hands of all responsibility for their ineffectiveness in pursuing one or several objectives.

On the other hand, it must also be recognized that the expansion in the political and social tasks assigned to state-controlled companies has provided theoretical justification for management's heavier reliance on political conditioning by accentuating the need to co-ordinate the objectives of the various enterprises among themselves and with the more general objectives of the state.

The reduction in the pressure to produce positive commercial results necessitates frequent capital injections and drives away private investors unless there are well-founded prospects of profitability. This results in the ownership of state-controlled companies becoming even more concentrated in the hands of the majority shareholder (the state), bringing into question the very reason for the state-controlled companies' existence and the distinction between these and traditional public enterprises. Economically, they are almost identical to public enterprises; as we are reminded by Marzano and Marzovilla (1988: 63), they represent 'surreptitious forms of nationalization, and yet they are not subject to the controls that apply to public enterprises in the strict sense'.

In the course of this development, which was also re-examined for us by Stillitano and Virno (1987) and by Ravazzi (1987), the role of endowment funds progressively changed; whereas originally they were the most appropriate vehicle for investment by state-controlled companies, they became simply a means of covering losses, partly because in the great majority of cases funds were paid to the companies without any conditions as to their use.

From this stems the conviction, evident in many of our studies, that nowadays the distinction between public enterprises in the narrow sense and state-controlled companies is no longer very meaningful, despite recent attempts by the latter (and also by some public enterprises, such as the State Railways) to regain managerial independence and restore their efficiency. From our perspective, the two groups thus form the aggregate public corporations; they are certainly not perfectly homogeneous, but nor are the state-controlled companies themselves or the group of state holdings which used to own them.

This judgement obviously has no normative value. In other words, having demolished 'the pretence of preserving the private-sector nature of state-controlled companies, in which the public sector should have only a capital interest but no substantial influence over their management criteria,' (Leccisotti, 1979: 16) we do not intend to state that such enterprises should remain part of the public sector. Quite to the contrary, the scope for possible deregulation or privatization, either complete or partial, will be examined below for all types of public corporation (including public enterprises in the narrow sense).

1.3. *Indirect public intervention*

The considerations set out so far relate only to budgetary intervention, predominantly of a direct kind, by the long hand of the state over the invisible hand of market forces. Perhaps even more prevalent in Italy is indirect intervention via the regulation of the private sector, which does not always have an immediate impact on the public purse; this consists in a plethora of rules and regulations aimed at prescribing or fostering certain forms of behaviour, results, conditions, requirements, prohibitions, or economic rights, the only apparent contradiction being the absence, until very recently, of legislation to protect competition in this quintessential *Rechtsstaat*.

It was only recently that Italy passed anti-trust legislation. Elsewhere this has long been recognized as essential for the proper functioning of the economy. Legislation to protect competition sets general rules to prevent monopolies or oligopolies from exploiting a dominant position and obstructing the entry of potential competitors into the market, thus reducing market efficiency to the detriment of consumers. The very existence of such a law also limits the scope for excesses in discretionary government action that is inconsistent with the behaviour of private agents and appears to be ineffective or unjustified; by implication, it therefore recognizes the legitimacy of market mechanisms and their effects.

It is almost superfluous to recall that such an approach contrasts with the attitude displayed by Italian economic policy-makers when they seem to maintain that competition in this or that sector can be guaranteed by the presence of public corporations or when they impose a higher level of economic regulation than in other countries.

As far as indirect intervention in Italy is concerned, there can be no doubt as to the mass of economic regulation of the private market on the part of the public sector: on monitored and administered prices, on pay and working conditions, on the cost and availability of capital, through barriers to entry (the distributive trade, taxes) and vice versa, through requirements to provide certain services (credit, education); all with overlapping objectives with regard to resource allocation, income redistribution, economic stabilization, and development.

In addition, Italy makes equally frequent, but perhaps more

justifiable use of so-called social regulation, which, at the theoretical level, is distinct from economic regulation in that it does not relate to public control over the price or volume of goods and services but to other aspects, such as quality: take, for example, the setting of minimum standards (for food and environmental quality), the requirement for producers to inform users of the quality of a service and the ability to meet demand without excessive risk (a requirement that is used today to justify the restriction of supply by granting authorizations and licences or requiring registration in professional registers), the designation of goods worthy of special protection (merit goods) which every citizen has a right or duty to enjoy or not to enjoy, as the case may be (for instance, the requirement to have certain vaccinations or the ban on narcotic drugs).

All these forms of economic or social regulation (cf. Pandolfelli 1986, 1987*a*, 1987*b*, 1988*a*, 1988*b*) will be discussed at length in later chapters. What is already clear, however, is that the paradox of excessive regulation, on the one hand, and the absence up to the recent past[6] of any law to protect competition, on the other, is only apparent, as Romani (1988*a* and 1988*b*) reminds us; the working of competition is acknowledged to be particularly important, and is therefore legally protected where there is a widespread conviction that the citizen-consumer is best served by the impersonal mechanism of competition, which leads producers and final users to achieve social welfare by pursuing their own self-interest.

If, by contrast, the political philosophy of the country is based on the notion that ethical-altruistic planning is needed to achieve social welfare, it will appear necessary for the public authorities to control all aspects of economic life: it is then a short step to the illusion that the common interest is directly protected by public intervention, so that legislation favouring the indirect mechanism of competition is superfluous or even harmful in that it may directly constrain the state's ability to direct economic life.

1.4. '*The prisoner's dilemma*' and altruism

Of course, competition does not always ensure the greatest social welfare; the so-called market failures then emerge. These are

---

[6] In 1990 a law was passed (M. 287 of 10 October), according to which an antitrust body was created in Italy to ensure competition, avoid concentrations, and inhibit the abuse of dominant positions.

frequent, and demonstrate why the unbridled pursuit of self-interest sometimes does not lead to a social optimum, as in all instances of the 'prisoner's dilemma', where the dominant strategy for each individual implies an outcome that would be dominated by agreement to co-operate. This does not mean, however, that economic pseudo-solidarism is normally preferable; there are at least three sets of reasons for this, as has already been explained elsewhere (cf. Padoa Schioppa, 1989a).

First, upon closer examination altruism and self-interest may coincide if long-term rather than short-term individual interests are considered, since in repeated games it is necessary to win credibility and a reputation as a reliable player. In such circumstances the 'prisoner's dilemma' is resolved, because co-operation becomes the dominant strategy from the point of view of the greatest self-interest, an outcome to which altruism (but other motives as well) might also have led.

Secondly, altruism achieves an outcome that is socially preferable to that induced by selfish motives only if we have perfect information on the fellow citizen with whose welfare we are concerned, a prerequisite that is difficult to verify. Otherwise, solidarity is not enough, as keenly demonstrated by Ricossa (1988: 146).

Altruism is spontaneous and effective on the small scale, directed towards someone we know or meet and whose needs we perceive clearly because they are revealed by a direct personal relationship that can easily develop into sympathy or even love. This kind of assistance also has a place in society at large, but it cannot satisfy the need for solidarity generated by a very widespread and complicated division of labour between persons who are interconnected only very indirectly and often without their knowledge (in the sense that they do not know who individually represents the final link in the chain of social relationships). Society at large has defeated poverty not by emulating St. Martin, who gave half of his coat to a poor man, but by manufacturing millions of whole coats at a price within everyone's reach.

Finally, in many circumstances solidarity, which is assumed to inspire, at least partly, the actions of the state, may even have socially undesirable consequences. This is true, for example, whenever attempts to protect the weaker party in a relationship give him too many guarantees and safeguards that narrow the opportunities open to him and others like him by reducing market flexibility. In such cases, economic policy leads to excessive regulation or sanctions that actually become the cause of serious disequilibria, even if it is motivated by the best of intentions to intervene in favour of one's neighbour.

For that reason, Hayek's statement that perhaps the greatest discovery ever made by mankind was that men could live together, in peace and to their mutual benefit, without having to share common concrete objectives[7] apart from the rule of law, still generally holds true.

---

[7] Quoted in Ricossa (1988: 146). This problem is described for us by Boccaccio (1988).

PART II

The Classical Reasons for Market Failures

Pure Public Goods and Externalities

There are two dominant instincts in the human psyche: the one is purely individual, the Ego pure and simple; the other is an instinct for sociability, which subordinates personal pleasure to the welfare of others and drives the individual to sacrifice himself for fellow human beings. As a reaction against pagan utilitarianism, Christianity strove to base human society solely on the instinct for sacrifice, and it was a delusion; but it is just as much a delusion to want to base it exclusively on individual egoism. All progress will depend on the reconciling of these two extremes.

(L. Franchetti and S. Sonnino, *La Sicilia nel 1876*, 1876)

2

Free-Riding and Private versus Social Cost Benefits

2.1. Pure public goods

Subject to all these caveats, let us examine the various kinds of market failure observed in Italy and the means devised to overcome them. The analysis will follow a textbook procedure in order to verify systematically whether the conditions cited to justify public action actually exist, that is to say conditions that prevent the market from achieving an efficient (Pareto[1]) optimum or cause the achievable (Pareto) optimum to be considered socially undesirable.

Leaving aside the factors we have already described briefly above, which are associated with the 'prisoner's dilemma' and are in turn specific examples of more general instances of imperfect information and market incompleteness, the main reasons why the market may be unable to achieve a Pareto optimum, according, for example to Stiglitz (1986), stem from the existence of pure public goods, externalities, and natural monopolies.

In addition, there are two reasons why a Pareto optimum that the market may be able to achieve may not appear entirely desirable from the social point of view: these arise either from an initial allocation of resources that calls for redistributive measures, or from insufficient pursuit of utility by individuals (an element in the Paretian social-objective function), so that paternalistic intervention with regard to merit goods becomes desirable, as if individuals were not perfectly 'capable of understanding and intending'.

Among the normative justifications for public intervention in the economy, the one most frequently and traditionally adopted in the literature concerns so-called pure public goods, the existence of which therefore provides a classical reason for failure of the market.

---

[1] A Pareto optimum would be achieved in all circumstances in which it would be impossible to increase the utility of some individuals without reducing that of others. As many alternatives are conceivable, all equally efficient but differing from one another in terms of the distribution of individual welfare, economic policy can choose whichever is socially preferable.

Pure public goods (internal security, public order, defence, justice) have the two properties of non-rivalry and non-excludability in consumption, properties that lead to predictable 'free-rider' attitudes among individuals. Since individuals would systematically seek to make 'others' bear the cost of a good whose benefits they could not avoid enjoying, public intervention becomes necessary to make up for the insufficiency of output that would undoubtedly result if the market as a whole were left to its own devices.[2]

With regard to these goods that undoubtedly come within the agenda[3] of state intervention, we note that regulation is abundant, but implementation is insufficient, leading to the impression that Italy is a country where legislation is pervasive but following laws (as expressed by Franco Modigliani) is optional. In fact, one should deplore, among other things, the paucity of funding in this field, indicated both by an inadequate level of public expenditure on pure public goods and by a downward trend in such spending, as revealed in the item 'Traditional area' in Table 1.3.

The resulting deterioration in the quality of our system of defence, justice, and public order is inevitable and is illustrated by the feeling of ordinary men and women that they are not adequately protected against those fundamental social risks that historically underlie the social contract into which they have entered. One example from the legal system is sufficient to make the point: the average time for a case to be tried is extremely long in Italy, whereas it is obvious that speed is a necessary, although not sufficient, condition for delivering justice, especially if the accused is innocent.

---

[2] As Samuelson (1966: 1224–5) recalls, 'no decentralized pricing system can serve to determine optimally these levels of collective consumption. Other kinds of "voting" or "signalling" would have to be tried. But, and this is the point sensed by Wicksell but perhaps not fully appreciated by Lindahl, now it is in the selfish interest of each person to give *false* signals, to pretend to have less interest in a given collective consumption activity than he really has. . . . The failure of market catallactics in no way denies the following truth: given sufficient knowledge, the optimal decisions can always be found by scanning over all the attainable states of the world and selecting the one which according to the postulated ethical welfare function is best. The solution "exists"; the problem is how to "find" it.'

[3] Agenda is the term used to describe what has to be done, while non-agenda is applied to what the public sector has to avoid, as discussed in Padoa Schioppa and Padoa Schioppa (1984).

2.2. *Positive and negative externalities*

Similar considerations apply to goods that create large negative or positive externalities, in other words goods whose costs or benefits to society cannot be fully internalized by individuals via the price system, with the result that the private costs and benefits of the goods do not coincide with their social costs and benefits. In these circumstances, a non-market interdependence between economic agents arises, which reveals the market inability to perform its function.

Some of the newly emerging needs that have sprung mainly from negative externalities warrant particular attention. We are referring especially to the problems of the environment;[4] this has ceased to be a non-economic good in limitless supply at zero cost that had to be dominated and exploited, and has now become a scarce good that needs protection because it frequently suffers harm.[5] Writing from this new standpoint, Baumol and Oates (1988: 1) recall that

economic agents imposed external costs upon society at large in the form of pollution. With no 'prices' to provide the proper incentives for reduction of polluting activities, the inevitable result was excessive demands on the assimilative capacity of the environment. The obvious solution to the problem was to place an appropriate 'price', in this case a tax, on polluting activities so as to internalize the social costs.

Economic policy-makers in Italy seem less aware than their opposite numbers in other countries that such externalities exist and need to be addressed through effective public action.

A look at unpublished OECD data, collected for us by Pochini (1988), is sufficient to convince us that this is true: whereas some European countries (France, Germany, the Netherlands, Belgium, the United Kingdom) already apply forms of environmental taxation on atmospheric and acoustic pollution and solid waste, in Italy the only environmental emission taxed at present is water.

---

[4] Economic theory links the environmental issue more to the concept of externality than to that of public goods, as the environment always has the property of non-rivalry but not always that of non-excludability.

[5] The dual approach to environment also exists in modern thinking, as shown by the fact that in the early 1970s, precisely when the Club of Rome saw the environment as one of the 'limits to growth', the UN Stockholm Conference and the Council of the EEC were warning of the dangers of environmental exploitation and calling for adequate prevention of further ecological damage.

From a theoretical point of view, there are also two other ways of protecting the environment, which are not necessarily mutually exclusive: the regulation of requirements and prohibitions regarding environmental standards, and the creation of a market in licences or rights to pollute. Given the legal and administrative inclination of Italy's political class, it will come as no surprise to learn that the only environmental protection measures enacted in Italy so far are a series of bureaucratic controls established under various pieces of legislation (ranging from the Galasso Law, which imposed constraints on the use of urban and rural land, to the Merli Law, which introduced uniform, nationwide standards for emissions of each individual water pollutant).

In general, as Stazi (1988: 49) reminds us, 'the environmental standards do nothing to encourage polluters to improve their environmental record, as they block the development of new production and purification processes and permit the completely free discharge of polluting emissions within the set limits'.

More often, however, it is not the regulation of standards but the administrative procedures for achieving them that are open to criticism. In this regard, the analysis of Pochini (1988: 9) states that 'identical emission standards for everybody demonstrates the low efficiency and effectiveness of regulation. They do not, in fact, minimize the total cost to the community of cleaning up pollution.' For this to be a minimum, 'in accordance with the corrective measures adopted, all the firms involved should bear the overall planned reduction in pollution, by equalizing their marginal purification costs, which are certainly not identical'. In other words, adds Pera (1991: 70),

the setting of identical standards for all firms producing a certain type of pollution regardless of their specific characteristics . . . fails to take account of the fact that the cost of reducing pollution may differ widely from one firm to another, so that the cost of uniform standards is higher than necessary. . . . It would be preferable to reduce pollution in sectors where it could be done more cheaply, while permitting greater pollution by firms for which the cost of reduction would be higher.

Hence, only if the regulation of environmental standards complements rather than replaces the other two methods of protecting the environment by economic means is it likely to be efficient and effective, at least in a second-best system. A good example would be the introduction of an environmental tax levied at a uniform rate in proportion to discharges of pollutants.

Another example would be the supervised creation of an artificial market in rights to pollute. This solution, suggested to us by Stazi (1988), is based on the finding (originally made by Coase, 1960) that the failure to internalize the social costs and benefits of externalities is due entirely to high transaction costs: these prevent economic agents from achieving a social optimum that is to their mutual benefit in a private market. The dual nature of the problem is obvious: leaving ethical considerations aside, if a factory discharges waste into the water it harms those who want to swim, but at the same time those who want to swim in pure water harm those who want to use the water for productive purposes.

The state could therefore create a fictitious market by issuing a number of permits to pollute, equal to the predetermined standard for environmental degradation. Each individual (in our metaphor, each swimmer and each firm) would have to purchase pollution rights up to the point at which the marginal cost was equal to the marginal benefit obtained; at that level the resulting pollution would be the amount previously set and the allocation between the users would be optimum. The artificial market created by public intervention would thus internalize the externalities and eliminate the divergence between private and social marginal costs and benefits.

Natural Monopolies

When the philosopher says that moral freedom is compatible with any economic order whatever, he is speaking the truth as far as heroes, thinkers, and anchorites are concerned. These individuals are spiritually and morally free in any economic order, even the most conformist and mortifying. . . . If there are economic orders, such as communism and monopolistic capitalism, that tend by their very nature to reduce men to mere instruments, the meanest links in an iron chain of work and production, if these economic orders tend, by their invincible character, to stamp a uniformity on all men, to make them wake up, move, enter certain places of work that might be regarded more as places of punishment, always at the same time and to perform the same acts, why claim that moral freedom can prosper in any economic order?

(L. Einaudi, *Tema per gli storici dell'economia: Dell'anacoretismo economico*, 1937)

3

Contestable Markets and Government Failures

3.1. Contestable markets

Although economic-policy measures in favour of pure public goods and goods with high externalities are limited in Italy, the same cannot be said of so-called natural monopoly markets, where declining average and marginal costs made possible by increasing returns to scale and scope inhibit competitive market solutions. Indeed, if firms were to set prices equal to their marginal costs, which in the above-mentioned circumstances are necessarily lower than their average costs, they would make losses rather than profits.

In Italy the enlarged public-sector and state-controlled companies appear to exert strong direct and indirect influence over prices and volumes in those markets with the characteristics just described: from local or national surface-transport networks to air transport, from telecommunications to the postal service and electricity. The supposed existence of a natural monopoly in these public utilities has led to the creation of public legal monopolies that hitherto have not been brought into question in Italy, unlike other countries.

The close correlation established in the past in Italy between natural monopolies and public legal monopolies is open to at least four critical observations. First, the existence of a natural monopoly should not suggest the need to create a public legal monopoly if the natural monopoly is contestable, as in such a situation private agents would independently achieve a second-best social optimum. Secondly, even if the natural monopoly were not contestable, the advisability and scale of public intervention should be evaluated in the light of possible government failures, which may make it preferable to allow a market to operate with little public interference. Thirdly, even if competition *in* the market were destructive,[1] it would be necessary to maintain competition *for* the market

[1] 'Destructive competition' is present if (1) in the market the most efficient production technique entails high fixed costs, so that there is a difference between

of a non-contestable natural monopoly. Finally, even where a non-contestable natural monopoly called for public intervention, such intervention might conceivably be carried out through a regulated private firm rather than through a public corporation.

Taking the first aspect, increasing returns to scale and scope[2] are a necessary but not sufficient condition for supposing that an unregulated private firm would exploit its natural monopoly to extract the maximum surplus from consumers. In point of fact, its pricing policy depends on the degree of contestability of the market, which in turn is determined by the potential competition from new enterprises. Hence, where the natural monopoly is contestable, prices are set at a level at which it is not advantageous for an outside entrepreneur to enter the market, because he would make a loss by undercutting the incumbent as prices would barely cover long-run average costs.

In this regard, economic theory recalls that it is not so much the scale of investment that constitutes a potential barrier to entry but the fact that it gives rise to sunk costs, which are irrecoverable. In particular, where a network is involved, investment is certainly irreversible, so that competition would be inappropriate as it would become destructive.

3.2. Government failures

The second caveat concerning the link between natural and legal public monopolies stems from concern that even if the non-contestability of a market suggests the need for public intervention, it still has to be demonstrated that this is a better or even optimum solution for the consumer, from the point of view of both static and dynamic efficiency. We are reminded of this by Pera (1988*b* and 1991) in various research papers produced for our group.

In static terms, the costs of legal public monopolies may be high. First, they might induce some inefficiency, since the profit motive is removed and the moralizing effect of a non-soft budget constraint short-and long-term operating costs; (2) demand is highly variable, so that firms in the market must 'on average' be overcapitalized; and (3) in periods of strong demand operators from other sectors can enter the market. Competition could then depress prices to a level below that required to ensure the optimum amortization of fixed plant, and the market, if left to itself, would not allow the most efficient technique to prevail (cf. Kahn, 1971).

[2] More precisely, in technical terms one should speak of the subadditivity of the cost function.

is absent; secondly, legal public monopolies potentially distort resource allocation if they favour certain production factors over others or if they do not apply criteria of incentive compatibility that encourage optimality in the presence of asymmetric information; finally, the country pays dearly for economic policies that in theory are invoked to resolve a problem of a non-contestable natural monopoly but which in fact are motivated more by the desire to serve vested interests than by any concern with general ones.

From a dynamic point of view, legal public monopolies may weaken the innovative drive that reduces average and marginal costs, due to their bureaucratic management; moreover, in the forced absence of potential competitors, they make it difficult to perceive changes in the degree of market contestability induced by increases in the scale of production or by technological changes.

These types of static and dynamic government failures and the forms of contestability of natural monopolies discussed above explain many foreign countries' experiments with privatization and deregulation aimed at increasing the role of the market in the supply of goods and services that in the past were provided by a public legal monopoly.

These experiments, in sectors where competition has been partially re-established, usually show an improvement in productive efficiency, which in general is reflected in lower costs. They also have significant positive effects from a dynamic point of view by generating an incentive to widen the range of services and introduce technological innovations.

Similar assumptions also apply to Italy; a number of case studies, such as the one on the cement industry carried out for us by Nahmijas (1988), show that in sectors where public corporations and private enterprises operate side by side, the former are generally less efficient than the latter.

This lower efficiency may be attributed to a number of causes, but not necessarily to the existence of social objectives, as efficiency is measured in terms of the level of costs for given economic results. It goes without saying that a public corporation can continue to operate in a competitive sector only if it has the capacity to adapt to the principles and practices applying in that market. Otherwise there would be justification in the view of those who hold that public involvement in such sectors should be drastically reduced in favour of widespread privatization.

It is therefore well to specify the conditions that must be met if the efficiency criterion is to impinge really heavily on public corporations operating in sectors where competition actually or potentially exists. First, their access to the product market should not be favoured (or restricted) by barriers, protective measures, or preferential conditions. Secondly, their access to finance and intermediate inputs should be set on a competitive basis. Finally, public corporations should be given complete freedom to take technical decisions, so as to bear full responsibility for their operating results.

3.3. Should we liberalize natural monopoly markets?

From the point of view of Italian economic policy, it is important to understand which natural monopolies operate in a contestable market (so that public intervention appears not only unnecessary but actually harmful owing to the artificial barriers it erects to potential competition) and in what circumstances government failures in dealing with natural monopolies cause the market greater harm than the ills it was supposed to cure. Both cases call for significant deregulation or privatization.

As we shall see, we shall raise more questions than we can answer, and other countries' experience with liberalization will not always help us to analyse the situation in Italy (cf. Pera, 1991). In the telecommunications sector, for example, what do we learn from privatization and deregulation in other countries, especially the United States and the United Kingdom? As the dynamic effects of reintroducing some competition into the telecommunications market appear to be clearly positive everywhere (and a key factor in the decision to liberalize by normally recalcitrant countries, such as Japan), should we conclude that this natural monopoly is contestable, or that the greater efficiency achieved in the sector indicates a previous government failure? But does not the experience of these countries also show that considerable, perhaps higher, regulatory problems continue to arise even after privatization, because of the danger that the very existence of highly dominant enterprises will neutralize the effort to instil greater competition (Vickers and Wright, 1989a)? Does a new problem emerge after deregulation with regard to the standardization of equipment and transmission modes, which so far has remained unresolved?

The electricity industry is a non-contestable natural monopoly, but would it not be possible to hive off some parts that do not properly have anything to do with a network? Although it seems inevitable that electricity distribution will be dominated by a single supplier, would it not be beneficial to introduce competition into electricity generation and transmission?

Is the postal-services market really non-contestable, and is it correct to speak of a 'postal network'? Does not the popularity of private couriers serving both domestic and international destinations, local dispatch riders, and broad substitutes for the postal service, such as fax and electronic mail, prove the contestability of the market or the existence of government failures? Would not the user be better served by a competitive market bound only to maintain the secrecy of correspondence, the primary original argument in favour of nationalizing the service?

Although the rail-transport sector is predominantly non-contestable, would it be conceivable for a public agency to operate only the network and to lease the rolling stock to private carriers to transport freight and passengers over medium and long distances? Would the coexistence of the state and the market be sustainable in this sector, considering that only a public operator would have the obligation to provide a service over unprofitable lines?

Is the air-transport sector contestable, given the relative ease with which aircraft routes can be changed, especially in a market that now extends beyond the borders of European nation states? Is such an ease sufficient for contestability or is it not necessary to ensure a free access (or a differently regulated access) to airports' slots as well, so that the incumbents are really subject to actual and potential competition as happened after deregulation in the USA? And how is contestability affected by competition between close substitutes, such as high-speed rail transport and air transport within a small country such as Italy? But would a deregulated air-transport sector adequately meet safety requirements or at least the need for complete and symmetric information, which a market left entirely to its own devices may well not guarantee?

It is not always easy to give a documented reply to these questions. By way of example, we present one here that was formulated within our reseach group with regard to the advisability of a partial liberalization of the Italian air-transport sector. As Pandolfelli (1991: 247–8) reminds us, a recent study by Assoutenti shows that domestic and international regulation have reduced the development of international air connections, especially within Europe, for which there is unmet demand from business travellers. The study indicates, among other things, that some of the largest cities in Northern Italy have direct flights to an average of fourteen other European cities, whereas other cities in Europe with a comparable population and level of economic development have connections to an average of thirty-two cities. . . . The Assoutenti case is also supported by other considerations. First, the partial liberalization of interregional and international air services from and to Italy, realized in the second half of the 1980s has been followed by a substantial increase in flights to Italy by foreign carriers (from sixteen routes in 1986 to fifty-eight in 1988, of which only 30 per cent are operated by Italian carriers); secondly, many foreign-airline companies immediately exploited the greater capacity offered in Italy by significantly increasing their share of total seats (Air France increased its share from 44.9 to 48.1 per cent, British Airways from 42.9 to 48.8 per cent and Iberia reached almost 55 per cent). Moreover, between 1987 and 1988 the main foreign carriers increased the pairs of national and Italian cities they served by around 24 per cent (from sixty-six to eighty-two, whereas Alitalia increased the number of cities served by 11 per cent over the same period).

One could add that, since 1988, the EEC has introduced a number of changes in the European air-transport legislation with the purpose of promoting actual (not potential) competition in the access to the market and in air fares. By early 1993 the fare and access liberalization process should be completed, with the partial exception of cabotage (which refers to routes within a single EEC country). The implications for the Italian flag carrier (Alitalia) of this liberalization process are already evident, although partial. As indicated by Ajmone Marsan and Padoa Schioppa (1992: 19) when examining the price-setting by Alitalia within the EEC in 1990, 'it is possible to observe how an average fare reduction, under the pressure of competition, takes place through a downward widening of the fare spectrum with a range that is larger, the more elastic the demand. In fact, fare variability is higher on tourist routes and wherever competition is harsher. On the other hand, on other medium-range routes, the impact of competition is strongly reduced or even non-existent. In non-EEC Europe, typical signals of regulated markets are observed: a higher number of carriers on a route usually betrays the route's attractiveness and therefore leads not to a reduction but to a rise in fares thanks to a *de facto* collusion between airlines.'

4

Competition for the Market and Regulated Private Enterprises

4.1. Competition for the market

Re-examining the problem of the link between natural and legal public monopolies, we should add that even where public intervention is preferable to counteract market failures due to a non-contestable natural monopoly, safeguards to prevent any abuse of a dominant position remain of vital importance. Such abuse could arise, for example, if a network operator claimed the right to compete with other enterprises in the provision of services over the network, either directly or via associated firms. Moreover, the practice of exclusive network operation should be subjected to periodic review, because network economies depend to a large extent on the size of the market; as the market expands, the co-existence of several competing networks may become compatible with economic efficiency.

Where a legal public monopoly proves to be justified, identifying ways of forcing the monopolistic enterprise to operate efficiently poses a further problem. Certain automatic mechanisms that ensure some form of potential competition appear to have an important role to play in this respect. We shall examine two of these here.

We will look first at the advisability of establishing a certain level of virtual competition by liberalizing the production of goods and services for personal consumption. The possibility for firms or groups to produce, for their own exclusive use, goods and services subject to a legal public monopoly (energy, for example) would provide a powerful spur to efficiency on the part of the monopolist. Moreover, the legal monopolist's right to protection would be limited by his ability to keep costs down at least to the level at which an enterprise could produce the same good or service itself without the advantage of the economies of scale or scope enjoyed by the monopolist.

We are thinking secondly of the possibility of introducing

competition for the market, especially in the case of relatively small legal public monopolies. This could be done, for example, by awarding the franchise to supply a given service for a certain number of years to the firm that undertook to offer consumers the best terms. This method would give rise to considerable problems, however (asymmetry of information between enterprises already holding the franchise and those competing for it, the possible discouragement of investment by firms concerned at the possibility of losing the franchise in the future, difficulties in drafting technically complete contracts), so that in practice it would be suitable only for very simple services. The more efficient techniques involving tenders, procurements concessions, auctions, or various forms of franchise-bidding will therefore have to continue to be studied very closely.

4.2. *Public corporations or regulated private enterprises?*

Ultimately, even when it is decided that public intervention in natural monopoly markets is appropriate, there still remain two options with regard to the form such intervention should take, the choice between a public corporation and a regulated private enterprise—and the preference between incentive and dirigistic methods of control.

As far as the former problem is concerned, the choice between public corporation and regulated private enterprise stems from two different considerations, one relating to productive efficiency and the other to relations with the regulatory body.

There is a general (though doubtful) presumption that a private enterprise, even one subject to regulation, is more efficient owing to the greater control exercised by shareholders. Indeed, other countries have begun to reassess the role of public enterprises in managing natural monopolies and have moved towards regulated private enterprises. This shift is currently justified by the consideration of the efficiency implications of the different forms of ownership.

In addition, it is widely believed that public enterprises can more easily circumvent the constraints imposed by regulators. Given the difficulty of this issue, it is best to focus on the relationship between the regulator and the regulated. As a starting point, it seems appropriate to distinguish the setting of political objectives and control activities, which are the responsibility of the regulator, from the attainment of those objectives in accordance with criteria of efficiency, which is the responsibility of the regulated. The distinction is theoretically relevant, even though in practice it is blurred in countries where public enterprises play an important role in the production of public-utility services, that is to say in the majority of European countries. Historically, it seems that because public enterprises have a better knowledge of the market and production techniques than the regulators, they manage to set their own charges and determine the volume of output, while the regulatory body is left with few powers of supervision. It is generally believed that this privileged situation often leads public enterprises to pursue their own objectives, for example to the benefit of their managers and staff, at the expense of efficiency and the public interest.

As a consequence, regulatory arrangements are gradually being strengthened in a number of countries, often accompanied by a restructuring of the management of enterprises responsible for natural monopolies, in order to make a better separation between regulation and the setting of objectives on the one hand and the provision of instruments and production on the other.

It should therefore come as no surprise that this reshaping of the relationship between the regulatory body and the regulated enterprise is taking place in parallel with a growing preference for regulated private enterprises.

The choice between dirigistic and incentive methods appears to have many implications, especially for the level of charges as well as the quality of services provided by non-contestable natural monopolies. In particular, a number of pricing techniques have been devised to encourage regulated enterprises to behave properly. Among these, the proposal to regulate not the level of charges but their growth rate on the basis of the expected rate of increase in productivity and costs appears to be fairly successful. The device in question is the RPI-X or price-cap formula.[1] The regulatory body

---

[1] As explained by Vickers and Yarrow (1988: 206), RPI − X means that within a multi-product natural monopoly 'the price index for a basket of services increases by no more than the rate of general price inflation − X'. This is because the formula is a proxy for the welfare objective of achieving equality, in a dynamic sense, between the price of the basket and the natural monopolist's average cost. If the rate of price inflation is approximately equal to the rate of growth in nominal input costs, X stands for the rate of growth of productivity due to technological innovations or

forecasts the rate of growth in the operator's productivity and then permits it to raise charges by the targeted rate of change in input costs less the rate of productivity growth. The operator therefore makes a net gain if it is able to increase productivity by more than forecast; if it fails to meet the forecast it incurs a relative loss. Experiments in this direction in the United States and the United Kingdom provide significant examples of price-setting based on incentive methods.

At the same time, the procedure for charging for the services of non-contestable natural monopolies must be transparent. The operator should provide users with a detailed record of consumption, as is the case with telephone bills in many parts of the world (but not in Italy), and should be obliged to pay some form of compensation to users who have received substandard service. From this point of view too, more effective control would protect the public interest by preventing the operator's inefficiency from being 'compensated' by high charges and/or poor standards of service.

Relating these questions to the situation in Italy, we note with Pera (1988*b*, 1991) that Italy lags well behind other countries in the reform of the system for regulating non-contestable natural monopolies when it comes to strengthening the supervisory agencies, the use of incentive methods to achieve the objectives, and the choice of regulated private enterprises rather than public agencies.

In particular, Italy has always left the operation of natural legal monopolies to public corporations and has never used incentives to attain collective objectives; moreover, the regulatory bodies are very weak by comparison with the companies they regulate, whether they be public enterprises such as the State Railways and ENEL or state-controlled companies holding an exclusive franchise. The regulatory bodies are ministerial agencies that for the most part check legitimacy rather than merit and which in any case often have neither the tools nor the skill to make a serious evaluation of the regulated companies' production, investment, and pricing policies. Moreover, the control over pricing policies that was given to the Interministerial Committee on Prices (CIP) in 1984 relates primarily to the effect on the inflation rate, the CIP being ill-equipped to tackle questions of micro-economic efficiency.

changes in demand; indeed, an upward shift in demand allows, *ceteris paribus*, for a decrease in average costs, simply because the cost function is subadditive for a natural monopolist.

In the light of the wealth of experience in other countries, a system should therefore be created that has sufficient human and material resources to continuously monitor the operations of public corporations or regulated private enterprise; this could be done by modifying the structure and responsibilities of the secretariat of the CIP so that it became a technical body for supervising charges. The supervisory procedures would have to be radically revised, replacing the present *ad hoc* investigations by semi-automatic regulatory mechanisms.

5
Utility Charges and the Quality of Public Services

5.1. Public-utility charges

In setting public-utility charges, it is important to avoid on the one hand the Scylla of prices held excessively low for fear of competition, which would have to be avoided if it threatened to become destructive, and on the other the Charybdis of prices kept excessively high by the absence of competition.

From an allocative point of view, charges for natural monopolies should as a rule cover average long-term costs. If the natural monopoly is non-contestable, the problem of pricing is the same, whether the services are provided by a public corporation or a regulated private company, whereas the market will achieve similar results if the monopoly is contestable. The relationship between prices and average costs of public utilities is less clear if public corporations in the market of the non-contestable natural monopoly are causing specific distortions due to government failures.

The theory itself presents many ambiguities, but the situation in Italy in this regard is even more difficult to determine, as it is complicated by a number of factors. First, the prices of many types of good are administered or monitored in Italy, and not only those in which there is a natural monopoly.[1] Secondly, administered or

[1] According to definitions laid down by ISTAT, the prices subject to control (sometimes called 'political' prices) are, besides public-utility charges, those referring to administered 'goods and services, rents and monitored goods. The component indices contained within these categories are the following: administered prices—on milk, salt, sugar, tobacco, bread, kitchen matches, wax matches, some medicines; public-utility charges—on postal communications, financial services, rail transport, railway sleeping-cars, telephone communications, domestic air transport, lake and lagoon shipping, bus services, urban transport, motorway tolls, taxis, car insurance, furniture removals, funeral transport, museum entrance charges, electricity, mains gas, drinking-water, radio and television licences, hotel rooms, camp sites, lotteries and football pools; monitored prices—on pasta, beef, bottled gas, LPG for vehicles, kerosene, heating and diesel oil, non-prescription medicines, detergents (for washing machines, washing by hand, dishwashers, dishwashing by hand, delicate fabrics), laundry soap, super-grade petrol, regular-grade petrol, daily newspapers. Unregulated goods and services are all other items included in the ISTAT consumer price basket.

monitored prices are not based exclusively on considerations of allocative efficiency aimed at reducing or even eliminating monopolistic distortions. Distributive motives lead the authorities to set average charges and those for particular categories of user without reference to cost, and often without any analytical basis, as will be argued in section 18.2. Macro-economic objectives—in particular, the control of inflation and fluctuations in relative prices—may lead to tariff changes based on neither allocative nor distributive criteria. Italian economic policy-makers seem to watch the relationship between consumer prices and administered or monitored prices particularly closely and therefore control the latter mainly with a view to combating inflation. This is revealed, for example, by the evidence collated in Fig. 5.1, drawn from Ministero del Bilancio e della Programmazione Economica (1989).

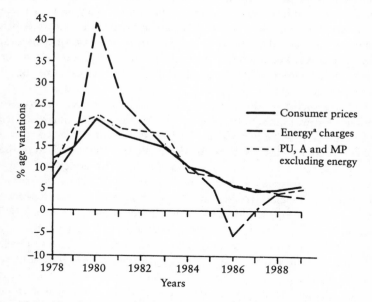

Fɪɢ. 5.1. Trends in consumer prices, energy, public-utility charges (PU), administered (A) and monitored prices (MP)

[a] Goods and services included in the PU, A, and MP basket and associated with the energy sector (electricity, mains and bottled gas, petrol, LPG, heating oil and diesel fuel, kerosene).

Source: Ministero del Bilancio e della Programmazione Economica (1989).

At the analytical level, the link between the setting of utility charges and the dynamics of consumer prices has been studied in various papers produced within our research group. Rubino and Visco (1987) show, through an examination of sectoral inputs and outputs, that the full effect of a change in utility charges is around one and a half times as large as the direct impact alone. Cuckierman and Padoa Schioppa (1986) note that in Italy variations in the price of one of the goods of greatest public concern in the sectoral input–output table,[2] namely energy, are responsible for substantial shifts both in the general price level and in the structure of relative prices, given differences in energy inputs in the various branches of activity.

Public control of the variability of relative prices and the control of inflation thus become joint objectives of macro-economic pricing policy and are at least partly divorced from other micro-economic goals of an allocative or redistributive kind. Policy-makers therefore confine themselves to identifying the tariff adjustments which, for a given desired increase in revenue from the sale of a natural-monopoly service, minimize the impact on the economy's production costs, which are particularly high in the case of public transport and electricity supply.

Alternatively, in the absence of optimal allocative criteria for pricing natural-monopoly services, the public sector can set prices with the sole objective of 'cushioning' shocks of various kinds. A paper prepared for us by Guiso and Visco (1987) indicates that utility charges could be used to counter the price effects of temporary and unforeseen disturbances coming only from the supply side; other policies would have to be employed to tackle similar disturbances from the demand side. If one wanted to select sub-optimal rules to link public-utility charges to unregulated prices, in a context of uniform-wage indexation, a rule of 'no feedback' should be preferred to a rule of proportional charges. It should not be forgotten, however, that if the result of this approach is that utility charges do not cover average costs, the sector will accumulate growing deficits that may eventually become unsustainable.

---

[2] This records exchanges of goods and factors of production according to sectors of origin (rows) and sectors of destination (columns).

5.2. *The case of telephone and electricity charges*

Let us now move on to examine the system of charges in certain Italian case studies of natural legal monopolies, beginning with the telephone monopoly analysed for us by Pupillo (1988*b*, 1991).

Despite the fact that the number of telephone subscribers in Italy more than doubled between 1973 and 1986, telephone ownership in relation to the population remains far lower in Italy than in other EEC countries (33.3 per cent, compared with 45.7 per cent in Germany, 44 per cent in France, and 39.7 per cent in the United Kingdom), and displays wide geographic differences. Indeed, the regional figures range from 65 telephones per 100 inhabitants in Liguria to 27 per 100 in Calabria, with the South about ten points below the national average.

More generally, possession of the telephone varies in Italy according to the type of household, determined by the level of education and age of the head of the household and the number of family members. From the point of view of socio-economic and demographic characteristics, the critical categories as far as telephone ownership is concerned appear to be single persons aged 65 or over and families with incomes of less than Lit. 1,500,000 a month.

International comparisons of the level of telephone charges must be interpreted with caution, given the limitations of the comparative methods usually adopted, but they do show that in Italy monthly equipment rentals for residential users are among the lowest in Europe, while installation fees and long-distance call charges for business users are in the medium-to-high range and international call charges the highest.

Table 5.1 shows that there is no reciprocity as far as international call charges are concerned; despite bilateral agreements within Europe, it is almost always more expensive to call a foreign country from Italy than vice versa. Moreover, in the last decade revenue from the telephone service has increased at an annual average rate of about 20 per cent, far exceeding the average growth in traffic, which has risen by little more than 5 per cent.

The analysis carried out by Pupillo (1988*a*, 1988*b*, 1991) on the cost structure of the service provided by the telephone companies SIP and ASST demonstrates that, whereas costs and revenues for local traffic are broadly in balance, there is marked cross-subsidization

TABLE 5.1. International telephone-call charges, 1987 (cost per minute in Lit., net of taxes, at average 1987 exchange rates)

Country	From Italy	To Italy
Austria	1,219	898
Belgium	1,398	1,157
Denmark	1,398	702
Finland	1,604	n.a.
France	1,219	971
Germany (Fed. Rep.)	1,219	830
Greece	1,219	872
Ireland (Republic)	1,604	1,485
Netherlands	1,398	929
Norway	1,604	1,137
Portugal	n.a.	1,470
Spain	1,398	1,415
Sweden	1,604	1,095
Switzerland	1,219	1,044
United Kingdom	1,398	776
USA	3,629	n.a.
AT&T	n.a.	1,965
MCI	n.a.	1,861
US Sprint	n.a.	1,764

Source: Pupillo (1991).

between the revenue from long-distance calls and the costs of installing and maintaining the basic telephone service. Many foreign observers consider the degree of cross-subsidization between different services and types of user to be excessive in comparison with other European countries; efforts to reduce it are being made not only by official institutions such as the EEC (which made suggestions in this vein in its Green Paper on telecommunications) and the Ministry of Posts and Telecommunications (Ministero delle Poste e Telecomunicazioni, 1985) in view of the creation of the single telecommunications market in 1992, but also by the market itself, where the development of private networks by large users and the use of satellites are exerting pressure for a rebalancing of telephone charges.

According to Pupillo (1991: 173),

the hypothesis on which one should work is therefore that of a scale of charges that takes account of the present regional differences in telephone ownership and reduces the present disparity between charges for access to the network and those for long-distance and international calls. Instead of giving a blanket subsidy, pricing criteria should be identified that would benefit primarily those areas and categories of user considered critical from the point of view of access to the telephone network and would encourage the use of the telephone instead of penalizing it. This can be done by making the scale of charges more flexible according to type of user.

The estimates given with regard to installation costs, despite being incomplete because they relate only to provincial capitals, provide useful indications for identifying particular groups that might be offered greater subsidies.

A number of measures could be taken to encourage the use of the telephone, such as: (a) reduction of international and long-distance call charges, given the growing demand for such services and the potential new demand that different price conditions would generate: since 1981 long-distance traffic has grown by an average of 7.5 per cent a year and international traffic by 13.5 per cent (STET, 1988); (b) wider use of metered charging for local calls. Since telecommunication costs seem to depend less and less on distance and increasingly on the duration of the call, charges should reflect this more strongly in order to generate revenue for the basic service.

The other case-study of charges for an Italian natural monopoly examined in greater detail in the course of our research relates to electricity. As Giordano and Rubino (1991) remind us, the present scale of charges is the result of a chain of developments that for convenience can be divided into three phases: the period from the end of the Second World War to nationalization of the industry, from 1962 to the first oil shock, and from 1973–4 to the present, characterized by the introduction of the 'thermal surcharge.' Apart from this, one of the most important innovations in electricity pricing policy in the 1980s appears to have been the introduction of multiple time-band charges for industrial users based on peak-load pricing criteria to accentuate the degressive nature of the scale of charges.

As with telephone charges, allocative criteria are overlaid or replaced by redistributive objectives; until the beginning of the 1970s ENEL's decisions appear to have been guided by social considerations aimed at sustaining the real income of particular groups of users.

After the first oil crisis, however, ENEL's pricing policy was adjusted in an attempt to reconcile the pursuit of social policy objectives with the elimination of the public-enterprise losses. During this phase electricity charges were raised and the entire structure of charges was overhauled. This firmly established the binomial nature of the two-tier tariff structure; there was a fixed portion—a capacity charge calculated on the user's plant capacity in kilowatt-hours—intended in principle to cover capacity costs, in other words the fixed costs arising from the existence of generating plant, and a variable portion based on consumption (in some cases broken down into a number of bands) to cover usage costs, in other words the variable costs of electricity generation and distribution.

Charges are also differentiated according to the main characteristics of demand, such as the voltage and capacity required, the duration of capacity utilization and the consumption time-bands, with a breakdown according to major categories of consumption (public lighting, domestic consumption, industrial, commercial, and agricultural consumption).

The change in the level and structure of electricity charges had a significant impact on electricity demand, as noted by Giordano and Rubino (1991: 218).

Contrary to some expectations, however, this effect is greater in the case of household demand than in that of industrial demand. Moreover, in recent years there has been a slight increase in the 'relative tariff' effect in the industrial sector, where the restructuring of electricity charges has been more far-reaching.

The main lesson for pricing policy that can be deduced from our investigation is therefore that it would be beneficial if pricing criteria aimed at modulating demand were extended to a wider range of users. . . .

Recent policy changes by ENEL appear to indicate moves in this direction; in the Report on the Annual Accounts for 1987, the proposal to extend multiple time-bands to further categories of user is justified on the grounds of the benefits that modification of the production processes of heavy electricity users may bring by encouraging them to restrict their consumption at times of high electricity demand.

This more innovative pricing policy appears to be consistent with the increased importance placed on energy conservation.

Energy saving is becoming a primary objective in the changed framework for energy policy in Italy following the rejection of nuclear energy in the 1987 referendum, pending the possibility that the Single European Market after 1992 will oblige the country to have second thoughts on the subject. Among the main forms of primary energy, nuclear energy entails very high externalities that certainly extend beyond the borders of the nation state and possibly even those of the EEC by reason of its characteristics and the associated risks; in an integrated Europe it is therefore no longer possible for policy on energy matters, especially with regard to nuclear energy and energy saving, to be decided at national level, as has already been indicated elsewhere (Padoa Schioppa, 1990e).

5.3. The case of quality standards for railways, postal services, and telephones

The volume and charges of services provided by legal natural monopolies cannot be analysed without also examining the question of productivity and quality of public utilities. As we shall seek to show, productivity and standard of service are closely interconnected although they remain logically distinct, as the former relates to the efficiency of production and the latter to the extent to which the product meets users' needs.

Little economic research has been carried out in Italy on either of these dimensions of the problem. Exceptions to this rule are the studies of the Italian situation by Nomisma (1987), Cananzi (1988), and FORMEZ (1987), which identify four areas of more acute inefficiency in the services provided by public utilities: air and rail transport, telecommunications, and the postal service. In the words of Nomisma (1987: 132–4),

trends in labour productivity in five branches of public utilities provided for the market . . . show that productivity growth is generally lower in Italy than in other countries, but also that the disparity differs widely from one branch to another. The largest differentials to our disadvantage were recorded in 1985 in air transport (70 points in relation to the sixteen main IATA companies), rail transport (between 37 points in relation to Spain and 20 points in relation to Germany) and telecommunications (38 points in relation to France). The disparity is less marked in the case of the postal service (ranging from a maximum of 21 points in relation to the United Kingdom to an advantage of around 1 point in relation to France) and electricity generation and distribution, where Italy comes midway between France and the United Kingdom.

The differences between branches relate not only to the scale of productivity disadvantages but also to their origins. Taking a long-term view, we can distinguish three cases in which Italy's poor productivity is the result of (1) a sort of employment hysteresis that prevents employment being reduced in line with the level of activity (as in the case of the State Railways); (2) the adoption of staffing policies that provide for the rate of increase in the number of employees to equal or exceed the growth in traffic (as at Alitalia in the 1970s and in the postal service throughout the period), and which therefore implicitly accept stagnating or declining productivity; and (3) differences in the mix of activities demanded by the market, which cause demand for different services provided by one and the same producer to grow at different rates (as for the number of consumers and the volume of energy consumed in the case of ENEL and for the number of telephone subscribers and the volume of traffic in that of the telecommunications industry) and which therefore lead to differences between the countries observed.

In more recent years signs of an improvement have begun to emerge in those branches where an explicit decision to stabilize employment levels has made it possible to raise productivity at rates close to the rate of growth in output; among the branches where productivity growth used to lag behind, this is certainly true of Alitalia, which has reduced employment slightly but constantly since 1983, and of Italcable, SIP, and ASST, where employment has remained more or less stable since 1984.

In the other branches, however, there is no sign of a reversal of the trend; the contraction in the input of labour at the State Railways since 1983 is less than proportional to the decline in the volume of traffic, while the number of staff employed by the postal service continues to increase at a consistently higher rate than the volume of traffic.

As far as standards of service are concerned, the report by Nomisma (1987) adds that the majority of public-monopoly producers do not even bother to establish adequate means of measurement. The gross inadequacies that sometimes come to light are therefore a symptom of an endemic undervaluation of this dimension of the production of public services.

Partly in response to these considerations, we aimed to gather further empirical evidence with regard to the quality of public utilities provided by natural legal monopolies, with particular reference to the railways, the postal service and the telephone service.

At the State Railways, the most serious problems of quality appear to relate to the organization of the service and its utilization.

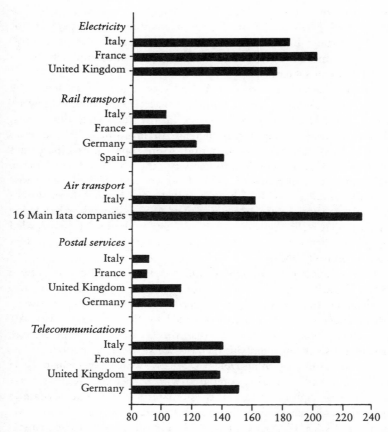

Fɪɢ. 5.2. International comparison of labour productivity in five public-utility services, 1985 (1970 = 100)

Source: Nomisma (1987).

On the basis of information drawn from the Ministry of Transport (Ministero dei Trasporti, 1988) and from Patrizii and Zollo (1985), we consider the first alarming item to be the fact that in 1987 as much as 72.7 per cent of the State Railways' total current revenue of Lit. 14,976.5 billion consisted of transfer payments from the Treasury, whereas only 21.3 per cent came from the sale of the service to users. Fifteen years earlier the proportions had been virtually the reverse—28.3 and 63.5 per cent respectively. The structure of expenditure, on the other hand, remained unchanged over the fifteen-year period, with staff costs accounting for 73 per cent of total spending; in 1987 the railways employed a total of 215,650 staff, plus another 1,750 recruited in that year under publicly subsidized training schemes.

Another sign of the crisis in the rail service is the fact that value added per employee rose by only 7.7 percentage points between 1972 and 1985 and by 4.7 points in the following two years, despite a nearly fivefold real increase in investment by the State Railways over the fifteen-year period. More sophisticated indicators of technical or economic productivity (the former, for example, being measured in terms of units of rail traffic per employee) show an even smaller rise in labour productivity. Furthermore, absenteeism was running at 11.35 per cent in 1987; although it has fallen in recent years, it appears to be on a par with the levels recorded by private firms during their most difficult period between the first and second oil shocks.

Excess capacity is substantial and has risen over the last fifteen years. Capacity utilization in passenger services, expressed as the ratio of demand (the number of passenger-kilometres travelled) to supply (the number of seat-kilometres provided by the Railways), was 38.5 per cent in 1987; this was lower than the 1972 level of 40.2 per cent, despite a rise of four points in the last two years of the period.

The situation regarding freight services—which represent only 35 per cent of rail transport, compared with 65 per cent for passenger services—is slightly better in absolute terms and in its dynamics over time; the capacity–utilization rate was 58.8 per cent in 1987, compared with 47.6 per cent in 1972. The substantial excess capacity implicit in these figures can certainly not be ascribed mainly to the need to cater for peak demand; it is due primarily to waste, which could be drastically reduced by reorganizing the service, a process that may have already begun in the 1990s.

Train speeds and delays in relation to published arrival times are the most important quality indicators we examined. Here too, it is not so much the mediocre level of service that is striking but the deterioration over the last fifteen years. Average journey speeds, which almost invariably are below 100 kilometres per hour, were often lower in 1987 than they had been in 1972. Average delays are about seven minutes, twelve minutes in the case of mainline trains.

International comparisons reveal why the Italian rail service is regarded as overstaffed and inefficient; if the number of staff per kilometre of line in Italy in 1986 is taken to be 100, the United Kingdom manages with 77, Germany with 74, and France with 50, while an index of economic labour productivity with Italy as the base 100 shows the United Kingdom on 146, Germany on 176, and France on 193.

The parallels between the railways and the situation in the postal service are rather striking. The common opinion that, here too, overstaffing and low productivity are not the least of the causes of poor service seems to be borne out by the figures and analysis published by the Post and Telecommunications Ministry itself.

According to the latest information available (see Direzione Centrale dei Servizi Postali (1988) and Onofri *et al.* (1987)), in 1987 a letter posted in Milan to an address in Italy took an average of 8 days to be delivered; a letter addressed to Rome took just as long if it was posted in a provincial capital, but 9.3 days if it was posted in a smaller town. All the quality indicators for the Italian postal service have deteriorated over the years and are worse than those for many other countries, such as the United Kingdom and Germany, where three-quarters of all letters were delivered within a day.

In the judgement of the Post and Telecommunications Ministry itself, the combination of poor service and low productivity, in both absolute and comparative terms, and the deterioration over time are attributable to three factors. First, the poor professional standard of the staff, which is too large overall and irrationally deployed owing to internal rigidities and the absence of sufficient wage incentives. Secondly, the virtual absence of managerial skills, computerization, and personnel-management techniques necessary to the scale and importance of the postal service. Thirdly, institutional constraints imposed from outside the Ministry that ultimately cause difficulties inside (e.g. the refusal of public-transport firms to carry mailbags following the regionalization of public transportation).

This analysis is extremely significant, not only because it constitutes a clear admission of government failures by a public enterprise that it has always been thought should be entrusted with a natural and legal monopoly, but also because in all probability it can be extended to many other cases of poor public services produced in similar circumstances.

In the case of the telephone service in Italy, our evaluation is not very different from those set out above with regard to the railways and the postal service, in spite of the fact that the labour input is less important in telecommunications. According to official data from STET (1988), quality has declined for a fairly long period in many respects, with an acute state of crisis in the late 1970s and early 1980s; in recent years, as the telephone company recovered its financial health, a massive effort was made to improve standards of service; however international comparisons, where they can be made, show that the quality of the telephone service in Italy is below that provided in the other European countries except Spain and Greece.

One need only look at the average time a subscriber has to wait to have a telephone installed. In Italy it took an average of three months from the time of application in 1968, but ten months at the beginning of the 1980s and five months in 1986; by contrast, in 1986 it took an average of less than four months for a telephone to be installed in Austria, just over three in the Netherlands, two weeks in Belgium, France, Germany, and Switzerland and a matter of days in the United Kingdom. As indicated by SIP (1992), since 1989 the Italian situation has improved. Installation waiting time declined from 72 days on average in 1989 to 17 days in 1991. However, the latter figure confirms that the quality of the telephone service in Italy is still below the best European standard, as in the UK 83 per cent of applications in 1991 were satisfied within 8 days.

PART III

The Modern Reasons for Market Failures

It is necessary to distinguish between actions and actors. If the actions are not good, industriousness on the part of actors will be valueless, but if actions give grounds for reasonable hope, good actors can certainly be found. . . . If it were not for an unforgivable waste of time, it could almost be considered a good outcome to obtain poor results from imperfect studies . . . for poor results reinforce the importance of good preparation.

(C. Cattaneo, *Saggi di economia rurale*, 1839)

6

Imperfect Information, Market Incompleteness, and Strategic Intervention

6.1. 'Strategic' sectors

So far, we have examined a number of classical causes of market failure in Italy stemming from the existence of pure public goods, externalities, and natural monopolies; they offer an equal number of reasons for direct or indirect public intervention in the market.

We must now discuss the other reasons invoked to justify public action in the economy. Still following the textbook procedure proposed by Stiglitz (1986), we should address two other types of market failure that prevent the achievement of a Pareto optimum, namely market failures due to imperfect information (to which even disequilibria in the labour market might be attributed) and those caused by market incompleteness (in the fields of insurance and finance, for example); it will be recalled that we have already maintained that instances of the 'prisoner's dilemma' also derive from a combination of these two factors. We should also discuss two undesirable aspects of the Pareto optimum the market may achieve, with reference to merit goods and redistribution.

We shall deal with these four cases in the context of the general concept of strategic goods in a situation of market incompleteness. Imperfect information is so common that it does not seem to constitute a separate, specific reason for market failure, as the preceding pages indicate. On the other hand, the category of incomplete markets is also so vast that it can encompass all forms of market inadequacy, from those that impede Pareto-optimal solutions to those which are Pareto-efficient but socially undesirable. As to the political category of 'strategic' goods, it has to be recognized that this is virtually a catch-all group unless subject to some form of qualification.

Indeed, the concept of a 'strategic' market is used with great frequency by Italian policy-makers with reference to both inputs and outputs. It may be applied, for example, to inputs that are particularly prominent in the sectoral input–output tables (such as hydrocarbons, fertilizers, or bank credit produced and distributed by public corporations or regulated private firms, but also labour and capital, the private supply and price of which are at least partly regulated). 'Strategic' outputs are those that favour the achievement of essential aggregate-supply objectives, such as sectorally or regionally balanced growth. Finally, goods and services are 'strategic' if they satisfy essential aggregate-demand objectives, such as redistribution, the welfare state, or stabilization, which in Italy are the responsibility of government through social-security transfers, collective consumption, tax revenues, and regulatory activities.

As one can imagine, it would be no easy matter to compile an exhaustive list of sectors that have been declared by Italian politicians to be 'strategic' being labelled 'of significant national interest' (from energy to steel and chemicals) or 'relevant to our balance-of-payments position' (from food to oil products).

It is also difficult to make a conceptual summary, however, as some ad hoc thought has been followed by policy-makers in their use of the notion of a 'strategic' sector; like the notion of merit goods, it appears to define an *ex ante* reason for public intervention in the economy but often merely provides an *ex post* justification for public interference in the market, even when this clearly strays into territory that elsewhere has been called the 'non-agenda'.

6.2. Market incompleteness

We therefore intend to identify, among all the public measures for the production, consumption, transfer, redistribution, and regulation of 'strategic' goods in Italy, those to which market incompleteness can be seen to apply, with the necessary implication that private and public operators coexist in the same sector.

Even qualified in this way, the range of strategic goods (in the strict sense, and hence without quotation marks) also includes many, perhaps too many, imprecisely delineated areas of 'modern' market failures. One example will serve to clarify the point. Let us suppose that the shortcomings of the credit and insurance sectors reveal incompleteness in these strategic markets and hence market failure, and let us take the case of old-age pensions by way of illustration. In those circumstances, it is not clear whether the pay-as-you-go scheme simply offers a type of financial asset with an index-linked deferred yield that the private sector would not be prepared to issue at similar prices,[1] or also imposes forced saving on 'short-sighted' individuals who, like the grasshopper in the fable, would not otherwise put aside sufficient resources for their old age (saving being a merit good), or is even being used to satisfy other redistributive objectives, themselves perhaps strategic for different reasons, in order to guarantee a dignified standard of living for needy old people.

We shall therefore not attempt to categorize, even briefly, all the strategic measures that point to market incompleteness. Instead, we shall confine ourselves to examining certain key issues in particular areas: as regards strategic measures involving aggregate-supply objectives, we shall concern ourselves with the Mezzogiorno and industrial restructuring; with regard to strategic intervention concerning the scale of productive inputs, we shall discuss employment and unemployment, private investment and financial restructuring; and for strategic measures relating to aggregate-demand objectives we shall deal with the welfare state (with particular reference to health, social security, and education), income redistribution (via public expenditure, tax revenues, and administered prices) and the main problems raised by a public debt that may tend to become unsustainable over the long term.

There are therefore several significant areas our examination will not cover. Some of these omissions are due to the consideration that our approach is more real than monetary (for this reason the banking sector, for example, will not be examined), while others stem from the fact that certain public measures in sectors that do not appear to be incomplete are described as 'strategic' but do not, according to our analysis, meet the necessary requirements (such as rescue operations in industries producing goods that are certainly not necessities such as the Christmas cake called *panettone*); yet other omissions are due to the fact that many interventions in sectors of dubious 'strategic' importance but displaying undoubted government failures are destined for an early grave or are already

---

[1] This problem is examined in detail in Padoa Schioppa (1990*c*, 1992*a*). With reference to Italy, it should be noted that neither the low cost of indexed old-age pensions nor the redistribution between and within generations made possible by the public pay-as-you-go social-security system could be matched by an identical private scheme. This is because 'if the young still to be born, who will have to pay for our future pensions, could step out of the contract, we, who pay for today's old-age pensions, could no longer cash our credit from the present elderly, because they will be dead. That is why the Government has to intervene with a social contract compelling the parties to honour their commitments' (Padoa Schioppa, 1990*c*: 9).

in the process of extinction as a result of privatization,[2] as in the case of the car factory in the South, Alfasud, controlled in the past by the state holding, IRI.

[2] In this regard Pera (1988a: 13) reminds us that 'the strategy of selling shareholdings or entire enterprises has been only one aspect of the strategy of industrial and financial restructuring of the public corporations'.

PART IV

Strategic Intervention in Aggregate Supply

The Mezzogiorno

This research was carried out over a period of more than three years, from the beginning of 1897 to April 1900. Almost all the data it contains are unpublished: in fact, a large proportion are unpublished not only for the years under examination but also for the years before. The statistical part of the *Yearbook of Public Finances and the Treasury* has not been published for ten years, and, with few exceptions, the Financial Administrations no longer break down even the data on taxes according to province. Hence any research into the geographical distribution of state revenue and expenditure runs into endless difficulties.

(F. S. Nitti, *Scritti sulla questione meridionale*, 1900)

7

Direct Public Investment and Public Support for the Disposable Income of Households

7.1. *Regional distribution of state expenditure*

The first strategic intervention we wish to explore relates to measures to reduce regional disparities, with particular reference to the problems of the Mezzogiorno.

No Italian economic-policy document fails to assert the public sector's involvement in efforts to overcome the country's so-called economic dualism, and yet the first thing to strike the researcher is the lack of sufficient empirical evidence to judge the extent to which this concern is translated into observable facts. In the course of the analysis that follows, it will also emerge that the available information is ambivalent and difficult to interpret. Nevertheless, with very little hesitation we shall be able to argue that public action in the Mezzogiorno can be criticized on at least four counts, namely that it is too biased towards supporting demand rather than increasing supply in the South, that public investment may promote not only the development of the infrastructure but also the growth of the criminal economy, that financial assistance to private firms, though considerable in size, is of low effectiveness owing to the tenuous link with actual real investment and with the growth in value-added, and finally that public dirigistic regulation is excessive, aggravating disequilibria in the labour market.

We shall return to these aspects at the end of Chapter 8, but let us begin by assessing the volume and type of public expenditure directed towards the South by comparison with the rest of the country and then compare it with government revenue collected in the various regions. In other words, we would first like to establish the budgetary impact of the Southern problem.

It may seem strange, but no official policy document or specialist publication from institutions specifically concerned with the question (such as the Association for Industrial Development in Southern Italy (SVIMEZ) or the Mezzogiorno Development Agency (Agenzia per il Mezzogiorno)) reports this essential information in full, although some (but not all) of the components of public expenditure and revenue are known; for example, we have information on investment by state-controlled companies, but not by the enlarged public sector broken down by region.[1]

As a result, the reconstruction of state expenditure in 1988 by region (Table 7.1), which follows the lines of a previous work by the Institute for Research into Regional Economics (IRER, 1986), is to some extent not only arbitrary on account of the subdivision we have made into five categories but is also certainly incomplete, as it ignores state expenditure that cannot be broken down according to region and also fails to satisfy the main objective, which is to analyse the wider public-sector aggregate including state-controlled companies.[2]

Subject to these limitations, it is interesting to observe in Table 7.1 that the state expenditure which can be broken down on a regional basis does not appear to be distributed in a way that clearly favours the Mezzogiorno; indeed, the South's 34.67 per cent share is lower than the proportion of the population living in the area (36.49 per cent), so that per capita state expenditure appears to be lower in the South than in the Centre–North, both including and excluding Latium. At the same time, and in a sense paradoxically, the proportion of state expenditure is greater in the South than in the rest of the country if measured in relation to the Mezzogiorno's value-added, which is only one-third that of the Centre–North.

The five categories into which we have subdivided the state expenditure that can be broken down by region are the following: expenditure to support households' disposable income, interest on the public debt, direct expenditure to boost value-added, transfers to public or private enterprises, and transfers to local authorities. In per capita terms, the Mezzogiorno does not emerge at an advantage in any category except the last and, in a sense, the first if we exclude Latium from the Centre–North in view of the high proportion of state expenditure that is clearly concentrated in that area (due to the presence of the capital, Rome). Moreover, as Table 7.1

---

[1] It should also be noted that many regional historical series display a break in the mid-1980s as a result of the changeover to the new regionally disaggregated national accounts. ISTAT has already bridged the gap at national level, but is only in the process of doing so for the regional figures.

[2] See the notes to Table 1.4 for an explanation of these distinctions.

shows, this result is obtained only by excluding interest on the public debt from expenditure to support households' disposable income, a move we consider plausible but uncertain, as we do not in fact know whether the interest is received by households or firms and whether or not it constitutes remuneration of a factor of production.[3]

In particular, contrary to what one might have expected, it is striking that state transfers to enterprises and direct state expenditure to boost value-added—and within this item direct investment—are lower in the Mezzogiorno in per capita terms. One should, however, avoid reaching hasty and simplistic conclusions on this basis, because the state is only one component of the public sector. It is well to recall that although state transfers cover a large part of local-authority spending and thus approximate closely to their capacity to influence the economy, the same is not true of state transfers to public and private enterprises.

From this point of view, the figure given in Table 7.1 does not reflect the overall effort of the enlarged public sector and state-controlled companies in the South, particularly in the investment field; indeed, we know from the aggregate data on Italy as a whole (Table 1.4) that in 1988 investment by general government touched Lit. 37,309 billion (with direct state investment accounting for only Lit. 4,240 billion of this), investment by the enlarged public sector came to Lit. 53,281 billion, and that by state-controlled companies to Lit. 14,811 billion.

7.2. Direct public investment

In beginning to estimate the extent to which the above figures on direct state investment that can be broken down by region under-estimate total public investment in the Mezzogiorno, we observe that investment in this area by state-controlled companies alone exceeded Lit. 4,000 billion in 1988 (Table 7.2), a substantial amount by comparison with direct state investment (Table 7.1), although broadly comparable with this if measured as a proportion of the corresponding total investment in Italy—in both cases, the percentage directed to the South is less than one-third and well below the level required by legislation (60 per cent from 1971 onwards).

[3] See the discussion in Sections 1.1 and 18.1 on this point.

Table 7.1. Geographic distribution of state expenditure (1988), population (1988), and value-added (1987)

Areas	Expenditure to support households' disposable income				Interest on the public debt	Expenditure with direct effect on value-added			Mezzogiorno Total
	Wages and salaries	Pensions	Other transfers to households	Total		Purchases of goods and services	Direct investment	Mezzogiorno Development Agency	
	Billions of current Lit.								
Centre–North, excl. Latium	30,200.307	54,251.348	3,392.900	87,844.691	22,941.9090	14,595.8120	1,499.95730	15.2903	16,110.623
Latium	8,175.340	8,810.580	1,505.440	18,491.390	3,144.4100	1,816.7200	159.97100	202.5970	2,179.290
Centre–North	38,375.547	63,062.018	4,898.340	106,336.080	26,086.3190	16,412.5320	1,659.92830	217.8873	18,289.913
Mezzogiorno	22,620.011	34,617.068	2,584.073	59,821.103	6,000.1573	4,685.7373	811.16611	2,942.1124	8,439.018
Italy	60,995.658	97,679.086	7,482.413	166,157.180	32,086.4760	21,098.2700	2,471.09440	3,159.9997	26,728.931
	%age composition of each type of expenditure according to area								
Centre–North, excl. Latium	49.51	55.54	45.34	52.87	71.5	69.18	60.71	0.48	60.28
Latium	13.40	9.02	20.12	11.13	9.8	8.61	6.47	6.41	8.15
Centre–North	62.91	64.56	65.46	64.00	81.3	77.79	67.18	6.89	68.43
Mezzogiorno	37.09	35.44	34.54	36.00	18.7	22.21	32.82	93.11	31.57
Italy	100.00	100.00	100.00	100.00	100.0	100.00	100.00	100.00	100.00
	%age composition of total expenditure in each area according to type of expenditure								
Centre–North, excl. Latium	14.86	26.69	1.67	43.21		7.18			
Latium	20.84	22.46	3.84	47.13		4.63			
Centre–North	15.82	26.00	2.02	43.84		6.77			
Mezzogiorno	17.58	26.90	2.01	46.49		3.64			
Italy	16.43	26.31	2.02	44.76		5.68			

Areas	Total transfers to enterprises				Transfers to local authorities			Total state expenditure ascribable by area	Population	Value added (at factor cost + imputed banking services)
	Public		Private	Total	Regions	Provinces & municipalities	Total			
	State-controlled companies agencies & ENEL	Autonomous government agencies								
Centre–North, excl. Latium								0.74	0.01	7.93
Latium								0.41	0.52	5.56
Centre–North								0.68	0.09	7.54
Mezzogiorno								0.63	2.29	6.56
Italy								0.67	0.85	7.20

	Billions of current Lit.								Thousands	Billions of current Lit.
Centre–North, excl. Latium	161.6273	11,540.110	1,903.9655	13,605.719	42,862.312	19,931.857	62,793.701	203,296.640	30,964	619,658.2
Latium	25.1860	2,298.720	188.2240	2,512.130	8,872.010	4,034.540	12,906.500	39,233.720	5,088	97,836.3
Centre–North	186.8133	13,838.830	2,082.1895	16,117.849	51,734.322	23,966.397	75,700.201	242,530.360	36,052	717,494.5
Mezzogiorno	70.1867	6,378.609	968.3567	7,417.146	33,423.169	13,576.439	46,999.387	128,676.810	20,711	233,846.5
Italy	257.0000	20,217.439	3,060.5462	23,534.995	86,157.491	37,542.836	122,699.590	371,207.170	56,763	951,341.0

									%age of total	%age of total
									54.55	65.14
									8.96	10.28
									63.51	75.42
									36.49	24.58
									100.00	100.00

%age composition of each type of expenditure according to area

Centre–North, excl. Latium	62.89	57.08	62.21	57.81	50.33	53.09	51.18	54.76	54.55	65.14
Latium	9.8	11.37	6.15	10.68	10.42	10.75	10.52	10.57	8.96	10.28
Centre–North	72.69	68.45	68.36	68.49	60.75	63.84	61.70	65.33	63.51	75.42
Mezzogiorno	27.31	31.55	31.64	31.51	39.25	36.16	38.30	34.67	36.49	24.58
Italy	100.00	100.00	100.00	100.00	100.00	100.00	100.00	100.00	100.00	100.00

%age composition of total expenditure in each area according to type of expenditure

									Total state expenditure ascribable by area	
									per head of population	ratio to value-added
Centre–North, excl. Latium	0.08	5.67	0.94	6.69	21.08	9.81	30.89	100.00	6,565.580	0.32808
Latium	0.06	5.86	0.48	6.40	22.61	10.28	32.89	100.00	7,711.030	0.40101
Centre–North	0.08	5.71	0.86	6.65	21.33	9.88	31.21	100.00	6,727.240	0.33802
Mezzogiorno	0.05	4.96	0.75	5.76	25.97	10.55	36.52	100.00	6,212.970	0.55026
Italy	0.07	5.45	0.82	6.34	22.94	10.11	33.05	100.00	6,539.600	0.39019

Notes: The table has been compiled by adopting the parameters for the regional distribution of state expenditure used by IRER (1986) for 1982 and applying them to the new regional accounting data on state expenditure in 1988, drawn from Senato della Repubblica (1989). The regional estimates were then reaggregated for larger areas. As in other figures and tables below, Latium can be separated from the Centre, which comprises Emilia-Romagna, Tuscany, Umbria and Marche, a different classification to that used by ISTAT; the North-East therefore comprises Trentino-Alto Adige, Friuli-Venezia Giulia and Veneto, while the Mezzogiorno can be divided into two groups: the South-West (Campania, Basilicata, Calabria, and the Islands) and the South-East (Abruzzo, Molise, and Puglia), which together correspond to the ISTAT definition of the Mezzogiorno used here. The five major categories into which state expenditure is broken down are composed as follows: expenditure on income support includes staff expenditure (wages and salaries paid to state employees), pensions (to former state employees plus finance to social-security institutions), and other transfers to households. Interest on the public debt is a separate item, as it represents transfers to both households and enterprises. Expenditure with a direct effect on value-added comprises purchases of goods and services, direct investment and transfers to the Mezzogiorno Development Agency, and the State Railways; and current and capital transfers to private enterprises. Finally, transfers to local authorities also include loans to the Deposits and Loans Fund, universities, hospitals, and local health authorities.

Sources: Calculations based on Attanasio and Padoa Schioppa (1991); Senato della Repubblica (1989); IRER (1986); ISTAT, unpublished data of the new regional accounts.

TABLE 7.2. Investment in the Mezzogiorno by state-controlled companies

Years	Billions of current Lit.	% age of total investment in Italy by state-controlled companies
1960	118.8	29.93
1961	164.9	32.30
1962	267.4	36.87
1963	331.0	43.37
1964	329.8	43.09
1965	285.9	41.00
1966	240.9	38.88
1967	254.8	37.25
1968	264.0	33.14
1969	329.6	36.59
1970	610.6	46.08
1971	924.9	52.20
1972	1,138.9	54.75
1973	1,125.3	46.89
1974	1,016.7	38.32
1975	1,148.2	37.12
1976	1,164.1	32.38
1977	1,162.0	30.42
1978	1,140.6	28.98
1979	1,294.4	31.45
1980	1,991.3	35.50
1981	2,346.5	33.97
1982	2,993.3	36.29
1983	2,961.5	32.87
1984	3,161.7	31.02
1985	3,756.0	31.38
1986	4,115.0	31.34
1987	4,264.0	30.24
1988	4,158.0	28.07

Source: *Senato della Repubblica*, various years.

If we now attempt to quantify investment in the South by general government as a whole and by all public corporations[4] (Table 7.3), we note from the latest data available from the Training and Research Centre for the Mezzogiorno (FORMEZ), which are unfortunately no more recent than the end of the 1970s, that investment by state-controlled companies amounts to only one-fifth of total public investment in the area.

The largest flow of capital appears to come from bodies in the enlarged public sector excluding ENEL, which, according to the figures shown in Table 7.3, invest more in the Mezzogiorno than in the rest of the country, so that overall public investment in the area amounts to 43.5 per cent of the national total. If this percentage continued to apply in more recent years, we would have to conclude that overall public investment (i.e. by general government and public corporations) is higher in the South than in the Centre–North both in per capita terms and in relation to value-added.

We have no way of knowing in which branches of activity such

TABLE 7.3.   Public investment in Italy and in the Mezzogiorno, 1978

	Mezzogiorno (A)		Italy (B)		A as %age of B
	billions of current Lit.	%age	billions of current Lit.	%age	
Investment by enlarged public sector excluding ENEL	4,258.9	73.3	8,023.0	59.1	53.1
State-controlled companies	1,140.6*	19.4	3,935.6*	29.0	28.98
ENEL	493.0*	8.3	1,615.0*	11.9	30.5
TOTAL	5,892.5	100.0	13,573.6	100.0	43.5

Data from the old national accounts.

Sources: Parmentola (1983), except for starred items which come from *Senato della Repubblica*, (1979).

[4] This concept is defined in Sections 1.1 and 1.2.

investment is concentrated, but from the nature of the enterprises concerned and the information available (on state-controlled companies, for example) it seems possible to deduce that public investment relates predominantly to infrastructure and public works as well as basic and heavy industry. This certainly does not mean that the traditional disparity in infrastructure between the various areas of the country has now been eliminated. On the contrary, Table 7.4 illustrates the marked imbalance that still exists in the provision of infrastructure, particularly in the energy and telecommunications sectors, and the dramatic contrast in housing quality between the South and the rest of Italy. These deficiencies are confirmed in the analysis by Di Palma (1986) for the EEC Report *The Contribution of Infrastructures to Regional Development* (Biehl, 1986).

7.3. Public support of households' net disposable income

Let us now try to make a more complete reconstruction of the total public support for the net disposable income of households in the South in order to ascertain whether it confirms the conclusion Table 7.1 appears to suggest, namely that in per capita terms state expenditure on wages and salaries is slightly higher in the South than elsewhere (except Latium) while other items are lower. Let us further see whether it is confirmed that public expenditure to support households' net disposable income is the largest item of public spending in the South (it corresponds to 46.49 per cent of state disbursements in the area) and accounts for a greater share than in the Centre–North (where it constitutes just over 43 per cent of the state total).

Staff costs depend on the number of staff and their average wage (as well as social-security contributions paid for them, which we shall ignore here as we wish to concentrate on the take-home pay of public employees). As to the number of employees, if we examine general government as a whole rather than just the state sector, we see from Tables 7.5 and 7.6 that the number of employees in non-marketed services[5] in the Mezzogiorno as a percentage of the national total is approximately in the same proportion as the region's share of the total population; hence the rate of public employment is no higher than in the Centre–North.

---

[5] Most of the staff in non-marketed services are employed by the government.

TABLE 7.4. Infrastructure networks (1984) and poor-quality housing (1981)

Infrastructure networks

	Unit of measurement	Mezzogiorno	Centre–North	Italy
Railways				
Electric traction	km/100 km^2	2.1	4.3	3.4
TOTAL	km/100 km^2	6.5	6.6	6.6
Roads				
Motorways	km/100 km^2	1.7	2.2	2.0
State	km/100 km^2	17.1	13.8	15.1
Provincial	km/100 km^2	35.5	34.8	35.1
Municipal (non-urban)	km/100 km^2	29.9	58.8	47.0
TOTAL	km equiv./100 km^2	31.0	37.1	34.7
Telecommunications				
Connectable telephones	no./100 inhabitants	2.3	3.4	3.0
Telex facilities	no./100 local units surveyed in 1981 Census	1.0	2.0	1.7
Energy				
Natural gas pipelines	km/100 km^2	3.8	7.3	5.9

Poor-quality housing

	Total dwellings (in '000s)		Poor-quality dwellings			
			In '000s		As %age of total dwellings	
	Mezzo-giorno	Centre–North	Mezzogiorno	Centre–North	Mezzogiorno	Centre–North
Total urban areas	1,180.0	3,791.0	333.9	515.5	28.3	13.6
Total major cities	738.6	2,652.0	236.1	378.4	32.0	13.3

Source: SVIMEZ (1986).

However, if we measure the relative importance of public employment in the Mezzogiorno differently by setting it in relation to the number of private-sector employees in the area, we see that in 1987, for example, it accounted for 31 per cent of total employment, well above the figure of 25 per cent for the rest of Italy. Indeed, the regional analysis carried out by Attanasio and Padoa Schioppa (1991) shows that from 1986 onwards the ratio of public employees to total employees in the South-West (the poorest area of Italy) was the same as in Latium, where most government offices are located. The comparison of the relative importance of public employment in the various regions would be even more enlightening if the percentages were calculated in relation to the non-agricultural private sector.[6]

Still using the data contained in Attanasio and Padoa Schioppa (1991) as a basis, it can be deduced that the average wage of public employees in the Mezzogiorno is higher than in the rest of Italy with the exception of Latium, not so much in absolute terms but more in relation to the average wage of private-sector employees. It should therefore come as no surprise that income paid to households in the Mezzogiorno in the form of the wages and salaries of general-government employees (net of social-security contributions) amounted to 33.57 per cent of the national total in 1986, slightly lower than the proportion of the population living in the area but far higher than the area's share of total value-added (Table 7.7).

As to old-age, survivors', and disability pensions (OSD) paid to private- and public-sector employees in the various areas, the empirical evidence analysed in detail in Padoa Schioppa (1992*a*) and summarized here in Tables 7.7 and 7.8 shows that 24.10 and 30.45 per cent of total public expenditure on pensions to the private and public sectors respectively was disbursed in the Mezzogiorno; these shares are not much different from the area's contribution to total value-added but far less than the proportion of the population living there, which was 36.05 per cent of the national total in 1985.

At first sight, therefore, the Mezzogiorno does not enjoy a relative advantage on this score. However, a clear advantage does emerge in terms of the ratio of contributions to pensions in the

---

[6] In this respect too there is a clear disparity; although the total number of employees in the Centre–North is more than double that in the Mezzogiorno, the Centre–North has fewer agricultural workers in absolute terms.

OSD scheme, as shown in Table 7.8, since the rate of social-security contributions is far lower in the Mezzogiorno than in the rest of the country.

It has to be understood, however, that this result, which is calculated for the entire national pension system for private- and public-sector employees, covers many different and even contrasting situations that emerge in the old-age and survivors' sector on the one hand and in the disability sector on the other.

We shall return to the first point at greater length below when we discuss the welfare state in Section 16.1; however, it already seems obvious that the modest total value of national old-age and survivors' pensions paid in the Mezzogiorno reveals the situation of a population with lower employment levels and hence, over the years, lower retirement rates (but with almost identical unit pensions): in 1985 the number of public old-age pensions paid to private-sector employees in the Centre–North was five times higher than in the Mezzogiorno and the corresponding figure for public employees was more than double.

It follows that the ratio of contributions to old-age pensions is higher in the South than in the Centre–North, despite lower contribution rates in the Mezzogiorno. By contrast, national disability pensions are equally distributed in the various areas of the country, with the result that the ratio of contributions to disability pensions is more than three times higher in the Centre–North.

It may seem amazing that there are around two recipients of disability pensions for every old-age pensioner in the Mezzogiorno, whereas almost the reverse ratio obtains in the Centre–North, as shown by Table 7.8. The reason lies partly in the demographic and employment trends mentioned above, but primarily in the fact that disability pensions are disguised forms of unemployment benefit, as demonstrated by the far higher ratio in the Mezzogiorno between the total amount of such pensions and the area's value-added.

For similar reasons, one should not be surprised at the finding by Bodo and Sestito (1989) that the number of Southern employees receiving benefits from the Wage Supplementation Fund (Cassa Integrazione Guadagni) and working zero hours is rapidly approaching the figure for the Centre–North, despite the very small number of Southern workers in sectors covered by the Fund, as indicated in Tables 7.5 and 7.6.

This entire discussion shows us that no assessment of net income

TABLE 7.5. Employment by geographical area and branch of activity (annual averages in '000s)

Branch of Activity	1970	1972	1974	1976	1978	1980	1982	1984
Centre–North								
Marketed goods and services:	11,957.1	11,614.5	11,845.3	11,816.3	11,892.8	12,113.8	12,094.0	12,109.6
Agriculture, forestry and fisheries	1,815.6	1,597.1	1,515.2	1,387.6	1,327.0	1,261.8	1,150.4	1,126.7
Industry	5,906.2	5,716.5	5,831.2	5,778.5	5,738.2	5,790.8	5,591.1	5,226.8
Industry excl. construction	4,688.8	4,624.8	4,778.5	4,763.6	4,724.7	4,751.6	4,560.0	4,270.3
Energy products	130.4	127.0	131.7	138.2	137.4	139.4	141.0	139.7
Industrial manufactures	4,558.4	4,497.8	4,646.8	4,625.4	4,587.3	4,612.2	4,419.0	4,130.6
Engineering and metal products	1,614.6	1,627.3	1,742.7	1,740.8	1,728.0	1,766.1	1,638.8	1,519.2
Other industrial products	2,943.8	2,870.5	2,904.1	2,884.6	2,859.3	2,846.1	2,780.7	2,611.4
Construction	1,217.4	1,091.7	1,052.7	1,014.9	1,013.5	1,039.2	1,031.1	956.5
Services	4,235.3	4,300.9	4,498.9	4,650.2	4,827.6	5,061.2	5,352.5	5,756.1
Non-marketed services	1,775.2	1,925.6	2,078.1	2,192.1	2,269.9	2,316.8	2,370.9	2,437.2
TOTAL	13,732.3	13,540.1	13,923.4	14,008.4	14,162.7	14,430.6	14,464.9	14,546.8

Mezzogiorno

Marketed goods and services:	5,048.4	4,937.6	4,954.4	5,008.5	5,065.4	5,109.1	5,074.0	5,083.4
Agriculture, forestry, and fisheries	1,789.4	1,741.9	1,658.8	1,632.4	1,592.0	1,498.2	1,355.6	1,283.3
Industry	1,786.8	1,717.0	1,754.6	1,772.6	1,781.8	1,795.2	1,817.9	1,724.2
Industry excl. construction	970.9	970.7	1,039.3	1,068.8	1,071.3	1,095.4	1,095.0	1,035.7
Energy products	45.0	46.6	47.3	53.3	53.6	55.6	55.0	54.3
Industrial manufactures	925.9	924.1	992.0	1,015.5	1,017.7	1,039.8	1,040.0	981.4
Engineering and metal products	147.3	172.7	218.9	232.7	239.3	253.5	253.1	226.6
Other industrial products	778.6	751.4	773.1	782.8	778.4	786.3	786.9	754.8
Construction	815.9	746.3	715.3	703.8	710.5	699.8	722.9	688.5
Services	1,472.2	1,478.7	1,541.0	1,603.5	1,691.6	1,815.7	1,900.5	2,075.9
Non-marketed services	827.3	898.3	971.2	1,028.1	1,068.9	1,123.2	1,189.1	1,195.8
TOTAL	5,875.7	5,835.9	5,925.6	6,036.6	6,134.3	6,232.3	6,263.1	6,279.2

Source: ISTAT, *Annuario di contabilità nazionale*, vol. xiv, bk. 2, (1986).

TABLE 7.6. Employees and self-employed by geographical area and branch of activity (annual averages in '000s)

Branch of Activity	1983		1984		1985		1986		1987	
	Employees	Self-employed	Employees	Self-employed	Employees	Self-employed	Employees	Self-employed	Employees	Self-employed
Centre–North										
Marketed goods and services	8,166.2	4,959.8	8,081.6	5,015.5	8,178.6	4,981.3	8,244.1	5,052.3	8,296.0	5,068.6
Agriculture	217.1	1,277.9	222.0	1,211.6	195.1	1,146.5	211.1	1,143.9	203.6	1,119.6
Industry	4,650.4	1,041.1	4,415.2	995.6	4,354.7	997.6	4,318.8	1,022.2	4,308.4	1,009.9
Services	3,298.7	2,690.8	3,444.4	2,808.3	3,628.8	2,837.2	3,714.2	2,886.2	3,784.0	2,939.1
Non-marketed services	2,566.2	0.0	2,620.6	0.0	2,666.0	0.0	2,684.4	0.0	2,713.3	0.0
TOTAL	10,732.4	4,959.8	10,702.2	5,015.5	10,844.6	4,981.3	10,928.5	5,052.3	11,009.3	5,068.6
Mezzogiorno										
Marketed goods and services	3,162.3	2,154.3	3,146.5	2,209.4	3,185.1	2,227.5	3,157.6	2,261.2	3,120.2	2,316.9
Agriculture	610.3	690.0	570.4	682.5	589.2	649.9	555.5	651.6	549.0	641.0
Industry	1,319.1	337.3	1,283.6	310.2	1,259.6	302.1	1,225.3	305.3	1,194.0	294.4
Services	1,232.9	1,127.0	1,292.5	1,216.7	1,336.3	1,275.5	1,376.8	1,304.3	1,377.2	1,381.5
Non-marketed services	1,315.7	0.0	1,399.3	0.0	1,372.2	0.0	1,386.7	0.0	1,408.8	0.0
TOTAL	4,478.0	2,154.3	4,485.8	2,209.4	4,557.3	2,227.5	4,544.3	2,261.2	4,529.0	2,316.9

Source: ISTAT, unpublished data of the new regional accounts.

TABLE 7.7. Items indicating the general government's support for households' disposable income 1985–1986

	Centre–North		Mezzogiorno		Italy	
	billions of current Lit.	%	billions of current Lit.	%	billions of current Lit.	%
Value-added (1986)		74.81		25.19		100
Population (1986)		63.79		36.21		100
Wages and salaries (1986) paid by general government	54,112.100	66.43	27,351.370	33.57	81,463.470	100
Public pensions (1985) paid to employees of:						
Private sector	41,257.638	75.90	13,097.940	24.10	54,355.578	100
Public sector	12,191.438	69.55	5,337.927	30.45	17,529.365	100
Taxes (1986) paid to general government:						
Private sector employers social security contributions	64,300.6	83.53	12,681.6	16.47	76,982.2	100
Personal income taxes	55,540.659	79.82	14,039.423	20.18	69,580.082	100
Net indirect taxes	52,180.184	80.54	12,610.897	19.46	64,791.081	100

[a] Old-age, survivors' and disability, (OSD) pensions.

Sources: Padoa Schioppa (1992*a*) for data on OSD pensions; calculations based on Attanasio and Padoa Schioppa (1991) for data (from old regional accounts) on taxes and value-added; Attanasio and Padoa Schioppa (1991) for population data.

support in the Mezzogiorno would be complete if it failed to take account of relative taxation levels in the various parts of the country. In percentage terms, not only are social-security contributions lower in the South than in the Centre–North owing to the additional relief granted to the Mezzogiorno and the lower tax base on which they are calculated (the wage bill), but direct and indirect taxes as a proportion of the national total are also lower than the area's relative share of the population and value-added, as illustrated by the last columns in Table 7.7.

The reason for this is the same: the average rate of personal income tax is lower in the Mezzogiorno owing to the progressivity of direct taxes, and the tax base is narrower by virtue of the lower incomes of households in the area; net indirect taxes are lower in this part of the country, not only because the VAT tax base (at factor cost) is smaller but also because the average VAT rate is lower in the Mezzogiorno, given the higher proportion of consumption of basic necessities in this area.[7]

[7] Indeed, in the year under consideration, there existed four rates in the VAT tax schedule, the minimum being 2%, the maximum being 38%. A deeper analysis on

TABLE 7.8. Number and value of OSD pensions to employees and ratio of contributions to pensions, 1985

	Centre–North	Mezzogiorno	Italy
Private-sector employees			
Old-age pensions:			
Unit value ('000s Lit.)	7,660	6,449	7,461
No. ('000s)	3,155	619	3,774
Contributions to Pensions ratio	0.619	0.747	0.637
Disability pensions:			
Unit value ('000s Lit.)	5,857	5,448	5,683
No. ('000s)	1,723	1,275	2,998
Contributions to Pensions ratio	0.893	0.263	0.632
Survivors pensions:			
Unit value ('000s Lit.)	4,069	3,483	3,914
No. ('000s)	1,718	620	2,338
Contributions to Pensions ratio	0.712	0.468	0.647
OSD pensions:			
Contributions to Pensions ratio	0.701	0.441	0.637
Public-sector employees			
Old-age pensions:			
Unit value ('000s Lit.)	12,584	12,973	12,668
No. ('000s)	756	310	1,066
Contributions to Pensions ratio	0.896	1.017	0.928
Survivors pensions:			
Unit value ('000s Lit.)	12,584	12,973	12,668
No. ('000s)	756	310	1,066
Contributions to Pensions ratio	0.964	0.900	0.931
OSD pensions:			
Contributions to Pensions ratio	0.911	0.987	0.929

Source: Padoa Schioppa (1992*a*).

therefore indisputable that the public sector provides net support for the incomes of households in the Mezzogiorno; this is already evident on the expenditure side if measured in relation to value-added, but it stems mainly from lower government receipts in the Mezzogiorno if valued in per capita terms. Overall, as asserted more than ten years ago by the specialist on the Mezzogiorno, Graziani (1979: 63),[8]

although the economy of the South is no longer strictly speaking a really poor economy and despite the fact that it has industries owned by independent financial groups, it still bears the stamp of a publicly subsidized economy.

the different consumer baskets of the South and the Centre–North is contained in Section 18.3.

[8] See also the more recent work by Giannola (1986).

8

Subsidies for Enterprises and Dirigistic Regulation

8.1. Tax concessions and unit labour costs

We shall now analyse in greater detail the other types of public support of some significance granted to the Mezzogiorno, as shown in Table 7.1, in particular subsidies for enterprises, concentrating especially on tax concessions. The first column of Table 8.1 shows the data collected for us by Del Monte and Vittoria (1988) on capital grants and interest subsidies to firms in the South and relief from social-security contributions granted over the twenty-five years from 1959 to 1984 (at 1988 prices).

Two facts emerge clearly: first and foremost, that the total figure for capital grants and interest subsidies (which were broadly equal over the period as a whole) is modest but far from derisory, as confirmed by the available information on each year in the 1980s (Table 8.1) and by the comparison with the figure on contemporaneous subsidized investment and subsidized loans; secondly, leaving aside other forms of tax concession enjoyed in the Mezzogiorno (such as the one on reinvested profits), that relief from social-security contributions over the period 1959–84 amounted to a substantial sum (more than double the combined total of capital grants and interest subsidies over the same period) but, according to our estimates,[1] was equivalent to total public investment in the Mezzogiorno in just the two years 1987–8.

Undoubtedly, *additional*[2] contribution relief in the Mezzogiorno over and above that accorded nationwide ensures that labour costs per employee are lower than in the Centre–North; in the Mezzogiorno they are currently around 80 per cent of those in the

---

[1] Our estimates were obtained by extrapolating to 1987–8 the percentage shown in Table 7.3 for public investment in the Mezzogiorno in relation to the national total and then applying it to total Italian public investment in the two years in question.

[2] An examination of the effects of general relief from social security contributions is deferred to Sections 12.3 and 12.4.

TABLE 8.1. Grants and financial and fiscal subsidies to the Mezzogiorno (in billions of 1988 Lit.)

	1959–84	1980	1981	1982	1983	1984	1985	1986	1987	1988
Capital grants[a]	7,928	632.9	824.8	868.8	824.9	428.3	907.9	546.4	747.4	913.9
Interest subsidies[a]	8,870	439.7	553.2	667.0	530.4	244.7	544.4	305.7	303.0	373.5
TOTAL	16,798	1,072.6	1,378.0	1,535.8	1,355.3	673.0	1,452.3	852.1	1,050.4	1,287.4
Subsidized investment[b]	n.a.	1,896.0	2,409.2	2,556.3	2,232.8	1,192.2	2,599.7	1,526.6	1861.5	2,316.1
Subsidized loans	n.a.	547.2	780.6	860.3	675.1	341.9	748.7	489.7	606.4	715.2
Social-security-contribution relief	38,117	n.a.	n.a.	n.a.	n.a.	n.a.	n.a.	n.a.	n.a.	n.a.

Notes

[a] Including contribution to rents for individual annual data from 1980 to 1988.
[b] Fixed investment eligible for capital grants, hence excluding the cost of purchasing land and stocks of raw materials, which are eligible only for subsidized loans.

Sources: Del Monte and Vittoria (1988) for 1959–84; SVIMEZ (1989) for 1980–8.

TABLE 8.2. Unemployment rates by age group and sex (unemployed persons as a %age of the relevant labour force)

Year	Male			Female		
	14–19 years	20–4 years	25–9 years	14–19 years	20–4 years	25–9 years
Centre–North						
1978	21.3	15.1	4.3	33.0	17.3	9.4
1979	22.0	13.4	3.9	34.3	17.7	9.2
1980	19.9	13.0	4.1	33.1	17.2	9.2
1981	23.6	14.0	4.7	35.5	18.7	10.1
1982	27.4	15.5	5.1	40.0	21.0	10.6
1983	30.1	17.0	6.5	44.9	23.4	12.3
1984	32.3	17.6	6.3	48.5	27.4	11.7
1985	34.4	18.4	6.2	47.4	28.2	13.3
1986	30.9	17.4	6.4	44.1	28.4	14.4
1987	29.5	16.9	6.7	42.7	27.6	15.0
1988	24.3	15.1	6.5	39.8	25.0	14.6
Mezzogiorno						
1978	31.2	23.5	8.6	51.5	41.0	21.7
1979	34.3	25.8	9.3	53.3	40.2	22.3
1980	33.6	27.6	9.9	54.3	43.0	23.3
1981	36.9	29.4	9.9	58.3	46.6	27.3
1982	41.4	30.5	11.4	58.1	47.6	28.2
1983	43.8	31.3	12.3	61.1	49.2	30.5
1984	42.1	32.5	13.3	63.9	52.7	32.4
1985	43.0	35.0	14.1	67.8	53.9	34.1
1986	47.3	36.9	16.6	65.7	57.2	37.5
1987	51.8	41.9	20.3	68.4	61.4	42.6
1988	52.1	44.6	22.3	69.0	64.3	45.7

Sources: ISTAT, 'Rilevazione delle forze di lavoro. Media annua: Nord-Centro Mezzogiorno', *Supplemento al Bollettino mensile di statistica*, various years.

zogiorno they are currently around 80 per cent of those in the Centre–North, compared with approximately 50 per cent in the early 1950s (Figure 8.1).

Until 1970 this labour-cost differential reflected differences in

[3] The previous Interorganizational Agreement of 1961 had already reduced inter-regional differentials in contractual wages to a maximum of 20%. Moreover, in

TABLE 8.3. Employment rates by age group and sex (employed persons as a %age of the relevant resident population)

Year	Male			Female		
	14–19 years	20–4 years	25–9 years	14–19 years	20–4 years	25–9 years
Centre–North						
1978	26.6	58.4	84.3	23.1	52.2	52.3
1979	27.0	62.2	84.9	22.9	51.8	53.8
1980	28.5	63.0	83.5	22.7	54.3	53.9
1981	26.2	65.6	83.5	21.9	54.3	55.7
1982	24.8	63.4	81.3	19.9	53.2	55.5
1983	22.0	59.9	80.5	17.6	51.6	55.9
1984	19.5	58.0	78.6	15.8	47.9	56.3
1985	17.9	57.1	77.9	15.1	47.7	57.3
1986	18.4	56.9	77.7	15.1	47.8	57.6
1987	19.1	56.5	79.9	15.0	48.0	57.8
1988	21.1	60.6	85.2	16.1	53.1	62.6
Mezzogiorno						
1978	19.6	46.8	75.7	9.3	22.8	31.2
1979	19.7	45.9	78.2	9.3	24.9	32.8
1980	19.7	44.8	78.9	9.4	24.9	33.3
1981	18.5	45.7	77.4	8.4	23.4	30.8
1982	16.8	46.0	77.0	8.2	22.0	31.9
1983	16.1	44.5	74.2	7.4	22.1	32.7
1984	15.2	41.5	73.1	6.2	19.5	30.8
1985	14.3	38.6	73.3	5.9	18.8	30.0
1986	12.7	37.6	69.3	6.1	18.5	28.6
1987	11.9	34.3	65.7	6.0	17.4	28.0
1988	13.3	38.0	69.6	6.4	17.9	26.7

Sources: ISTAT, 'Rilevazione delle forze di lavoro. Media annua: Nord-Centro Mezzogiorno', *Supplemento al Bollettino mensile di statistica*, various years; 'Popolazione e bilanci demografici per sesso, età e regione', *Supplemento al Bollettino mensile di statistica*, various years; *Statistiche demografiche*, various years.

employers' and trade-union organizations tended to eliminate by laying down a single minimum national wage and a single cost-of-living adjustment and providing for a gradual standardization of all contractual wage components throughout the country. Whereas in this way the existing 'wage cages' (*gabbie salariali*) were abolished, it is significant that the same period saw the adoption of the first measures to grant relief from social-security contributions in the Mezzogiorno, which date from the end of 1968.

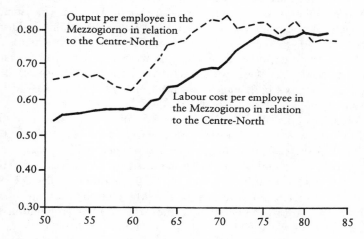

FIG. 8.1   Labour cost per employee and output per employee in the Mezzogiorno in relation to the Centre–North in industry, excluding construction

Source: Siracusano *et al.* (1986).

Given the different trends in labour productivity in the two parts of the country (Figure 8.1), labour costs per unit of output are now identical throughout Italy, whereas at the beginning of the 1950s unit labour costs in the Mezzogiorno were only 70 per cent those in the Centre–North.

In reality, this analysis is still at too high a level of aggregation and thus conceals significant differences in productivity, labour

commenting on its presumed effects, Lutz (1961: 385) stated that the wage rate 'in these Southern provinces will, however, be only 13–15% below the rate in the *bulk* of the Northern provinces, since the rates set for the latter are in most cases 5–8% below the top rate'.

costs per employee and labour costs per unit of output, even within
the two major geographic areas. Figure 8.2 illustrates the point we
are making. Whereas from the beginning of the 1960s onwards the
North-East recorded marked growth in productivity and labour
costs per employee in relation to the North-West (traditionally the
most highly developed area), Latium showed an opposite trend, with
a relative fall in both variables, while the other areas in the Centre
kept pace with or outstripped the North-West in terms of productivity and gradually approached the level attained in that area as
regards labour costs per employee. The South-West has consistently
brought up the rear, with the South-East only slightly ahead; during
the twenty-seven years under examination neither of these areas has
achieved anything other than a temporary productivity gain in relation to the North-West, while they have both shown a spectacular
relative increase in labour costs per employee, which has had a
dramatic impact on unit labour costs.

Small wonder then that employment rates have remained far
lower in the Mezzogiorno than in the Centre–North, and as little
as half in the case of young people and women, while the regional
disparity in unemployment rates has actually worsened, especially
for the more vulnerable sections of the population. Tables 8.2 and
8.3 show that young women in the Mezzogiorno not only face
almost as large differentials in employment rates in relation to
their peers in the Centre–North as in relation to men of the same
age in the Mezzogiorno, but also have far higher unemployment
rates than males of the same age in the Mezzogiorno (and *a fortiori* in the Centre–North).

8.2. *Labour-market disequilibria and dirigistic regulation*

Such labour-market disequilibria appear to be the inevitable consequence of falling demand for labour in the South due to rising relative unit labour costs and a continuous absolute and relative
expansion in the supply of labour, fuelled by consistently faster
natural population growth than in the Centre–North, which from
the mid-1970s onwards was no longer eased by substantial migration flows (Table 8.4). A number of other factors also played a
part; we shall return to these at the end of Chapter 8.

In our interpretation, the main blame for these disequilibria
must be laid on the excessive dirigistic regulation in favour of the

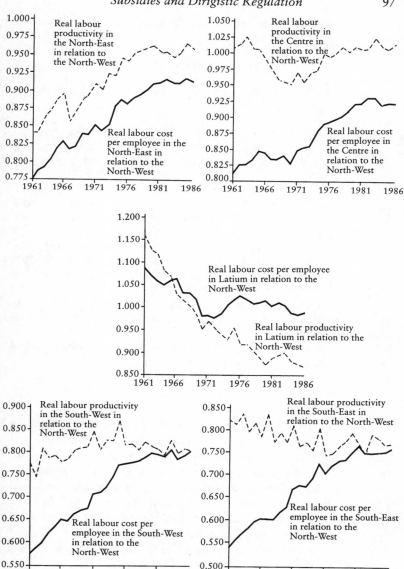

FIG. 8.2. Differentials in labour productivity and labour cost per employee in various areas in relation to the North-West

Source: Calculations based on Attanasio and Padoa Schioppa (1991).

TABLE 8.4. Changes in the resident population due to natural growth and migratory flows (in '000s of persons)

	Period	Of which:			
	1951–72	1951–60	1960–72	1972–85	1951–85
Natural growth					
Mezzogiorno	5,435.1	2,436.9	2,998.2	2,040.4	7,475.5
Centre–North	3,698.0	1,347.8	2,350.2	161.6	3,859.6
Italy	9,133.1	3,784.7	5,348.4	2,202.0	11,335.1
Migratory flows[a]					
Mezzogiorno	–3,951.2	–1,586.0	–2,385.2	–497.2	–4,448.4
Centre–North	2,258.9	657.5	1,601.4	541.2	2,800.1
Italy	–1,692.3	–928.5	–763.8	44.0	–1,648.3
Effective change[b]					
Mezzogiorno	1,483.9	850.9	633.0	1,543.2	3,027.1
Centre–North	5,956.9	2,005.3	3,951.6	702.8	6,659.7
Italy	7,440.8	2,856.2	4,584.6	2,246.0	9,686.8

[a] Migratory flows have a positive (a negative) sign in an area if the number of immigrants to that area is higher (is lower) than the number of emigrants from that area.

[b] The effective change is the algebraic sum of the change due to natural growth and the one due to migratory flows.

Source: SVIMEZ (1986).

Mezzogiorno over the last two decades. This stemmed from the aim of providing equality of opportunity by means of legal and administrative instruments that were indifferent to market reactions and were designed to protect the weak instead of strengthening them, thus giving rise to automatic mechanisms that backfired on those they were intended to safeguard. The fact that dirigistic regulation rested on a mistaken understanding of equality of opportunity will become clear when it is seen that it was inspired neither by the principle of giving to each according to his needs nor that of giving to each according to his worth.

Only by viewing the problem from this angle can one understand why public dirigistic regulation encouraged the reduction of regional nominal-wage differentials (by enshrining the private sector's agreements between the two sides of industry in law, and setting uniform public-sector salaries for the entire country), why it later allowed regional net nominal-wage disparities to be squeezed (through the progressivity of direct taxes) and why in addition it interfered with the price mechanism (by favouring the Mezzogiorno in some publicly and privately produced goods and services) in order to boost the net purchasing power of wages in the Mezzogiorno while at the same time freezing labour costs in the region by granting additional relief from social-security contributions.

In truth, the slower rise in the households' consumption deflator of the Mezzogiorno relative to the Centre–North[4] evidenced by Table 8.5 is not entirely ascribable to price regulation, as it is not due solely to public measures affecting certain collective services (for example, motorways are toll-free in many areas of the Mezzogiorno but not in the Centre–North) and certain private goods (for instance, rents on both offices and residential property are lower in the South); it is also due partly to other market factors, such as the lower labour cost in the underground economy or the lesser importance the Southern regions attach to non-food consumption, the most expensive and fastest growing item in the basket of consumer goods.

What is certain is that the web of laws and public regulations greatly contributed to the disproportionately large rise in net real wages in the Mezzogiorno, as illustrated in Figure 8.3. In particular, ignoring the underground economy, net real wages in the South-West were well below those in the Central and Northern regions in the 1960s, but by 1976 they had caught up with those in the North-East and by the end of the decade had even overtaken those in the North-West; they are now on a par with net real wages in the Central regions, which are the highest in the country, with Latium in the lead.

The reduction in net real-wage differentials between regions from the mid-1970s onwards and the burgeoning state safety-net for the unemployed in the Mezzogiorno had a disruptive effect on the area's equilibrium in that they removed incentives to migrate to the Centre–North, while the two oil crises and the elimination of

---

[4] The smallness of price rises in the Centre is attributable entirely to the containment of prices in Latium, which in turn is a function of the high proportion of administered prices in this region, as indicated in Attanasio and Padoa Schioppa (1991).

TABLE 8.5. Households' consumption deflator

Year	North	Centre	Mezzogiorno	Italy
1960	68.85	68.16	69.55	68.89
1961	70.08	69.71	70.56	70.13
1962	73.69	73.65	74.15	73.80
1963	78.82	78.72	79.74	79.04
1964	82.94	82.71	83.71	83.10
1965	85.53	85.56	87.53	86.07
1966	88.18	88.14	89.61	88.55
1967	91.16	90.67	91.94	91.26
1968	92.43	92.29	93.10	92.57
1969	95.14	95.06	95.55	95.23
1970	100.00	100.00	100.00	100.00
1971	105.80	105.52	104.82	105.48
1972	112.62	112.32	111.39	112.23
1973	126.24	125.19	126.80	126.17
1974	153.31	151.44	151.89	152.54
1975	180.78	176.95	178.70	179.42
1976	214.76	208.21	208.94	211.82
1977	255.59	244.59	244.62	250.31
1978	289.30	275.90	274.83	282.55
1979	332.85	317.73	315.58	324.95
1980	400.80	382.01	378.69	390.83
1981	478.28	457.26	449.51	465.96
1982	559.33	534.67	527.54	545.43
1983	645.95	618.11	603.73	628.46
1984	719.31	685.59	667.61	697.91
1985	791.69	721.91	731.98	760.71
1986	837.01	765.66	775.39	805.07
1987	879.68	803.22	808.83	843.93

Sources: Cananzi and Fiorito (1986) for data up to 1984; for later years, our calculations on data from ISTAT, *Annuario statistico italiano*, (1989) for the consumer price index for the households of employees; Banca d'Italia (1989*a*) for the households' consumption deflator at national level; ISTAT, unpublished regional data on consumption. For the period 1985–7, given the national households' consumption deflator, the distribution among the three areas is assumed to be identical to that obtained from regional data on the consumer prices for the households of employees, aggregated according to area by taking the weightings obtained from households' consumption in each area. For 1985–7, it is therefore assumed that the proportion between the consumer prices for a particular area and national consumer prices is the same as that between the regional and national households' consumption deflators.

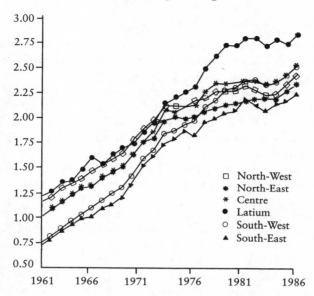

Fig. 8.3. Net real wages (nominal wages deflated by consumer prices and net of direct taxes) in the various areas of Italy

Source: Attanasio and Padoa Schioppa (1991).

the differential in unit labour costs have helped discourage private businesses from the Centre–North from investing in the Mezzogiorno: as illustrated in Attanasio and Padoa Schioppa (1991), internal migration practically came to an end in the mid-1970s, while, starting with the 1980s,[5] masses of immigrants began to arrive in Italy (even in the South) from the rest of the world.

[5] Attanasio and Padoa Schioppa (1991: 301–2) explain the decline in internal migration in Italy after a period of strong migratory flows in the 1960s and early 1970s as follows: 'Gross outmigration rates appeared to be strongly correlated with unemployment differentials. However, since the mid-1970s, this link seems to have been broken; we think that this might be partly due to the increase in the level of aggregate unemployment. We also think that three other factors constitute important explanations; these include: (*a*) A strong decrease in interregional net real-wage differentials coupled with an increase in the net real wage of the South-West relative to the Northern areas. . . . (*b*) A rise of various forms of Government transfers to the Southern regions, which can take the form of more frequent disability pensions, a higher number of tenured public-sector jobs and better pay relative to the private sector . . . (*c*) An increase in the fixed costs involved with the decision to migrate. The typical example here is the housing-rental price; the situation has been aggravated by

8.3. *Public and private investment*

Just as the *additional* relief from social-security contributions in the Mezzogiorno reduces labour costs per employee (and hence per unit of output) and, other things being equal, has positive effects on the demand for labour, so too the systematic policy of granting financial assistance to Southern firms has a beneficial effect, albeit a modest one,[6] according to the conclusion expressed in the research carried out for us by Del Monte and Vittoria (1988). They estimate that in just over thirty years this policy created 14 per cent of marginal manufacturing jobs and increased the value-added of manufacturing industry by an amount fluctuating between 4.7 and 13.4 per cent.

According to many observers (sometimes critical observers as Faini, 1982), a reason for the weak impact that public financial incentives have on employment and value-added lies in the composition of the investment they induce, which is biased in favour of production techniques or sectors (such as heavy industry) with a high capital intensity (or a high capital/output ratio), sectors and techniques that suffered a particularly sharp decline following the oil crisis of the 1970s.

However, total (private and public) per capita gross fixed investment in the Mezzogiorno increased considerably in proportion to that in the Centre–North up to the time of the first oil shock, declined during the rest of the 1970s, and then began to rise again, although the ratio remained below unity even in the best years (Figs. 8.4 and 8.5).

It is difficult to understand why, despite the ratio of total gross fixed investment to GDP being distinctly higher in the Mezzogiorno than in the Centre–North over the last thirty years, the rate of growth in value-added was not higher in the Mezzogiorno than in the rest of the country, so that the regional disparity not only stopped narrowing in the early 1970s but actually tended to widen.[7]

a rationed housing market, due to rent-control regulations. Finally, we think that the persistence of long periods of low migration rates, *ceteris paribus*, raises the cost of migrating.'

[6] Faini (1982), Bodo and Sestito (1989), and De Caprariis and Heimler (1988) also found the benefits of financial assistance and tax concessions to the South to be modest by comparison with the resources deployed.

[7] Various recent data and opinions are relevant in this connection, such as the

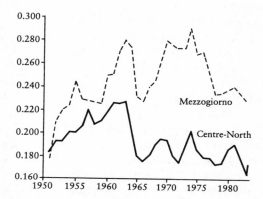

FIG. 8.4.   Gross fixed investment/GDP in the Centre–North and Mezzogiorno

Source: Galli and Onado (1990).

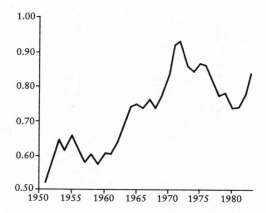

FIG. 8.5.   Ratio of per capita gross fixed investment in the South relative to the Centre–North

Source: Galli and Onado (1990).

SVIMEZ report (1987); the Ministero del Bilancio e della Programmazione Economica (1988); Banca d'Italia (1989); and Attanasio and Padoa Schioppa (1991).

The partial answer to this embarrassing question, documented in Galli and Onado (1990), lies in the fact that capital productivity is still far lower in the Mezzogiorno.[8] This calls for further explanation, however; we shall provide some indications below, drawn from our own and other research.

A recent EEC report on developing regions in Europe, including the South of Italy (Di Palma 1986: 381), maintains that this situation is due to deficiencies in infrastructure that cause a general fall in productivity. With regard to Italy in the second half of the 1970s, it states that 'in all quantified models one of the determining factor[s] for explaining development levels is the endowment with regional infrastructure'. The report concludes (pp. 399–402) that 'in most cases, the influence of infrastructure on income and productivity is statistically more significant than on employment. . . . There is a tendency that less developed regions are underutilizing and highly developed regions are overutilizing their capacities.'

Furthermore, according to other authors, all the investment in the Mezzogiorno induces no more than a small volume of further spending and is only partly successful in generating a multiplier effect on Southern income, owing to bottlenecks in the input–output supply of the Southern economy. The investment effect is mainly transmitted outside the Mezzogiorno during both construction and eventual operation, because most of the additional demand the projects create is met by non-local suppliers.

As we are reminded by Scandizzo and various co-authors,[9] who have used computable general-equilibrium models and social-accounting matrices for the various regions of Italy for the years 1970–86, the investment multiplier in the Mezzogiorno is reduced because the investments entail a partial reallocation of resources to the Centre–North, which has a more balanced network of industrial sectors, greater competitiveness, and a better ability to respond swiftly to variations in demand, whatever the cause. This does not mean—Scandizzo adds, in contrast to many other Southern specialists—that the regions of the Centre and North do

---

[8] Given that the investment/GDP ratio is higher in the South and the depreciation rate the same throughout the country, if the capital/output ratio were the same in all areas the rate of growth in Southern GDP would have to be higher. Only a higher capital/output ratio in the South than in the Centre–North can explain why this is not the case.

[9] See Fornasari *et al.* (1984), Scandizzo (1985, 1987*a*, 1987*b*, 1988), Scandizzo and D'Angiolini (1988), and Scandizzo and Tuccimei (1988).

not also suffer relative harm; they bear an opportunity cost, equal to the loss they sustain owing to the fact that public investment and publicly subsidized private investment are carried out in the Mezzogiorno instead of the Centre–North.

An often heard argument is that the Mezzogiorno lacks a spirit of enterprise able to exploit all the stimuli stemming from public investment and financial assistance to private enterprises. According to this opinion, the commodities in shortest supply in the South would be entrepreneurship, managerial skills, and 'animal spirits', with the consequence of an insufficient number of mutually integrated medium-sized firms.

From this point of view, our researches suggest that the efforts of the public sector have not only failed almost completely to instil an entrepreneurial spirit where it was lacking but in certain instances have accentuated the tendency to wait passively for solutions from on high (and from the centre of the country) rather than from within the economy of the Mezzogiorno itself. In this vein, Marzano and Marzovilla (1988: 28) remind us that 'although state-controlled companies have made a substantial contribution to the direct expansion of employment and to the industrialization of the Mezzogiorno, indirectly they have probably curbed part of the spontaneous development and job-creation associated with these processes'.

In this regard, Del Monte and Vittoria (1988) add that the policy of setting up large plants in the Mezzogiorno has generated a series of initiatives that have spawned a rash of new enterprises, but that these have quickly gone out of business. Consequently, this policy is likely to have increased the probability of company closures as well as company formations in the Mezzogiorno, sowing the suspicion that these public measures, far from permanently encouraging development, lay the basis for a policy of long-term welfare assistance.

Del Monte and Vittoria (1988) nevertheless reject the claim put forward by several observers that local firms had been discouraged by the arrival of firms from outside the area. Available empirical evidence, such as that from a sample survey they carried out in the Southern town of Caserta, shows that the opening of factories by non-local firms is positively correlated to the rate of growth in the region's gross domestic product and to the intensity of regional policy, and that the formation of local firms with more than ten employees is positively correlated to the intensity of regional policy and the number of non-local factories.

It is nevertheless a fact that the capacity of both local and non-local firms to create value-added is linked more to the growth of existing firms than to the formation of new ones. Interestingly enough, similar findings are confirmed by the snapshot of all Italian firms, carried out for us by the research group headed by Contini[10] on the basis of the archives of the National Social Security Institute (INPS) for the period 1978–83.

These data, which make it possible to analyse for the first time flows of company formations and closures in Italy, suggest the following general comments. Company-formation rates are surprisingly high, even in capital-intensive sectors; 90 per cent of the companies formed are very small, with fewer than six employees. A new company's chances of survival are fairly slim, given that 15 per cent of new firms do not reach their first anniversary and 30 per cent close within three years. This has serious consequences for output and employment, as the data show that the proportion of job-creation ascribable to the formation of new firms is small by comparison with that due to the expansion of existing ones (between 14 and 16 per cent); the percentage of jobs destroyed as a result of the closure of a firm by comparison with the contraction in employment in a declining enterprise is of the same order of magnitude.

8.4. Summary and regional policy proposals

To conclude this analysis of the scale and type of public intervention in the strategic area of the Mezzogiorno, we have to recall that, although the gap between the Centre–North and the South has actually widened in recent years, both parts of the country have experienced economic growth; in the mid-1980s real per capita value-added in the Mezzogiorno was twice as high as at the beginning of the 1960s and approximately equal to the level reached by the Centre–North twenty-five years earlier. Although this gives us, and others (from Sylos Labini, 1985 to Saraceno,

---

[10] In this connection see Contini and Revelli (1985a, 1985b, 1986a, 1986b, 1987, 1988), Battagliotti and Revelli (1988), Revelli and Tenga (1987, 1988), and Revelli and Vitelli (1988).

1983; from Siracusano *et al.*, 1986 to Giannola and Imbriani, 1988), grounds for cautious optimism, it also obliges us to answer the vexed question as to why the public sector has achieved so little in its attempt to counter market incompleteness in this part of Italy.

The data presented in the preceding sections enable us to state that this was not due to a lack of public resources in the Mezzogiorno. On the contrary, the public sector has spent a great deal on both direct investment and net payments to boost households' disposable incomes, and more in the South than in the Centre–North both per capita and in relation to value-added. Tax concessions and loan subsidies have been much more limited, but they have certainly not been trivial. Moreover, dirigistic regulation of the Southern market has been substantial.

In seeking to understand why the results achieved in the Mezzogiorno have fallen so far short of the objectives, it is necessary to re-examine not the scale of overall public intervention but its nature. Historically, we can observe four main types of intervention in the Southern economy; the most prominent, in budgetary terms, is public support for households' net disposable incomes, followed by direct public investment and public transfers to assist private investment, primarily through loan subsidies and tax concessions; finally, dirigistic regulation of the private market is very extensive.

These revealed public preferences have many implications for development. The public expenditure multiplier in the Mezzogiorno is bound to be lower if funds are used to increase households' net disposable incomes rather than gross domestic product. We believe that economic measures aimed at boosting demand in the Mezzogiorno without at the same time increasing supply are relatively ineffectual or even counterproductive as they raise Southern reservation wages. This is the consequence of using public transfer payments to households and, to a certain extent, collective consumption on wages and salaries, which in the short term can create little or no value-added if no commensurate service or commodity is supplied in exchange. This public action may concern persons officially in employment (such as workers receiving benefits for short-time working and public employees recruited more to provide a reservoir of votes than to increase domestic product) or hidden unemployed (such as perfectly healthy persons drawing disability pensions and students 'parked' in the universities, partly financed by student grants[11]).

We are not willing, however, to give full endorsement to the thesis of Giannola (1986: 238), stating that

a similar policy of public transfers [to the South] is clearly the preference of the strong regions [in the Centre–North], which in this way ensure support for their own levels of activity. It is no accident that this was the main strategy adopted at critical phases of the economic cycle, and in particular in the years of intensive restructuring of Italian industry.

We consider that the policy of direct public investment in the Mezzogiorno is not open to these criticisms; not only does it directly stimulate the supply of essential goods, such as public works and infrastructure, but it also generates positive externalities for the economy as a whole by raising productivity. Nevertheless, even this form of intervention, which generally enjoys widespread approval (cf. Savona, 1988), is not without its disadvantages.

It is becoming increasingly evident that the procurement contracts often used for implementing public investment allows firms associated with organized crime in the South (Mafia, Camorra, 'Ndrangheta[12]) to launder money, even without connivance from political quarters, which also takes place; as revealed by Centorrino (1984), for example, such firms do not need to submit selling prices comparable to those of their competitors, as they are financed cheaply by the underground's illegal funds, with the result that they are able to present bids that always appear attractive to the public sector and consistently win the contract. Moreover, even if profit margins are paper-thin, firms linked with organized crime derive great benefit from the possibility of legalizing their liquid 'dirty' money through expenditures connected with the contract, such as outlays for labour, raw materials, and intermediate inputs.

Furthermore, exchanges of favours between organized crime and politicians are probably numerous, as suggested in many recent trials. In this regard, Centorrino (1985: 13) recalls that

contacts between the Mafia and political circles are conducted on several levels, and at least two reasons emerge. Let us try to reconstruct them.

[11] In Italy, high-school graduates are attached to universities while searching for a job because university fees are extremely low and there is no admission test, hence entrance is essentially free.

[12] Three manifestations of the same criminal phenomenon, the Mafia being primarily Sicilian, the Camorra Neapolitan and the 'Ndrangheta Calabrian.

First, we must set out from the logical premiss that *mafiosi* deal and kill to enrich themselves and need especially to invest their illicit earnings in legal activities. . . . Second, there is the other side of the coin: according to the judges, the countless tales of senior officials, past and present Members of Parliament, chairmen of health boards, local-authority officials and mayors prove that they have had dealings with the Mafia to obtain votes or favours or just to be left in peace and provide the best example of the ease with which the Mafia manages to penetrate unsuspected areas of public and business life.

Since the development of the Mezzogiorno requires both an expansion in public capital and infrastructure and a reduction in the scope of organized crime, there appear to be few exits from the vicious circle described above. In our view, the solution to this most difficult of problems is not to block contracts for public investment,[13] or to award them to the highest bidder instead of the lowest, or to give preference to non-local firms that are probably more independent of the Southern underworld; rather, it lies in backing up direct economic measures involving public expenditure with stronger public-order measures and judiciary controls.

Moreover, the presence of organized crime entails an economic cost for the Mezzogiorno, not only on account of the unfair competition to the detriment of potential firms but also because of the intimidation and extortion practised on 'clean' private firms already operating in the area. We cannot ignore—warns De Rita (1984: 488)—'the extent to which the local economy can be adversely affected by the Camorra or the Mafia factor, which discourage "sound" productive investment'. One must therefore conclude that more effective action by the state with regard to public order, justice, and internal security in the South is now a *sine qua non* for both public and private investment there, and hence for growth in the area.

Moving on to examine financial assistance to firms in the South, both through interest subsidies and capital grants, we note that this too is open to distortions that are partly similar to those described in the discussion of direct public investment.

[13] This is the solution implied by those who affirm (Centorrino 1984: 45) that 'the distorted use of public expenditure in the Mezzogiorno is both a cause and an effect of the Mafia phenomenon. . . . All one can do is to note that the thesis commonly expounded in the literature, namely that public expenditure in the South had reduced tensions and created consensus, has been turned on its head.'

The discretionary procedures for granting assistance are a cause of inevitable waste of resources, given that the bureaucracy is often inefficient and not always immune to pressure or bribery. The links between the bureaucracy, political circles, and the business world weaken the Mezzogiorno's growth potential and at the same time, according to Graziani (1979: 65), strengthen the hand of the

bureaucratic administrative grandees, who in the Mezzogiorno are particularly numerous and influential. As we have said, the economy of the Mezzogiorno lives largely on transfers of funds from other regions, and these transfers are predominantly public money. As such, they come under the control of the local bureaucracy, which in the Mezzogiorno has even greater power than it enjoys in the other regions of the country. On the other hand, the bureaucracy is necessary to the political equilibrium of the Mezzogiorno, since it is responsible for distributing public expenditure in a way that preserves the political status quo.

The low effectiveness of financial assistance to firms operating in the Mezzogiorno is also partly attributable to two other reasons: the fact that it does not always translate into productive investment but may fuel liquidity or purely financial speculation rather than the flow of real capital, given that the procedures for granting assistance are not linked to the actual progress of the project; and the further circumstance that, by artificially reducing the cost of capital, it stimulates investment in technologies or sectors with a high capital/output ratio and modest multiplier effects, partly owing to the lack of an adequate network of mutually integrated firms supplying one another in different sectors.

Apart from non-economic measures to improve internal security and to raise the quality and honesty of public employees, two types of economic action could be taken to overcome these problems: appropriate changes in the mechanisms for granting financial assistance so that it became more automatic and less discretionary, and more closely linked to the actual progress of the project; and above all new types of transfer to enterprises intended not to reduce their costs but to increase their profits from real, observable investments. For example, it seems to us that adequate tax allowances that increased proportionately as profits rose (forms of regressive tax-based incomes policies, to which we shall return in Section 13.4) would discourage recourse to public funds for purely financial speculation and would reward the most efficient firms.

To resolve the last problem mentioned above with regard to the drawbacks of financial assistance to firms operating in the South, the focus of public measures to promote the development of the Mezzogiorno should be changed by directing fewer resources towards heavy industry and more to light industry, giving preference to labour-intensive techniques over capital-intensive ones, improving the quality of support to agriculture and tourism, paying equal attention to services, especially business services,[14] and encouraging the growth rather than the formation of enterprises, especially local ones.

Finally, as to the harm caused by the fourth type of public intervention in the Mezzogiorno, we concur with the formula of Savona (1988), whereby the response to the excess of legal and administrative procedures that establish specific rights or obligations in the South and are the source of so many disequilibria in the labour market should be to provide for 'less state and more market' in the South. This means encouraging or allowing the deregulation of wages, prices, and tax concessions while being aware of the political risk that such a policy will be interpreted as a means of abandoning the South to its fate instead of wagering on its ability to do better by its own devices over the long term.

Restoring flexibility to the labour market in the South necessitates abolishing a series of protective measures in the name of the very principle of equality of opportunity that had originally motivated them, with a number of implications for both general working conditions and pay. Politically, the most 'disturbing'

---

[14] All the recent literature stresses the role of business services; see for example FORMEZ (1989), and within that report especially Biondi (1989) and Ciciotti (1989: 34–5). 'The first problem is to identify the types of services to consider and, in particular, whether policy should focus on so-called advanced services. In our opinion, there are at least three reasons for not considering the activities of the advanced-services sector as the sole target of a business-services policy. . . . First, what may be defined as an advanced service . . . in one context may not be an advanced service in another, partly owing to the considerable practical difficulty in measuring the innovative capacity of firms, even a *posteriori*. . . . Secondly, one must not make the mistake of adopting a definition of advanced services that favours particular user sectors (manufacturing industry, for example) or excludes certain categories of supply (such as the traditional professions). . . . Thirdly, it should be remembered that there is a functional link between services produced within a firm and those purchased from outside; this means that policy should apply to services both internal and external to the firm; as they constitute an integrated system. . . . Moreover, and in our view this is the important element in an interventionist policy that sees business services as a strategic factor in socio-economic growth, the concept of services must be understood in a very wide sense; for example, it should also include the provision of adequately equipped commercial premises.'

implications are perhaps those relating to the latter, because once wages regained their allocative significance as an indicator of scarcity there would no longer be any reason, other things being equal, to expect them to remain uniform across the various regions of Italy, between the sexes or between different age groups.

A uniform wage can lead at one and the same time to excess labour demand for 30-year-old men in the Centre–North and an excess labour supply of women of the same age in the Mezzogiorno. If the wages of the latter group fell, however, demand for their services might increase and the supply diminish. Moreover, if 30-year-olds in the Mezzogiorno not only had less probability of work, as is the case today, but also faced the prospect of lower wages than their counterparts in the Centre–North, there would be an incentive for them to migrate to that area, a phenomenon which is almost completely absent today.[15]

Nor must the spectre of past waves of emigration continue to prevent Italian public opinion,[16] from understanding that mobility is sometimes psychologically difficult but more often a source of personal and social development and is appreciated as such, especially in more advanced countries like the United States, thus providing some solution to mismatching in the labour market.

To complete the picture, it may be added that the policy of granting general, and additional relief from social-security contributions in the Mezzogiorno cannot continue for much longer; by reducing labour costs, it can create an incentive for employers to move from the Centre–North to the South—albeit a moderate one, as we have seen—but it cannot encourage labour to move in the opposite direction, as net real wages tend to be the same. With a given labour-cost differential, the effects of reducing sectoral disequilibria in the labour market would be greater if cost differences were the result of wage dispersion rather than the disparities in social-security contributions, in view of the different impact on the consequence of labour supply.

Moreover, contribution relief is never granted permanently, with the result that it benefits employment rather less than a fall in

[15] As Sarcinelli (1989) recalls, in the absence of wage flexibility and labour mobility, two of the three fundamental requirements for being able to describe the Mezzogiorno as an optimal monetary area properly integrated with the rest of Italy are missing.

[16] See Lutz (1954, 1961, 1962) and the debate she inspired, e.g. Ackley and Spaventa (1962).

wages, since labour is a quasi-fixed cost in the short run and hiring is decided by firms with a long-term perspective.

In addition, contribution relief is a financial burden on the public sector, exacerbating its already large deficit. Since its impact on employment is very limited for a number of reasons, some of which are re-examined in Sections 12.3 and 12.4, it should be drastically reduced.

As seems obvious, deregulation of the Southern labour market implies re-creating a closer link between the individual real wage and productivity, the latter unfortunately being lower in the South than in the Centre–North, partly due to deficiencies in infrastructure that the public sector should rectify as quickly as possible.

It should be noted, however, that lower nominal wages in the South than in the rest of the country owing to lower productivity would not imply proportionally lower net purchasing power in the South, since the burden of direct taxes is lighter in the Mezzogiorno and the consumer price level is lower than elsewhere.

Finally, and in more general terms, the portion of wages linked to individual productivity—which at present is smaller than the parts determined by automatic indexation or by labour agreements (cf. Padoa Schioppa, 1986*b*)—needs to be expanded for reasons of both efficiency and equity throughout the country, and not only in the least developed regions: indeed, raising wages in proportion to individual productivity boost labour productivity by providing proper incentives, and correctly rewards merit. These aspirations are now beginning to emerge in Italy, as demonstrated by recent supplementary wage agreements at important private-sector companies (Fiat and Olivetti, for example), and even by innovations of this kind in the public sector (cf. FORMEZ, 1987), of which no one in Italy can now be unaware.

Industrial Restructuring

But it seems to me that although up to now the remedies have been studied very thoroughly, no one has yet said *who will apply them*. . . . It is a waste of effort to continue to give the state advice, because the state is incapable of heeding it. . . . We are left with the alternative to declare the problem insoluble or to call for the creation of a new state that would do what the present one cannot. . . . But who will make the revolution? The antithesis . . . between reforms and revolution is meaningless. It is like the antithesis . . . between evolution and revolution. . . . Give me a fulcrum, said Archimedes, and I will move the world; but he never found the fulcrum and the world remained peacefully in its place. . . . Millions of clever books can be written about the Southern problem, and the most effective and certain remedies can be devised for the ills of Naples and Sicily, but all this work will lead nowhere until a vigorous, constant, and consistent movement emerges in the Mezzogiorno itself to implement those reforms that for the moment are no more than the pious desires of academics. Is that possible? And in what way will it come about?

(G. Salvemini, *Scritti sulla questione meridionale*, 1899)

9

General Instruments of Industrial Policy

9.1. *The evolution of Italian industry*

Despite its particularities, the problem of growth in the Mezzogiorno is part of the more general problem of Italian development. This has been tackled in many of our studies, some of which try to identify the lines along which the Italian economy has evolved while others endeavour to show the effects various public policy instruments have on it.

The former include analyses carried out for us by Heimler and Milana, (see Heimler, 1984, 1987a, 1987b; Heimler and Milana, 1985, 1986; Milana, 1985, 1986 which show the increasing weight and the relative growth of industrial processing and manufacturing. This expansion is unique among the economically more advanced countries, in which there is a general tendency for the industrial share of value-added to contract.

Over the years, the composition of Italy's output has shifted more into line with that of the most developed countries, but the economy continues to be highly specialized in the traditional manufacture of textiles and clothing, leather goods and footwear, and non-metal mineral products. It is impossible to make an accurate assessment of the benefits of this specialization, or to predict future developments on the basis of experience in other industrial countries, since it is typical only of the Italian economy, which is backward in world trade in new high-technology goods.

The information gathered on the use and costs of factors of production makes it possible to analyse in depth the growth of the internal structure of individual branches of industry. Over time there has been a general reduction in unit requirements for all productive inputs, boosting productivity and reducing production costs. In recent years labour savings have been much greater than savings in other production factors, and this has led to a marked change in the relative intensity of factor use. Moreover, the reaction of Italian producers to the rise in energy prices has also been appreciable. Ten years after the first oil shock, the consumption of energy inputs would have been 33 per cent higher than the actual figure if technology similar to that existing in 1973 had still been in use. The energy savings have been achieved thanks to a change in the composition of inputs and a parallel increase in the use of machinery per unit of output.

Overall productivity appears to have increased less rapidly than labour productivity alone, although it rose steadily until the beginning of the 1970s. In the period after 1973 the rise in both productivity indexes slowed down, mainly in conjunction with the recessionary trends associated with the two energy crises.

Significant complementarity between labour and capital inputs, which has been found in eight out of nineteen industries, helps explain the marked shift in the use of production factors over the last ten years. The frequency with which the two primary factors appear to complement rather than replace one another should lead to a critical re-examination of a large part of industrial policy. The implications of variations in relative prices for the volume of demand may prove to be very different from those indicated by traditional analysis, which concentrates solely on the creation of value-added. Complementarity between labour and capital leads to a reduction in the use of both when the price of one of them increases. Owing to the inadequate statistical information available, it is not possible to distinguish imported intermediate inputs from those produced domestically. Nevertheless, aggregate indicators show a continual increase in demand for imports of intermediate goods, probably due to the substitution of such products for labour.

Indeed, as we are reminded by Heimler and Milana (1986: 28), historically

Italian producers reacted to increases in labour costs by substituting capital for labour, but in the sectors where the two factors are complementary they replaced both with intermediate inputs and imported materials.

The role of the relative prices of production factors, which is often neglected in analyses of the structure of Italian industry, is essential in explaining the changes that have occurred in demand. Restructuring within individual industries makes it possible to reduce production costs significantly; without it, the very survival of firms in domestic and international markets would have been jeopardized in the years of deepest crisis, given the considerable increases in labour costs at the end of the 1960s and the sharp variations in relative prices in the 1970s. Hence it does not appear that empirical evidence, combined with certain interpretative models of an econometric type, confirms the thesis that the structure of Italian industry has remained ossified over the years.

9.2. *Industrial policy and relative prices*

In the light of these observations, we can now offer some thoughts on the industrial policy pursued over the past twenty years and possible alternative action.

The observed replacement of labour by machines and intermediate inputs can be attributed in large part to the more rapid rise in per capita labour costs than in the prices of other production factors. Similarly, the substitution of machines and intermediate inputs for energy, which occurred mainly from 1973 onwards, was the direct consequence of the oil shocks.

A first reflection suggested by these effects thus relates to Italy's public policy for its contribution in setting relative factor prices, a policy that tends to keep the relative price of otherwise expensive factors artificially low on account of its counter-inflationary objectives. This influences the behaviour of firms and sometimes makes it difficult to properly adjust production techniques, thus imposing high costs on the entire economy.

One significant example according to Heimler and Milana (1984) came in 1979–80, when the CIP reduced the price of electricity for energy-intensive industries. The CIP's decision stemmed from the belief, now found to have been mistaken, that unit energy requirements were inelastic, so that if energy prices had remained at their market level these industries would have suffered higher cost increases than their foreign competitors. This partly removed the incentive for electricity-consuming companies to save more energy and for the electricity-generating sector to proceed to a full restructuring, which would have brought lower energy costs, as occurred in France, for example.

As to labour costs, an interventionist policy should take account of the demand elasticity, which in absolute terms is generally less than unity; an increase in this factor cost thus leads to a limited reduction in the quantity used and is passed largely on to selling prices. In view of the relative rigidity in the use of labour, producers respond to wage increases by reducing employment to some extent, increasing capital intensity, and using larger quantities of materials purchased from other sectors or from abroad.

As regards variations in interest rates, partly determined by the interaction of monetary and fiscal policies, it may be useful to evaluate their effects not only on aggregate demand and investment but also on input substitution. An increase in interest rates causes a rise in the user cost of capital, which in turn leads to the replacement of capital by other productive inputs. Here too, the complementarity between capital and labour, evident in numerous industries, means that an increase in the user cost of capital reduces the demand for both capital and labour and causes a parallel increase in the demand for intermediate inputs.

A rise in import prices due to a devaluation of the lira against other currencies can lead to a reduction in the volume of imported inputs. A slowdown in the processes of restructuring and input substitution as a consequence of such a policy reduces the scope for containing the rise in unit costs and inflation in general. Moreover, given that around 80 per cent of Italy's total imports are used in production, a deterioration in the terms of trade due to devaluation of the lira generates sooner or later increases in costs and domestic prices. In general, a protectionist policy aimed at containing imports can have adverse consequences on both prices and plant modernization and restructuring by delaying the adoption of up-to-date technologies that require increasing quantities of foreign products.

9.3. Industrial policy and technological progress

Let us now try to assess the effects of the industrial policy aimed at introducing innovative technology, by distinguishing (as proposed by Heimler and Milana) between technical progress geared towards improving the quality of production factors and that aimed at increasing the total productivity of the means of production.

Whereas the first type of technical progress is almost completely exogenous to the enterprise because it is embodied in the inputs it purchases and is at least partly determined by economic policy, the second type depends on the firm's capacity to reorganize production more efficiently. With regard to the first, the public authorities can act on several fronts, such as continuous education, vocational training, guidance, finance for research and development (R & D), or the promotion of socio-economic infrastructure conducive to improvements in labour productivity.

An educational policy that pays greater heed to the needs of the economy tends to improve the efficiency of the labour force and hence makes it easier to adopt technologies that require an ever higher level of expertise. The technological revolution that is taking place, which is based mainly on a substantial increase in automation, calls for a significant deepening of education, mainly by rationalizing and modernizing school and university curricula.

Looking at the research and development promoted within Italian enterprises, the analysis carried out for us by the Szegö group[1] notes that innovation in the Italian economy is financed predominantly by public funds, in a way that gives rise to serious distortions. In other Western countries, by contrast, other methods are used, such as tax incentives, public contracts, or funding via the capital markets. In addition, empirical evidence in Italy reveals what is in many ways a surprising lack of correlation between public measures in support of research and development and total private investment in R & D: between 1979 and 1985 public funding of enterprises fluctuated widely, whereas firms' commitment to research and development was constant. This leads Szegö to argue that firms formulate their innovation strategies regardless of public financial support.

The intensity of R & D efforts differs according to company size. As the majority of small Italian enterprises operate below the technological threshold, they are not able to benefit directly from research and development activities. Public funding therefore appears to perform a significant, but not decisive role, and only for larger firms.

Public measures regarding the socio-economic infrastructure are of great relevance to industrial policy, as has already been shown with regard to the problem of the Mezzogiorno. In the preceding sections we have mentioned the first statistical analyses (at both national and European level) aimed at measuring the implications that the existence or lack of infrastructure has for the market. It seems to us, however, that no attempt has yet been made in Italy to quantify the impact of changes in the efficiency of public

[1] Camerano (1987), D'Ecclesia and Camerano (1987), and Szegö (1993). See also Norton (1986) and Gabriele and La Camera (1986).

services on firms' costs, despite the fact that various qualitative studies on services such as transport, telecommunications, and postal services have clearly demonstrated the importance of the problem.

10

Discretionary Instruments of Industrial Policy

10.1. *Industrial policy and 'strategic' factors*

Whereas the industrial-policy instruments listed above are of a general nature and leave the market free to adjust, discretionary measures in specific sectors are aimed at creating a different industrial structure to the one the market would have established. Industrial policy in this second sense tends to channel the flow of private investment towards particular companies, sectors, and regions. It is often used when it is felt that the market is incapable of bringing about the adjustments in the industrial structure that are deemed necessary, as in the case of the Mezzogiorno.

If such an industrial policy is examined with reference to Italy, it is possible to identify three sub-periods in which different methods and objectives were employed, although the measures were always fragmentary and not part of a general framework of planned development.

The year 1975 was a turning point, signalling the end of the first phase in which incentives were provided without discrimination between industries. In view of serious disequilibria in the markets in energy products and in the prices of industrial inputs, a conviction had emerged during the first half of the 1970s that Italian industry needed to undergo profound structural change in order to cope with the sharp variations in relative prices and international competitiveness.

These concerns were fuelled by numerous analyses that underlined a certain (presumed) degree of rigidity in Italian industry and its inability to restructure itself and introduce technological innovations. These diagnoses were backed up by other, no less pessimistic, reports on the competitive prospects of Italian companies, based mainly on studies that took the product-cycle theory as their starting point. These described the international position of Italian industry as particularly weak, relying on technologically mature products and hence vulnerable to competition from newly industrialized countries that could use low-cost labour.

In this climate, a new philosophy of public intervention was taking shape, aimed at selecting 'winning' sectors and encouraging the abandonment of 'mature' products, which, according to the forecasts of that time, would find it increasingly difficult to survive. The new strategies should therefore have fostered a shift in production from some sectors to others and assisted the restructuring of existing manufacturing activities where possible. The lack of confidence in industrial firms' capacity for spontaneous renewal had thus caused public intervention to be focused, in theory at least, on action that would accelerate the change in the sectoral composition of industry. Presidential Decree 902 of 1976 on the National Incentives Fund and Law 675 of 1977 on the restructuring and reorganization of industry were the result of the new policy, which for the first time explicitly introduced a logic for intervention according to sector, as opposed to the traditional system of blanket incentives.

Nevertheless, the basic hypotheses underlying the dominant analyses of the second half of the 1970s were largely disproved by the facts. It is true that Italian industry continued to figure in the so-called traditional sectors, but its production methods had changed radically, thanks to the introduction of new technologies able to increase factor productivity and modify factor-input ratios. Italy had a growing trade surplus on manufactured goods, with exports increasing more strongly than imports. The last years of the period under consideration saw a growing international integration of Italian industry and a steady improvement in the competitiveness of the very sectors that had been identified as areas without prospects for growth or competitiveness.

More recently it has become clear that the changes that occurred in the 1970s and early 1980s affected all sectors to differing degrees, irrespective of the maturity of their products. This was due mainly to the fact that technological and organizational innovations in individual industries spread to other sectors as a result of sectoral interdependence. For example, innovations in new materials and services, such as data processing and telecommunications, had an impact on process innovations in more traditional industries (textiles and clothing, paper and printing products), which entailed a profound change in techniques and in the use of production factors, a reduction in costs, and an improvement in profit margins.

The accentuation of international competition during the 1980s caused public intervention in all countries to be concentrated more strongly on trade flows. In Italy, exports were aided by public subsidies for credit to finance exports of capital goods, while Law 227 of 1976 increased the subsidies available and reorganized the institutions responsible for granting export credit and export-credit guarantees.

In the 1980s industrial policy continued to be influenced by uncertainty about the prospects for the further development of the Italian industrial model. Measures therefore remained fragmented, and aimed at coping with emergencies or sectoral crises rather than achieving planned and strategic objectives of industrial growth.

A number of recent empirical analyses on incentives in the form of subsidized credit confirm that public assistance to enterprises has generally been inspired by a defensive logic aimed at promoting the reorganization of production in industries considered to be weak rather than supporting industries at the cutting edge, which would give a strong boost to overall growth. In the context of export assistance, the public commitment to subsidized credit has steadily increased, rising from 2.4 per cent of the value of total Italian exports in 1974 to around 4 per cent in the first half of the 1980s.

10.2. Industrial policy and multi-country comparisons

International data from OECD sources indicate that at present Italy, France, the United Kingdom, Switzerland, and Belgium have a relatively high ratio of export credits to exports (between 15 and 20 per cent) and are drawing away from Japan and the United States, which have the lowest ratios (between 5 and 10 per cent).

Available evidence indicates that Italy contrasts with some other countries (notably the United States and Japan) in the choice of instruments of industrial and trade policy. Whereas Italy appears to prefer specific and discretionary action on costs—reducing the cost of credit and, in some cases, the effective prices of capital goods—other countries seem to make greater use of instruments that cause less distortion of competition and free trade by acting directly on demand. In the United States the very limited use of credit subsidies reflects a free-market philosophy aimed at minimizing the distortion of competitive prices and the inefficient use of resources. In Italy, on the other hand, credit subsidies have come to predominate. In addition, in this country employment policies played an increasing role in the 1980s, especially through the use of the Wage Supplementation Fund and relief from social-security contributions.

There are also other characteristics that set Italy apart from other industrialized areas. In some countries the tendency to adopt forms of planned action in place of an industrial policy based on emergency measures is now gaining momentum, with the various strands of policy being integrated within a single, continuous strategy.

Close co-ordination between fiscal, tariff, and trade policies is sometimes enhanced by the existence of highly integrated institutions, such as the Ministry of International Trade and Industry (MITI) in Japan, where a single governmental machine makes it possible to effectively monitor the industrial system both within the country and in its activities in world markets. In Italy, by contrast, the institutional framework for industrial and trade policy is determined by a number of public bodies with interwoven and overlapping powers.

10.3. Some industrial-policy proposals

The powers and functions at present distributed in Italy among a number of bodies (interministerial committees, ministries, local authorities and agencies) should therefore be organized in a more co-ordinated manner. The new structure devoted to industrial policy should be based on the types of public intervention that are consistent with Italy's traditions and the general shape of her public administration, but it should also incorporate important innovations so as to make the country better equipped for the future.

As to industrial-policy instruments, Italy makes insufficient use of public-sector demand, at least by comparison with the other major industrial countries. The premiss for the development of direct public intervention must be the restoration of sound public finances; without this, it would not be possible to raise the quality of investment and collective consumption in accordance with long- and medium-term plans.

In present conditions, the constraint imposed by the budget deficit should not, however, be an insuperable obstacle to improving the quality of public contracts and modernizing the infrastructure. In addition, there is considerable scope for co-ordinating public-spending programmes among the industrial countries, as has already occurred in industrial-development projects decided at the EEC level. Participation in major aerospace programmes, technology development programmes, infrastructure projects, and land-use planning programmes still provides many important opportunities for promoting Italian industry.

However, as already recalled with reference to the Mezzogiorno, in the field of industrial policy too it is imperative to warn of the double danger of excessive public regulation of the market and the inappropriate choice of other policy instruments. As the Minister for Industry recognized in evidence to the Chamber of Deputies' Committee on Economic Activities on 13 October 1987, the significant modernization of Italian industry after the oil shocks is not so much the outcome of industrial policies as the spontaneous result of market reaction to the explosive increase in the cost of labour and certain imported raw materials in the 1970s, and from the 1980s onwards is also an expression of the self-restraint imposed on both employers and trade unions by Italy's membership of the EMS, reinforced by a non-accommodating monetary and exchange-rate policy.

The Minister was downright critical of the *specific* sectoral plans (Battaglia 1987: 4):

As well as highlighting the inadequacy of the specific sectoral plans as a tool and the inconsistency of the (mainly financial) instruments provided for under Law 675 on industrial reorganization, the document on industrial policy approved in April 1986 by the Senate Industry Committee at the end of a detailed inquiry emphasized that the targeted programmes had proved useless for selective structural intervention in industry owing to the difficulty of formulating programmes in such a way that they provided a systematic and coherent framework for action. The document also stated that support was concentrated mainly in sectors with a preponderance of large industrial groups, to the detriment of those with a large number of small and medium-sized enterprises.

No conclusion seems to provide a more fitting epilogue to our analyses than that reached by the former Minister for Industry (Battaglia 1987: 15):

On the basis of the data and assessments made so far, there appears to be a need for reconsideration, with the general objective of encouraging and reinforcing the changes now occurring throughout industry, which are aimed at improving efficiency and safeguarding competitiveness.

The rapidity with which structural changes can occur depends crucially on the capacity to intervene in sectors such as applied research and technological innovation and on the spread of new technology in industry. The strategic importance of these factors relates to industry as a whole, and not only to advanced sectors.

The ultimate objective of industrial policy should be to improve the working of the market in order to ensure the best possible operating conditions for enterprises and the most efficient use of factors of production, in accordance with the market's allocative function.

In this perspective . . . it appears essential to carry out a careful reorganization of the existing dirigistic regulations and . . . to eliminate all the regulatory and bureaucratic obstacles that hamper firms' activities.

In short, the policy of industrial rescue operations in response to exceptional events must be brought to an end and a system of ordinary intervention created to deal with crises, based on well-defined objectives, time scales, and instruments.

PART V
Strategic Intervention in Productive Inputs

Employment

After the occupation of the factories, the owners of Fiat suggested to the workers that they should codetermine the running of the firm and participate in the ownership. Naturally, the reformists were in favour. An industrial crisis was looming, and working-class families were worried by the spectre of unemployment. If the Fiat plan were to be accepted, there would be some security of employment for the workforce, and especially for the more politically active workers, who were convinced they faced the sack. . . . The Fiat proposal fitted into Giolitti's political plan. And what was this plan? The days of tranquil government by the bourgeoisie had come to an end even before the war. . . . After the bloody decade from 1890 to 1900, the bourgeois had to abandon a dictatorship that was too exclusive, too violent, too direct: southern peasants and northern workers had risen against them *simultaneously*, although not in any co-ordinated way. In the new century the dominant class inaugurated a new policy, of class alliances, of class-based political blocs, in other words of bourgeois democracy. It had to choose: between a rural democracy, in other words an alliance with southern peasants . . . and an industrial bloc uniting capitalists and workers . . . committed to a reformist policy on wages and trade-union rights. Not by chance, it chose the latter; Giolitti was the personification of bourgeois dominance, and the Socialist Party became the instrument of Giolittian policy.

(A. Gramsci, *Alcuni temi della questione meridionale*, 1930)

11

Public Employment, Unemployment Benefits, and Dirigistic Regulation of the Labour Market

11.1. Direct and indirect public action to combat unemployment

It would be impossible to understand fully the strategic motivation behind Italian economic policy without examining the state's constant commitment to tackle what is perceived as perhaps Italy's greatest structural problem and one that is growing worse, namely unemployment. As we have already shown in Tables 7.5, 7.6, 8.2 and 8.3, it is so closely bound up with the problem of the Mezzogiorno that we have already had to discuss it at length when dealing with that strategic sector in Sections 7.3–8.2.

According to ISTAT's latest reconstructions, which are reproduced in Tables 11.1 and 11.2, in 1988 the overall unemployment rate[1] was 12 per cent, but touched 18.8 per cent for women, 34.5 per cent for young women, and 21.6 per cent for men under 30 years of age, whereas ten years earlier it had been little more than half as high; the overall employment rate, on the other hand, remained virtually stable at 36–7 per cent over the same period, with a slight decline for men and some increase for women. The greatest disequilibria in the labour market, apart from those in the southern regions, are to be found among other weak groups that we have already mentioned, that is to say young people and women.

In an attempt at classification, it is useful to emphasize the four types of direct and indirect public action to combat unemployment. First and foremost is the creation of direct demand for labour within government and public corporations. Secondly, there are measures that cater for emergencies, even endemic ones, by providing unemployment benefits, both openly (via the Wage

---

[1] The official figures overestimate unemployment in that they ignore the underground economy, which many indicators show to be flourishing in Italy, especially in the Mezzogiorno, but at the same time they underestimate it because workers drawing benefits from the Wage Supplementation Fund are treated as employed; reclassifying them as unemployed would increase the unemployment rate by around 2 %age points.

Employment

TABLE 11.1. Employment and unemployment rates by sex

Year	Employment rates (%age)			Unemployment rates (%age)		
	Male	Female	Total	Male	Female	Total
1978	51.4	21.3	36.0	4.7	12.6	7.2
1979	51.4	21.8	36.2	4.9	13.3	7.7
1980	51.7	22.4	36.7	4.8	13.1	7.6
1981	51.7	22.6	36.7	5.4	14.4	8.4
1982	51.3	22.6	36.6	6.1	14.9	9.1
1983	51.0	22.7	36.5	6.6	16.2	9.9
1984	50.5	22.8	36.3	6.8	17.1	10.4
1985	50.4	23.0	36.3	7.0	17.3	10.6
1986	50.2	23.5	36.5	7.4	17.8	11.1
1987	49.7	23.7	36.4	8.1	18.7	12.0
1988	50.6	24.4	37.2	8.1	18.8	12.0

Sources: Calculations based on ISTAT (1985*a*) data for the years 1978–81; (1985*b*) for the years 1982–5; and *Statistiche demografiche*, various years, for 1986–7; 'Rilevazione delle forze di lavoro. Media annua: Nord–Centro–Mezzogiorno', various years for 1978–87; Banca d'Italia (1989*a*) for the general rates in 1988.

Supplementation Fund) and covertly (in the form of disability pensions or student grants). Thirdly, the state offers credit subsidies and tax concessions to increase the net advantage the private sector derives from employing labour. And finally, economic policy imposes dirigistic regulation of the private labour market as regards both wages (minimum wages, automatic increases, indexation) and legal rights or duties; in many respects, workers and employers are not free to determine the conditions for admission to the labour market (ban on employing children or firing women in the two months before and three months after childbirth), the criteria for hiring (by name or from the top of a list of candidates, for a fixed term or not), the limits on the provision of labour (working hours, leave entitlement, public holidays) or the circumstances in which employment can be terminated (prohibition of dismissal without due cause).

TABLE 11.2. Employment and unemployment rates by sex in the population under 30 years of age

Year	Employment rates (% age)			Unemployment rates (% age)		
	Male	Female	Total	Male	Female	Total
1978	50.0	32.8	41.5	19.1	20.0	18.1
1979	49.9	33.1	41.6	14.7	24.4	18.8
1980	50.6	33.5	42.1	14.6	24.7	18.2
1981	49.8	32.3	41.4	16.1	26.1	20.6
1982	48.1	32.1	40.2	18.0	28.2	22.4
1983	46.6	31.1	39.1	19.4	30.7	24.3
1984	44.8	30.0	37.5	19.7	32.8	25.5
1985	44.0	29.5	36.9	20.4	33.4	26.1
1986	43.6	29.6	36.7	20.6	33.8	26.8
1987	42.8	29.7	36.4	22.1	34.9	27.8
1988	47.0	31.9	39.5	21.6	34.5	27.4

Sources: Calculations based on ISTAT (1985*a*) data for the years 1978–81; (1985*b*) for the years 1982–5; and *Statistiche demografiche*, various years, for 1986–7; 'Rilevazione delle forze di lavoro. *Media annua: Nord–Centro–Mezzogiorno*', various years for 1978–87; Banca d'Italia (1989*a*) for the general rates in 1988.

11.2. Dirigistic regulation of the labour market

As we have already recalled in the analysis of the Mezzogiorno, the Italian labour market appears to be one of the most highly regulated, providing excessive automatic safeguards for some sections of the labour force but insufficient protection for others, which nevertheless sometimes emerge as more flexible and able to adapt to a flourishing market that is marginal, semi-clandestine, or even underground. In that sense, Padoa Schioppa (1988*b*: 75–6) asserts that

the assessment is complicated, because on the one hand it is true that legislation and the courts create deep divisions within the active population by regulating the labour market unequally, and thus paradoxically widen the gap between insiders and outsiders, and it is true that they cause distortions between sectors, geographic areas, and companies of different size and type, depending on their degree of protection. On the other hand, it is also true that the most creative section of the working population, the section with the greatest incentive for self-improvement and hence the most efficient, enterprising, and adaptable to constantly changing needs, is often the group that is apparently marginalized and least protected. But this group is in fact better integrated within small and very small production units, with a greater interest in their growth, and is less alienated, thanks to the variety of responsibilities it is given or to the distance from major cities which are sometimes unlivable in. Italy is an extremely interesting laboratory of examples of this kind, ranging from the new so-called Adriatic model to the traditional models applied in the knitwear industry of Prato (in Tuscany) and Carpi (in Emilia-Romagna), or in the underground glove-making industry in the Neapolitan hinterland.

Many examples could be cited to support this view of the inherently contradictory nature of the dirigistic regulation of the Italian labour market, starting with the Workers' Statute or the 1975 Interorganizational Agreement between employers and trade unions on uniform cost-of-living adjustments; created to protect the weaker party in the voluntary exchange—the worker versus the capitalist, the woman as opposed to the man, the probationer as opposed to the worker who cannot be dismissed, the Southern worker as opposed to the one in the Centre–North—in reality they undermined his position[2] by increasing the cost of his labour per unit of output.[3]

The case of working mothers provides an almost symbolic example of the distinctive rigidity of the Italian labour market caused by regulation that pays no heed to market reactions or to the perverse effects on the weak party it was supposed to protect. The 1971 Law on Motherhood (Law 1204 of 30 December) is unique in the legislation of industrial countries, in that it does not permit but requires women to be absent from work for two months before and three months after the birth of their baby, irrespective of need and on almost full pay; it subsequently facilitates the mother's absence from work, on reduced pay, during the first three years of her child's life.

[2] It should be remembered, however, that the implications of dirigistic labour market regulation and, in particular, of the 1975 Agreement can be interpreted differently; see e.g. the interpretation of Barca and Magnani (1989).

[3] For a critical, albeit rapid, examination of such legislation, which was introduced in Italy mainly in the 1970s, see Modigliani *et al.*, (1986) and Padoa Schioppa (1986*b*). The effects these laws and their interpretation by the courts had on the non-monetary component of labour costs are well known and were described in great detail in several of our analyses, especially by Crescenzi and Ravoni (1986), Dal Co (1984), Faustini *et al.*, (1986), Forlani (1985*b*), and Tronti (1987).

The Law was intended to prevent the dismissal of pregnant young women who needed to give up work for a prolonged period, and to provide equality of opportunity for women (both healthy and sick); however, in practice it exacerbated the exclusion of women from the market by increasing the expected cost of female labour relative to male, as discussed elsewhere (cf. Padoa Schioppa, 1977).

The resulting fall in female participation rates, which was observed in Italy up to the mid-1970s and was unique among developed countries, demonstrated that in fact the Law placed women at an even greater disadvantage by protecting their weakness rather than combating it; at the very time this was happening in Italy, all special protection for women (such as the ban on night work, heavy work, etc.) was being abolished elsewhere (in the United States, for example) in the name of the same objective of equal opportunity (cf. Padoa Schioppa, 1979a). It is no accident that during that period Italian women swelled the ranks of home workers, often in the underground economy, thus participating in the phenomenon known as 'productive decentralization'.

The situation of female workers in Italy is now better than it was, but not because Italy has followed the lead of other countries by deregulating and adopting a series of social policies designed to strengthen women (from the provision of crèches to old-people's homes); instead, further layers of protection have been added—the relative position of female workers has been improved by introducing the right to paternity leave as well as maternity leave!

In general, it is difficult to make a cross-country comparison of labour-market legislation and regulations, and different interpretations are possible, some of which even gave rise to differences of opinion within our research group. In this regard, Forlani (1985a: 73) reminds us that

the OECD countries can be distinguished according to stance: one group, which has a marked *laissez-faire* tradition and hence little inclination to provide strong forms of protection for workers upon recruitment, dismissal, or in unemployment, consists of the Anglo-Saxon countries and Japan (where one should nevertheless remember the dichotomy . . . between the one-third of the workforce who are 'workers for life' and the two-thirds who have barely any protection); another group, comprising basically the Scandinavian countries, provides particularly strong guarantees (more as regards economic protection in unemployment than measures to prevent dismissal); and other countries with their own individual arrangements.

As far as the areas of greatest regulation are concerned, Forlani (1985*a*: 74), whose judgements we do not always share, maintains that

as a result of recent Italian legislation (Law 863 of 1984 and previous decrees on training schemes and recruitment by name), the difference between hiring conditions in Italy and the unrestricted conditions prevailing in other countries is only apparent. Recruitment from lists following a FIFO system (first in, first out) cannot be considered a serious constraint, given its relatively low incidence and the circumvention of the rules as a result of direct switching from one firm to another.

Italy's position with regard to firing is, on the contrary, highly anomalous, being difficult and costly. This helps understanding why unemployment is very low among workers over 30 but extremly high among young people: Italy has the second-highest youth-unemployment rate in Europe, exceeded only by Spain.

It is hard to compare in a multi-country analysis the protection provided for absences from work, absenteeism, and strikes. Here more than in other fields, what counts is not only the law but also its interpretation by the courts and by public opinion which may vary considerably from one period to another even within the same country as a result of changes in the balance of power between different social classes. This explains why in Italy absenteeism is now treated much more severely than in the 1970s and is in fact far lower than it was then, without any changes having been made in the Workers' Statute; it was not until the 1980s that it was reduced to levels comparable to those abroad.

Moving on to the regulation concerning labour costs, Forlani (1985*a*: 74–6) states that

despite differences from one country to another, measures to reduce youth labour costs appear to be universal, although the prevalence of apprenticeships in Germany has a greater impact on average labour costs than the British Youth Training Scheme, for example. It is particularly difficult to make a comparative analysis of relief from social-security contributions. Incentives of one kind or another are provided in almost all countries. However, they generally appear to be applied more selectively than in Italy. . . . There are notable differences between the countries examined as regards the distribution of the cost of financing the system of unemployment assistance. In general, employers' contributions are higher than those paid by employees and vary according to the system of protection. In some cases, however, employers' and employees' contributions are equal (Germany) or the employers' share is actually lower (the Netherlands). The contribution systems in force penalize labour-intensive firms, since contributions are levied on salaries. The system adopted in Sweden is an exception, and for this and other reasons it would be well to analyse it in depth. Comparison with Italy is almost impossible; apart from the special case of Wage Supplementation Fund benefits, Italy's system of unemployment benefit is more ridiculous than sensible (Lit. 800 a day).

The system, however, has been recently changed, and unemployment benefits are no longer derisory.

11.3. Public employment and unemployment benefits

Touching briefly on the other categories of measures into which we divided strategic action affecting the labour market, we note in Table 11.3 that direct support for employment is reflected in the growth in the number of public employees in non-marketed services and, in broad terms, also in public corporations. Between 1970 and 1987 there was a net increase of 1,200,000 employees in government, a rise of more than 50 per cent, while employment in state-controlled companies rose by around 100,000 overall, despite the decline that occurred after 1980. Whereas in the 1960s the growth in public employment was in the central state administration, from the 1970s onwards it was chiefly in public enterprises and local administrations.

With regard to the second category of measures, namely those to cater for emergencies by providing support for the unemployed, it is worth discussing the system operated by the Wage Supplementation Fund in a little more detail.

The Wage Supplementation Fund came into being at the end of the Fascist era. Its scale of operations expanded enormously from the mid 1970s onwards in parallel with industrial restructuring and did not decline again until the second half of the 1980s, as illustrated in Table 11.4.

Traditionally, Italy does not have a universal system of unemployment benefits (especially for young people), but workers who are temporarily laid off for a variety of reasons may obtain ordinary or special benefits from the Wage Supplementation Fund;

TABLE 11.3. Public employment

Year	Employment in general government ('000s)	Employment in state-controlled companies ('000s)
1970	2,129.9	462.4
1971	2,235.7	531.6
1972	2,355.3	584.8
1973	2,465.2	617.9
1974	2,568.0	687.3
1975	2,656.0	706.7
1976	2,743.0	715.0
1977	2,819.0	710.7
1978	2,880.0	706.8
1979	2,933.0	712.2
1980	2,954.0	715.5
1981	3,013.0	714.9
1982	3,049.0	702.5
1983	3,080.0	706.8
1984	3,108.0	679.2
1985	3,120.0	653.1
1986	3,263.0	588.7
1987	3,309.0	564.7

Sources: ISTAT, *Annuario di contabilità nazionale*, 1987, for new national accounting data on general government from 1970 to 1985; ISTAT (1989); for data on 1986–7 Marzano and Marzovilla (1988) for data on state-controlled companies from 1970 to 1980; Ministero delle Partecipazioni Statali, various years, for data from 1981 to 1987.

these amount to 80 per cent of their gross wages (a higher percentage of wages net of tax and work-related living expenses). The payments are temporary in name only, as in fact workers can continue to draw benefits for many years.

The example of the Wage Supplementation Fund typifies a whole series of pronounced rigidities in the Italian labour market caused by the excessive protection given to some groups of workers coupled with an absence of safeguards for others. There is no parallel elsewhere in Europe. The only other scheme with a fixed replacement ratio between unemployment benefit and the wage the worker would have earned had he been working is the compensation for short-time working in Germany (*kurz Arbeit*), but the percentage is only 60 per cent and it is paid for a much shorter

TABLE 11.4. Hours compensated by the Cassa Integrazione Guadagni (Wage Supplementation Fund) (in '000s)

	1979	1980	1981	1982	1983	1984	1985	1986	1987	1988
Ordinary hours										
Agriculture	282	334	442	349	367	223	712	379	303	270
Industry excluding construction	56,133	106,694	185,272	189,412	226,037	194,444	117,066	97,787	85,189	59,681
Construction	1,596	1,472	2,711	2,620	2,073	3,122	3,417	3,125	2,944	2,190
Transport and communications	215	229	542	785	755	540	476	359	233	267
Tobacco growing	779	609	48	40	18	26	38	18	113	168
TOTAL	59,005	109,338	189,014	193,205	229,250	198,356	121,708	101,667	88,783	62,576
Total hours[a]										
Agriculture	318	365	549	499	730	574	1,166	805	838	592
Industry excluding construction	191,910	237,062	487,976	546,520	669,478	728,758	613,429	556,587	443,947	350,177
Construction	106,238	68,740	85,570	68,537	70,130	82,163	96,137	83,448	80,407	62,910
Transport and communications	313	362	1,624	1,933	4,918	1,418	4,876	5,674	3,329	1,985
Tobacco growing	779	609	2,026	1,974	1,262	982	1,022	843	459	950
Distribution	n.a.	n.a.	n.a.	n.a.	n.a.	n.a.	n.a.	n.a.	4,060	1,873
TOTAL	299,558	307,138	577,745	619,464	746,518	813,896	716,631	647,356	533,040	418,488

[a] Comprises ordinary and special benefits and the special scheme for the construction industry.

Source: Banca d'Italia, (1989*a*).

period. Everywhere else the replacement ratio of benefits to wages is variable and in all cases is less than 80 per cent.

11.4. *The Wage Supplementation Fund (Cassa Integrazione Guadagni)*

As illustrated in Padoa Schioppa (1988a), the system operated by the Wage Supplementation Fund is a veritable gift from government to both companies and workers: to companies, in that it enables them to shed excess labour through a gentle form of dismissal, and to workers, in that the sum they are paid for not working is almost as much as the net wage they would receive if they were employed.

This is not without consequences, for on the one hand, *ceteris paribus*, it increases the reservation wage of the labour force, and on the other it exposes firms and workers to moral hazard: as contributions to the Fund bear no relation to recourse to Fund benefits by individual workers and firms, workers and employers agree among themselves to keep wages relatively high (and consequently employment low). This harms neither the prosperity of the workers, whose unemployment benefits increase in proportion, nor the profitability of the firm, which makes productivity gains by virtue of the reduction in manpower, but operates solely to the detriment of the government, which disburses larger sums through the Fund.

It can thus be proved (cf. Padoa Schioppa, 1988a) that if, *ceteris paribus*, Italy adopted a system of unemployment benefits similar to those operated elsewhere in the world, with a variable rather than a fixed replacement ratio, employment would be higher than can be achieved by means of the Wage Supplementation Fund, without loss of welfare for either workers or employers. The reason for this lies in the fact that, under the present system, the trade unions are less inclined to accept wage cuts because this would have an impact on the value of both the hours worked and those not worked, given that unemployment benefits are proportional to wages. Indeed, the link the Fund creates between unit benefits and wages indexes public-transfer payments as well as the incomes of workers and firms. The Fund therefore propagates inflation by saving the market from having to pay the cost of the inflation caused by the behaviour of unions and employers and preventing the state from reaping the benefits.

It can be proved that behaviour to the detriment of the state induced by moral hazard would cease if contributions to finance the Wage Supplementation Fund increased in proportion to recourse by firms and workers, in accordance with the principle of experience-rating. In a sense, this would confirm the hypothesis originally proposed by Feldstein (1973) and reiterated by Topel (1983: 555), albeit with reference to the very different case of the United States of America, that 'methods of financing unemployment insurance can have important effects on the incidence of unemployment'.

Some observers maintain that the Wage Supplementation Fund is a brilliant Italian invention, as it gives the labour market an otherwise unattainable flexibility by eliminating the obstacles to the dismissal of workers and guaranteeing social security (80 per cent of gross wages) rather than simply providing assistance for the needy unemployed. In reality, as indicated above, in the short term the Fund perpetuates rigidities in the labour market because it offers palliatives to make them tolerable, and in the long term it perversely magnifies them.

The Venetian mask of Pantalone comes to mind in this regard, asserts Padoa Schioppa (1988a: 121); he is rich and greedy, but stupid, and always ends up footing the bill, harming not only himself but everyone else as well.

Nowadays Pantalone promises to pay a fixed portion of the hourly market wage as an hourly subsidy to workers who remain underemployed. With such a promise, he creates an incentive for both workers and firms to keep higher hourly wages and lower hours worked per head, at his own cost. If he understood that he systematically pays the consequences of a gentlemen's agreement between firms and their workers which goes against him, he would ask firms to bear the consequences of their behaviour through experience-rating taxation. Not only would Pantalone become richer, but employment would also rise.

11.5. Firing and hiring costs

Other rigidities in the Italian labour market also seem to favour workers over the short term, as proved in the perceptive essay by Bentolila and Bertola (1988) and the contribution by Bertola (1992) on the economic consequences of limiting the freedom of firms to hire and fire labour, with application to the situation in Italy. They demonstrate that restrictions on firing have three effects: on the variability of employment, on the average level of employment, and on company profits.

With regard to the first aspect, constraints on the firm's ability to dismiss workers increases the stability of employment with respect to changes in factors outside the firm's control, such as demand or the prices of raw materials. It is obvious that the firm is reluctant to make workers redundant and to pay the costs involved in response to a deterioration in market conditions if a recovery is expected or is at least possible; in cases of uncertainty, however, firing costs will also make the firm reluctant to recruit in response to positive developments.

Hiring costs have very similar effects in dynamic terms; if the professional training of new recruits is expensive, the firm is discouraged not only from hiring new staff but also from firing existing workers. By contrast, marginal employment subsidies increase the variability of employment, reducing the cost of recruitment and, by implication, dismissal.

As to the second aspect, it has been demonstrated, rather surprisingly, that hiring and firing costs actually increase employment in the short term, since the discouragement effect has a stronger impact on dismissals than on recruitment, owing to uncertainty and the high cost of reversing decisions. Moreover, in the short run, firing costs definitely increase the probability of (continued) employment of the firm's existing workers, who are insiders and hence the firm's main counterpart, although they reduce the probability that the unemployed, who by definition are outsiders, will find work. This has important implications for young people, housewives, and weaker regions.

Over the long run the situation is reversed, because both the low variability of employment and the average level of short-term employment are achieved at the expense of profitability, so that the firm is forced to deviate from the maximum-profit path. This increases the probability of company failures and reduces the likelihood of new firms being created, with adverse effects on permanent employment.[4]

---

[4] This aspect is clearly highlighted in the critique by Bodo (1993) on Bentolila and Bertola (1988), reproduced in Padoa Schioppa (1993*b*).

12
Incentives and Disincentives for Private-Sector Employment

12.1. Incentives for private employment

As we have seen, the unemployment benefits and firing constraints that currently exist in Italy appear to have serious and adverse implications. Here too, therefore, market flexibility must be increased by laying greater emphasis on public incentives to encourage employment in the private sector.

A number of interesting proposals for employment incentives were analysed for us by Cugno and Ferrero (1987). In their opinion, the most effective would be a subsidy proportional to the wage rate of additional workers; as this would be automatic in much the same way as the profit-sharing proposal recently reiterated by Weitzman (1983, 1984), it appears to have the attractive property of keeping employment high even if relative prices are distorted.

Other forms of subsidy for private-sector employment also warrant attention, although in reality they do not always act as an incentive; one is a general subsidy, whereby firms receive a fixed sum for each worker employed, another is a marginal subsidy, with firms being paid a fixed amount for each worker in addition to their initial workforce, and finally there is the block grant, a fixed overall subsidy offered to firms on condition that it is used to increase employment.

Some experiments with alternative ways of using the special benefits paid by the Wage Supplementation Fund are also relevant in this regard; the trial scheme operated by the Agenzia del Lavoro di Trento in the alpine region of Trentino-Alto Adige was analysed for us by Felli and Ichino (1988, 1993) on the basis of the results achieved in the years 1985–6. Under the programme, employers are offered a financial contribution that is conditional on their actively re-employing workers receiving Fund benefits, and is paid at different rates according to sex and the length of time the workers have been receiving benefits (higher for women and the long-term unemployed).

The effectiveness of the programme, which has been assessed in terms of the greater probability of re-employment as a result of the use of the Fund's special resources in this way, is beyond doubt; the scheme reduces the average period of workers' inactivity by 20 months. Although significant, this figure has to be seen in the light of the average period for which the sample of workers were in receipt of Fund benefits, which was no less than 44 months, with peaks of 94 months, despite right-truncation of the available longitudinal data. Since the subsidy paid by the Agenzia for each worker is less than 20 months' benefit, the analysis seems to indicate that the experiment may potentially improve the employment prospects of benefit recipients and generate savings for the Exchequer.

12.2. Labour sharing

The Wage Supplementation Fund could also be used to redistribute unemployment, so to speak, by rotating benefit recipients. The contra-indications of using the Fund as a job-sharing mechanism are considerable, as it prevents firms from weeding out less-productive workers. For that very reason, the principle of rotation is systematically defended by trade unions and attacked by employers, as illustrated in Padoa Schioppa (1988a). Accordingly, a firm emerges in a stronger position if it succeeds in winning trade-union agreement to Wage Supplementation without rotation, as explained by the Managing Director of Fiat, Romiti (1988).

Other forms of job sharing can be devised that not only redistribute the available work but also allow individuals to adjust their working hours and leisure time, something the working population prefers and which entails no cost to the public purse. Schemes of this kind were examined for us by Colombino (1986a, 1986b; 1986c, 1987, 1988), on the basis of local samples covering a total of more than a thousand individuals in Milan, Turin, and Bologna.

There are three main conclusions. First and foremost, in order to evaluate labour-sharing policies it is neither necessary nor sufficient to measure their effects on the aggregate observed unemployment rate; the impact on personal preferences must be measured directly. Secondly, there is ample scope for a redistribution of working time, especially among the female population, with beneficial effects on social welfare; in other words, it is possible to devise job-sharing policies that imply a net positive balance between efficiency and equity effects. Finally, the pattern of personal preferences is such that the consequences of job sharing in terms of efficiency and equity generally have opposite signs: efficient policies frequently lead to greater inequality and vice versa, as there is often a trade-off between efficiency and equity.

For example, a 'personalized' reduction in working hours coupled with the transfer of the released hours to the unemployed is efficient from an allocative point of view, but it reduces equality in the sense that the increase in welfare is greater for those who already enjoyed a relatively high level of welfare before the change. Vice versa, a universal and uniform reduction in working hours, accompanied by a similar transfer to the unemployed, is inefficient in allocative terms but increases equality. The choice between these two types of measure naturally depends on the social preference as regards the equity efficiency trade-off.

12.3. Relief from social-security contributions

The instrument that is most typically included in Italy among incentives for private-sector employment is undoubtedly relief from social-security contributions, for which both employers and trade unions persistently call on the grounds that it would reduce unit labour costs without cutting wages, and would thus boost employment.

Just as dirigistic regulation that creates inviolable rights or obligations can deviate from the original intentions and end up harming those it was supposed to protect, so too incentives in the form of contribution relief can have long-term effects very different from those observable in the short run.

Our analyses (Modigliani *et al.*, 1986, and Padoa Schioppa, 1990*a*, 1992*d*) confirm that over the last twenty-five years the abatement of social-security contributions has reduced labour costs in the very short term and has had a slight positive effect on employment, made even smaller by the slowness with which the demand for labour adjusts; over the long term, however, it has encouraged trade unions and employers to increase wages in almost the same proportion, so that the beneficial effects on labour costs and employment have been negligible.

This outcome is, in fact, consistent with the more general theory of tax forward or backward shifting, which conveniently distinguishes between the impact and incidence of a tax, between the persons initially affected by an increase (or reduction) in contributions and those who ultimately pay for (or benefit from) the tax change; in the case in point, it is mainly workers already in employment who ultimately gain from contribution relief, with job-seekers and firms deriving little benefit.

As indicated in Section 8.1, perhaps only the substantial *additional* relief granted to firms in the Mezzogiorno by comparison with that provided in the Centre–North produces a limited reduction in labour costs per employee in the South, but only modest employment effects in view of the productivity differential between southern firms and those in the rest of the country. It would therefore probably be wise to abandon the policy of remitting social-security contributions, because despite being desired and demanded by workers and employers the practice seems to have little positive permanent effect on employment and is very costly for the public purse.

12.4. *The tax-push hypothesis revisited*

The responsiveness of wages and salaries to other forms of taxation, in particular income tax, should also be re-examined in this context. When direct taxes in Italy were almost proportional,[1] as they were before the tax reform of 1973–4, workers displayed a degree of fiscal illusion, and claimed extremely modest wage increases for each (admittedly very small) rise in the average rate of direct (and indirect) taxation. However, the analysis by Padoa Schioppa (1990*a*) shows that, as a result of the switch to a highly progressive income-tax system, in the long term gross wages adjusted fully to changes in the average direct tax rate, given the strong substitution (or progressivity) effect combined with the weak income (or compensation) effect observable in workers' behaviour. Today wage bargaining appears to be concerned not with gross wages but with wages net of direct taxes.

This outcome, based on empirical evidence over the last twenty-five years, is a specification of a general case, in which the theoreti-

---

[1] The specific characteristics of the various types of income tax that existed before the reform and the changes they underwent are described in detail in Parravicini (1971).

cal implications of the shifting of direct taxation are theoretically uncertain, as the income and substitution effects may have the same or different signs and may be small or large; the other element that is ambiguous *a priori* is the budget policy accompanying the direct-tax measures, so that, in the words of Rosati (1987: 1) 'a change in direct taxes may be followed by a change in wages in the same direction, in the opposite direction or by no change at all, depending on the overall characteristics of the budget policy considered'.

In summary, let us recall the assessment contained in Padoa Schioppa (1992*b*: 82–4) on the effects of the impact and incidence of all the main forms of tax on wages in Italy.

Our estimates for Italy illustrate four economic-policy conclusions, some of which are not new (Tanzi, 1980) but are still controversial and sometimes run directly counter to the more generally accepted views (Giavazzi and Spaventa, 1989).

First, since the compensation effect is positive but slight, the shifting of increases in direct-tax rates onto wage demands would be very small if income tax were proportional, as essentially it was before 1974.

Secondly, as the progressivity effect is large and negative,[2] the long-run elasticity of wages to the average direct rate, (with the marginal tax rate moving together with the average) is now higher than it was in the past, and is in fact close to unity. Since the tax reform dispelled workers' fiscal illusion, it cannot be said that they submitted passively to fiscal drag, although it is true that the progressivity of the tax system and inflation were responsible for a tremendous increase in the tax burden in the years after the reform. Hence, it does not appear to us that considerations of equity should have led to the adoption of a policy later referred to as compensation to workers for fiscal drag. This had already been provided by wage negotiations, certainly not immediately or automatically but over the long term. . . . According to our estimates, Italian workers were 'amortizing' fiscal drag for about a decade (1975–84), and if over the long term they were prepared to accept reductions in net wages—as they did to some extent over the last ten years—this was because they were ready to moderate their wage demands in the face of rising unemployment. . . .

Nevertheless, we consider that although compensating for fiscal drag

---

[2] In two later papers making cross-country comparisons of tax effects on wages (Padoa Schioppa, 1992*d*, 1993*a*), some of these results were found to hold true for most large European countries, but only up to the beginning of the 1980s; for semantic reasons, however, what had previously been considered a negative progressivity effect (in Padoa Schioppa, 1990*a*, 1992*b*) was later labelled a positive progressivity effect.

could not be rationalized in terms of equity, it could be justified on grounds of efficiency; if the level of direct taxation falls and/or the degree of progressivity diminishes for a given average direct-tax rate—as undoubtedly is the case when fiscal drag is offset, even though other more transparent forms of tax indexation may be preferable—wages and labour costs decrease over the long term, to the benefit of employment.

Some Italian economists and policy-makers have noted, however, that compensating for fiscal drag has inflationary implications, in that it will cause a fall in tax revenue without any immediate countervailing reduction in public expenditure. A complete analysis of the inflationary effects of compensating for fiscal drag would go beyond the bounds we have set ourselves here, as it would require a parallel examination of aggregate supply and demand, as well as consideration of the consequences of tax changes on demand. We shall ignore the problems of aggregate demand and concentrate on those of supply. Our estimates lead us to assert that compensating for fiscal drag does not create inflationary pressures on aggregate supply, since the lower the average level and progressivity of direct taxes, the lower are nominal wages and prices and the more down-ward-shifted is aggregate supply. However, since presumably the fiscal measures increase aggregate demand, thus inflating the budget deficit, the effects on inflation are ambiguous a priori. The same is not true of unem-ployment, however; the effects are certainly positive, given the combina-tion of a definite reduction in aggregate supply and a probable increase in aggregate demand.

The fourth observation is that Italian trade unions continue to attach high importance to employment, so that unit labour costs are much less flexible than net real wages. This rigidity explains why relief from social-security contributions may stimulate some job creation in the short term but cannot increase employment more than marginally over the long term. It also demonstrates why Italian workers still suffer from fiscal illusion as consumers: although they are interested in real wages net of tax for a given employment level, they lose some of their purchasing power when there is an increase in the indirect-tax rate, and hence in consumer prices.[3] This obviously stems from the fact that the net real wage is only one of the workers' goals.

There is therefore no lack of excellent reasons for reconsidering the overall utility of relief from social-security contributions and for proposing a redistribution of the tax burden from direct to indirect taxation, as realized in other countries (see section 19.4).

---

[3] Changes in indirect taxes affect consumer prices, as these taxes are passed on completely, but they do not have positive employment effects because unit labour costs depend on producer prices at factor cost.

13

Classical–Keynesian Unemployment
and Incomes Policy

13.1. *Personal income tax and labour supply*

As well as affecting the rate of wage increases and thus employment, changes in the level and structure of taxation also influence
the supply of labour and, to a lesser extent, savings decisions. The
analyses carried out for us by Quintieri and Rosati (1986*a*, 1986*b*,
1988, 1990) show that progressive taxes harm workers not only
through their effects on the demand for labour, as we have seen,
but also by causing a contraction in the volume of labour they supply. Conversely, a reduction in the progressivity of personal income
tax accompanied by an increase in indirect taxation or wealth
taxes is shown to induce individuals to increase the amount of
labour they are willing to supply. For a given tax liability, it is
therefore possible to identify different fiscal policies that encourage
a rise in labour participation rates.

This effect is particularly marked for those sections of the population whose labour supply is more elastic to net real wages. From an
examination of the Italian data, which are broken down according
to sex and age group, it emerges that the female labour supply is
particularly responsive to changes in net real wages, with the highest
elasticity occurring in the central age groups. Empirical evidence
therefore indicates a lower marginal rate of substitution between
leisure and consumption for women than for men; more precisely,
the supply of primary workers (men in the central age groups) is virtually inelastic, while the parts of the labour force consisting of
younger and older men on the one hand and women on the other
have a higher elasticity with opposite signs. This provides further
confirmation of the heterogeneity of the labour market.

These facts show how fiscal policy can have significant effects
not only on the overall labour supply but also on its composition.
For example, a permanent tax increase tends to elicit a rise in the
male labour supply and a reduction in the female participation
rate. The decrease would be even more pronounced if the marginal

revenue were used to finance additional public expenditure on health and education, which are shown to have a negative impact on the female labour supply in view of the degree of partial substitutability with private spending of this kind.

13.2. *Taxes, liquidity constraints and saving*

This last remark highlights the links between individual decisions regarding the supply of labour on the one hand and private consumption and saving on the other. It is for that reason that we are dealing with the question here, even though it is connected only indirectly with the labour market. The common frame of reference is that of the life cycle and permanent-income hypothesis, which postulates that consumption (like labour supply) depends not on current income but on the resources available during an entire lifetime. However, if consumers cannot borrow enough to finance their desired level of consumption, the growth rate in aggregate consumption will be much more sensitive to changes in current disposable income than is suggested by the permanent-income hypothesis.

Our analyses indicate that this is the case in Italy, where the excessive sensitivity of consumption to current income appears to be attributable to imperfections in the markets for consumer credit and home loans. We are drawn to this conclusion both by Jappelli and Pagano (1987) (which is based on an international comparison across seven industrial countries), and by the analysis contained in Jappelli and Pagano (1988) (which uses micro-economic data to compare the situation in Italy with that in the United States). The research carried out for us by Jappelli (1987) and Jappelli and Pagano (1988), although based on very different methods, both conclude that a person is more likely to be subject to liquidity constraints if he is young, does not own a house, and lives in the Mezzogiorno.

It is not easy to give a valid response to those who argue that such liquidity constraints are irrelevant in Italy because families are able to make up for the imperfections of the financial markets by forming a kind of dynastic market or simply by showing solidarity with kith and kin. One would have to establish the extent to which *inter vivos* transfers were to family units that had been refused loans by financial intermediaries, and whether the transfers were sufficiently large to enable recipients to follow their desired consumption path. In contrast to other countries (see Cox and Jappelli, 1988) information on this aspect in Italy is only now beginning to become available, and is still patchy. In a sample survey taken in 1987, Guiso and Jappelli (1991) found that 15.6 per cent of families appeared to suffer liquidity constraints on their consumption. They conclude (p. 119) 'that private transfers help remedy capital-market deficiencies. Private transfers are in fact mainly targeted towards families which face binding credit constraints. However, we have also found that many liquidity-constrained households receive no transfer.'

If further investigation confirmed the presence of liquidity constraints, this would have numerous implications. At the very least, it would indicate a failure of the credit markets, causing serious distortions, with relevant implications for fiscal policy; the most important of these would be to increase the effectiveness of temporary fiscal measures (such as one-off taxes) by influencing consumer spending more than predicted by the permanent-income hypothesis, and to render inapplicable many of the propositions of the optimal-taxation theory, which postulates, for example, that taxes on income from employment are more appropriate than taxes on investment income, or that proportional taxes are preferable to progressive taxes in order to minimize distortions.

In conclusion, an increase in the progressivity of direct taxation would have non-neutral consequences on labour supply, wage increases, employment and also, via liquidity constraints, the saving rate.

13.3. *Classical and Keynesian unemployment*

Up to this point we have supposed that incentives for private-sector employment must be directed primarily towards reducing unit labour costs, on the implicit hypothesis that Italian unemployment is, in the words of Malinvaud (1978), of the classical type. In fact, our research group carried out various studies on this issue, which are very new for Italy, in order to ascertain the nature of unemployment more precisely: is it caused by insufficient final demand, excessive labour costs (or capacity constraints), or sectoral imbalances? As a result, we obtained (in Padoa Schioppa, 1990*b*; Orsi, 1988; and Ferrari and Orsi, 1988) quantitative estimates of the demand gap, of the wage (or productive capacity) gap and finally of the degree of mismatching, which explains the structural (or natural) rate of unemployment.

The most important fact revealed by these studies, which combine a theory of investment with an analysis of rationed markets and provide econometric estimates and economic-policy simulations, appears to be the following. Unemployment in Italy is not caused either solely by excessive labour costs for a given productive capacity or solely by insufficient final demand, but by both these factors; it also stems partly from sectoral and regional imbalances, which explain why the structural (or natural) rate of unemployment is now equal to about half the overall rate.

One of the causes of sectoral mismatching has already been mentioned in the chapters devoted to the Mezzogiorno, in discussing the fall in regional labour mobility. According to our estimates (Padoa Schioppa, 1990*d*, 1993*c*), other factors that explain the mismatch are, first, the rapid changes in the composition of non-agricultural employment and, secondly, the sharp growth in long-term unemployment, with all that entails in terms of discouragement, obsolescence of human resources, and marginalization of the affected workers.

As regards the other factors explaining unemployment in Italy, we note that, since unused capacity is available, Keynesian demand stimulation at given price and wage levels would raise employment rates; unfortunately, demand stimulation tends to drive up prices and wages, so that even though the majority of firms report they are hindered by insufficient demand, the bottlenecks' removal would not be enough to generate a substantial growth in employment.

Wage increases would boost productivity rather than the demand for labour. The classical component of unemployment in Italy does not therefore stem from a shortage of capital but from an inability to exploit the available capital fully to the benefit of employment, given the excessive elasticity of wages to output demand. This characteristic, which is sometimes defined as wage rigidity, has adverse consequences for employment, owing partly to the replacement of labour by other production factors when wages are rising, and partly to the erosion of incomes by rising prices, an effect that is magnified in an open economy such as Italy's. At present, therefore, productive capacity is not, nor can it be, fully exploited in order to absorb the available manpower by stimulating demand.

The conclusion, expressed in Padoa Schioppa (1990*d*: 441), is that

today's Italian non-structural unemployment is both Keynesian and classical, not only because some sectors register insufficient demand while others insufficient capital, but also because the aggregate economy requires both a higher final demand and a larger capacity to employ more labour, *at the same time*. A rising level of demand alone is not sufficient. It would bring about increases in wages and prices which would only lead to strong productivity gains and few enhancements in employment. If the full utilization of the productive capacity could however be obtained at given wages and prices, the permanent benefits for employment would be much more consistent. But these benefits cannot be granted if demand does not steadily grow. It therefore seems clear that a mix of expansionary demand (better if internationally co-ordinated) and contractionary supply management is the best policy-proposal to reduce Italian non-structural unemployment. Structural unemployment, on the other hand, needs to be fought in Italy through micro-policies able to diminish regional and skill imbalances, largely responsible for mismatch.

13.4. *Incomes policy to stimulate private employment*

Hence, it can be seen that demand management does not provide effective stimulus to employment in Italy unless it is combined with supply management that monitors the rate of increase in prices and wages on the one hand and investment on the other.

We shall defer discussion of the latter aspect to the two following chapters. As to wages and prices, however, we wish to state immediately that, from the perspective we have adopted hitherto, incomes policy is understood as a form of incentive for the market, not as a means of dirigistic regulation. Accordingly, wages and prices would be kept down by granting tax reductions or other concessions only in exchange for proven wage restraint, which would produce net benefits for both sides of industry.

An incomes policy appears to be an indispensable ingredient of any package of measures for boosting private employment in Italy, but it becomes unacceptable and ineffectual if it is imposed from above rather than based on free choices determined by incentives and trade-offs. As indicated in Padoa Schioppa (1986*b*), an incomes policy is bound to fail in Italy if it does not follow the trade-off approach proposed here; if the conflictual attitudes inherent in the Italian economy impede co-operative solutions at the micro-economic level, they will certainly nullify any decided in macro-economic forums. On past experience, agreements reached at the top are systematically ignored and evaded by both employers and trade unionists at the grass roots if they are not in tune with what individuals really want.

Many examples could be cited in this regard. Padoa Schioppa (1986*b*: 686–90) affirms, however, that perhaps the most significant example concerns the *scala mobile* (the automatic wage-indexation clause). It is

provided by comparing the *de facto* indexation of nominal wages with the *de jure* wage indexation, which was imposed by national agreements between employers and trade unions and then incorporated into law, as in the case of the Interorganizational Agreement of 1975. In 1975 the automatic element of wage increases was reinforced, and at the same time it was made more egalitarian, by stipulating an equal absolute adjustment for all wage brackets. This indicated that both the employers and the trade unions wanted to narrow wage differentials and eliminate or reduce industrial disputes at company level.

An examination of the non-automatic components of actual wage increases provides legitimate grounds for doubting that workers and employers at the grass roots complied with this objective set by their national leaders. Even after 1975, collective wage settlements and company-level supplementary wage agreements, including wage drift, explain almost half the growth in effective wages and never less than 40 per cent; before 1975 the proportion had been much higher still. Moreover, from then onwards wage drift was used consistently to counteract the narrowing of wage differentials due to uniform cost-of-living adjustments. Data on wage drift in the engineering and steel industries (the sectors with highest wages), and especially those for more highly qualified staff, are very revealing. It is no accident that even aggregate data show wage drift rising again in relation to the other components of effective wage increases from 1980 onwards, when the white-collar revolt against the too egalitarian 1975 Interorganizational Agreement came to a head in the 'march of the 40,000', in open conflict with the stance of the trade unions.

The final breakdown of the Interorganizational Agreement came when it was formally rejected in the referendum of 1985 (see Padoa Schioppa, 1986*b*, 1989b).

Incomes policy in the sense used here can therefore do no more than encourage the market to exercise wage and price restraint. The analysis directly corroborates the findings recalled above with regard to state incentives for private-sector employment; for example, it is clear that an appropriate incomes policy could consist in reducing income-tax progressivity for a given average tax burden. As well as offering other advantages, this would moderate wage demands and thus increase employment. As has been demonstrated elsewhere (cf. Padoa Schioppa, 1989*b*), even marginal employment subsidies can be granted via tax-based incomes policies.

Judging from the above conclusions, government action of this kind certainly offers greater potential for boosting private-sector employment than the instruments used hitherto in Italy. A summary of the foregoing analysis will reinforce the point.

We have established that the four main types of state intervention in the Italian labour market—public-sector employment, unemployment benefits, dirigistic regulation, and incentives for private-sector employment—are sometimes inadequate, sometimes excessive, and generally ineffectual.

We have noted that the dirigistic regulation of wages and working conditions and the incentives provided in the form of relief from social-security contributions are set out with the good intention of protecting the weaker parties in the labour relationship or reducing the cost of employing them; both forms of regulation, however, end up weakening them, so that they fail to achieve the objective of increasing employment, at least in the official economy, and may instead channel workers towards the underground economy.

As to the other two forms of public intervention in the labour market, we have to admit that public-sector employment offers little potential for growth in view of the huge public deficit and the tendency to privatization, while the other type of public measure used, namely unemployment benefits paid by the Wage Supplementation Fund, is no more than a palliative and may even be counterproductive.

Given the hope that productivity in the provision of public services will increase, the demand for labour in this field can rise only in so far as the public sector's direct involvement in the economy increases. This would clearly be undesirable, for the reasons expounded throughout this book, so that the rate of growth in public-sector employment should in fact slow down. Two points need to be made with regard to unemployment benefits; first, one must not forget that unemployment benefits are the least of the available evils rather than the greatest good, and secondly payments from the

Wage Supplementation Fund should be replaced by benefits with a flat (though adjustable) rate, proportional to the need rather than to the previous wage, and available to all the unemployed. As presently constituted, the Wage Supplementation Fund triggers perverse mechanisms that alleviate some of the imbalances in the labour market over the short term but exacerbate them in the long run. The same applies to the constraints on hiring and firing and the costs they entail.

There is therefore no option but to try to improve public incentives for private-sector employment by reducing the progressivity of direct taxation, introducing marginal-employment subsidies, perhaps through a reformed Wage Supplementation Fund, and concentrating in particular on incomes policy in the meaning of the term indicated above.

Private investment

When I was writing my book, the flirtation with the counter-reform, absolutism, hierarchical rules, sensual literature, and art was already beginning; and the story of my life has been an implicit protest against this. . . . The moral and political crisis in post-war Italy . . . consisted essentially in rejection of the moral ideal of liberty in favour of the other, morally blind, ideal of so-called 'activism'. . . . But the concept of liberty has no substance other than liberty itself, just as the substance of the concept of poetry is solely poetry; and it must be awoken in men's minds in the purity that is its ideal strength, taking care not to confuse it with needs and demands of another order, and also leaving it to the man of action to avail himself, within limits he must set himself, of the forces that are actually available and conducive to his purpose.

(B. Croce, *Contributo alla critica di me stesso*, 1934)

14

Real and Financial Aspects of
Private Investment

14.1. Investment and productive capacity

The second aspect of the supply-management policy on which we wish to focus concerns public measures to stimulate private investment, having already discussed investment by general government and public corporations.

Investment is one of the strategic public objectives, owing to the importance of capital in creating value-added and growth. Greater capital investment is necessary, because although output can be increased in the short term by changing the utilization rate of existing capacity and, to some extent, the number of workers and working hours, in the long term technical coefficients, wages and prices are perfectly adjusted, capital is at an optimum as a result of past investment, and potential capacity is fully utilized. At the same time employment, working hours, labour hoarding, and the use of every other means of production are at the desired levels, so that actual production coincides with potential production and employment is affected by the level of productive capacity.

This means that the policy of stimulating employment would soon encounter limits in Italy if it were not accompanied by vigorous growth in private investment. In principle, capital could replace or complement labour. Although historically Italy has witnessed 'a marked substitution of capital for energy and labour in the new machinery gradually introduced over the twenty years from 1963 to 1984, with damaging and far from temporary consequences for employment in view of the fixed technical coefficients embodied in the old machines' (Padoa Schioppa, 1992c: 73), it is clear that the very existence of technical coefficients identifies capital investment as a constraint that may impede an expansion in employment in the long run.

On this fine dividing line between a situation in which machines pose a potential threat to employment and one in which they offer potential benefits, final demand and the relative prices of produc-

TABLE 14.1. Private investment (in billions of current Lit.)

	Fixed investment	Change in stocks	Total gross investment
1983			
Italy	134,592.0	2,943.0	137,535.0
Centre–North	93,034.7	2,498.2	95,532.9
Mezzogiorno	41,557.3	444.8	42,002.1
1984			
Italy	153,357.0	13,909.0	167,266.0
Centre–North	105,704.0	12,026.6	117,730.6
Mezzogiorno	47,653.0	1,882.4	49,535.4
1985			
Italy	168,230.0	14,960.0	183,190.0
Centre–North	118,427.4	13,159.0	131,586.4
Mezzogiorno	49,802.6	1,801.0	51,603.6
1986			
Italy	176,762.0	8,718.0	185,480.0
Centre–North	125,321.3	7,484.4	132,805.7
Mezzogiorno	51,440.7	1,233.6	52,674.3
1987			
Italy	195,464.0	8,012.0	203,476.0
Centre–North	139,317.6	6,693.8	146,011.4
Mezzogiorno	56,146.4	1,318.2	57,464.6

Source: ISTAT, unpublished data of the new regional accounts.

tion factors play an important role.[1] Both have had a positive influence on private investment in Italy; the growth in final demand has affected private investment via the income effect, while the rise in the ratio of energy costs to the rental cost of capital (more than fourfold over the last twenty years) and in the ratio of labour costs to the rental cost of capital (almost threefold over the same period) has also induced a large increase in the capital/energy and capital/labour ratios for the new vintages via a substitution effect

[1] In principle, profitability should also be relevant to investment decisions, but it seems to be an explanatory variable of some importance only in Q-type models, applied to Italy for us by Schiantarelli and Ratti (1988).

that is non-zero but not exceptionally high and in any case applies only to new machinery.

Comparing Table 14.1 with Tables 1.1 and 1.2 shows that in the mid-1980s investment was far from modest in all areas of the country, although it needs to be increased further to generate adequate growth in productive capacity, especially in the more backward areas.

14.2. The financial structure of firms

We need to examine not only the real determinants of investment but also the financial determinants, because they have a combined effect on private-capital accumulation; this is the least explored aspect of investment behaviour in Italy.

In order to carry out such an analysis, we must first examine the financial structure of Italian firms and the way in which it has changed over the last twenty years.

In the period up to 1970, observes one of our research groups, Italian manufacturing firms tended to operate with a relatively low level of self-financing. The system was essentially what is usually called 'debt-based capitalism'.

The rapid rise in nominal interest rates, together with the decline in real-profit margins, translated into a change in the trend of discounted current values. At the very time when the public sector was increasing its absorption of financial resources, the manufacturing sector was using the remaining resources mainly to finance interest payments and not to increase investment.

As recalled by Milana (1992b: 12),

the financial structure of [Italian] firms appeared to be seriously unbalanced after the first oil shock: the ratio of debt to both invested capital and output seemed very high, and short-term debt was by far the largest source of finance. Debt-servicing was a substantial item of expenditure, even though low real interest rates and the fairly widespread use of subsidized credit eased its impact on operating results. During that period the particularly high level of corporate debt was one of the main obstacles to industrial growth.

In this new situation firms could no longer expand on the basis of borrowing from the banking system. This is borne out by the experience of the mini-boom of 1978–80, which was financed by profits accumulated during the same period. Meanwhile, firms that drew on their internal resources or issued shares in the capital market were able to internalize the costs without having to increase their debt. In the new circumstances, what can be called 'equity-based capitalism', therefore, displayed clear advantages over the prevailing 'debt-based capitalism'.

The transformation of the financial structure of Italian industry from the latter type of capitalism to the former implies not only a change in agents' behaviour and in the markets, but also a shift in the composition of the economy's financial assets, with the share of money (M_2 or M_3) falling and the volume of securities rising, with the exception of Treasury bills and Treasury credit certificates, which remained almost unchanged at around one-fifth of the total.

14.3. The firms' financial structure and the public debt

The ability of the Italian financial markets to meet the changing financial needs of firms was re-examined for us by Dal Bosco (1987). In an international comparison, he shows that many different combinations of financial assets are compatible with the sustained financial development of the corporate sector. For example, the share of the money supply M_2 in financial assets in Japan is roughly the same as in Italy, but in the United States it is barely half as high. Whereas the proportion of finance raised in the capital markets is greater in Japan than in Italy, in the United States it is three times higher. The significant difference is that no other developed country is experiencing such a large growth in the public debt as Italy.

These comparisons suggest that desirable shifts in the composition of financial assets are possible, although not necessary (as shown by the Japanese case), but that they may be difficult to achieve with a high and rising public debt. This raises the question of the relationship between the financing of the budget deficit and the financial structure of firms since the 'divorce' between the Bank of Italy and the Treasury in 1981, as a result of which the central bank no longer automatically acquires Treasury bills not taken up at auction.

Although the 'divorce' is often presented as neutral[2] in its effects

[2] Not only is the 'divorce' possibly not neutral, but it is also only partial owing to the automatic nature of the use of the Treasury's overdraft with the central bank; see in this sense the analysis carried out for us by Salvemini and Salvemini (1989).

on monetary policy, it may potentially produce significant substitution effects within the banking system. The banks' response to the initial reduction in banking intermediation, and hence in profits from these activities, was not to introduce innovations in financial assets and liabilities but to charge higher commissions on the larger volumes of Treasury bills and Treasury credit certificates traded and to offer higher interest rates on deposits; this made it more difficult for the government securities market to clear, raised interest rates, and hence stimulated banking intermediation.

The net effect of the 'divorce', assuming the central bank's monetary policy to be neutral, seems to have been to put pressure on bank balance sheets; this was eased not by increasing lending to manufacturing firms and offering financial innovations to the industrial sector but by competing with the Treasury for the public's deposits. The result was twofold: a reduction in the volume of loans and an increase in the cost of credit. Hence, the change in the central bank's operating procedures reinforced the adverse effects of the growth in public debt on the manufacturing sector.

14.4. The reduction in financial disequilibria

With all these limitations and constraints on the firms' financial structure as a result of the increasing supply of financial assets to cover the budget deficit, the 1980s saw a change in the ratio of debt to equity capital, the emergence of new forms of organization and ways of raising funds (as underlined in our research by contributions from D'Ecclesia and Szegö (1988) and Szegö (1993), among others), and even an alteration in the relationship between credit institutions and firms.

Indeed, as Milana (1992*b*: 12–13) reminds us,

despite pessimistic forecasts as to the Italian economy's chances of extricating itself from a situation that had now become too constraining, the financial disequilibria were largely eliminated, thanks to a number of favourable factors. Undoubtedly the most important of these was the slowdown in inflation, which enabled firms to restore their profit margins. At the same time, the more favourable conditions on the cost front (especially with regard to the prices of imported raw materials), the reduction in the amount of circulating capital required per unit of output and important government measures regarding subsidized credit and tax concessions contributed greatly to the restoration of financial equilibrium in the productive sectors.

The difficulties encountered in raising finance during the years of greatest pressure on operating costs forced firms to 'save' credit and to seek forms of rationalization that would enable them to reduce the ratio of debt to real capital. This gave firms greater financial flexibility, leading in recent years to a more pronounced shift towards new methods of financial management (the centralization of group cash flow, the formation of holding companies, the adoption of new financial techniques), which have enabled firms to change the ratio of short-term to medium- and long-term finance and to reduce the cost of capital by altering their relationship with the banking system.

14.5. *The ratio between firms' own funds and debt*

Another effect of the improvement in operating conditions and of financial restructuring of firms, continues Milana (1992*b*: 13–14),

was the rise in the ratio of own funds to debt. The main reason for the increase in the ratio was the reinvestment of profits in view of the structural inability of the Italian stock market to supply firms with equity capital.

It has nevertheless become clear that the chronic weakness of the stock market in Italy is more the result than the cause of the dearth of share issues. The issue of shares has been seen more as a threat to control of the firm than as an opportunity to develop and improve its financial structure. This attitude, which is typical of firms controlled by small family groups, is very widespread in Italy in view of the relatively high proportion of small and medium-sized enterprises by comparison with other advanced industrial economies.

Although recourse to the stock market has remained low, it has increased slightly in recent years, in the light of the substantial rise in share prices in all the industrialized countries. However, there appears to have been no fundamental change in firms' preferences in this regard.

Even in the future, it seems unlikely that the Italian stock market will be able to provide a significant source of finance, except of course in certain exceptional cases. It should also be pointed out that own funds cannot be raised from investors in the stock market if the firm's production activities entail high risk but do not offer a high rate of return over the short and medium term. An efficient stock market can certainly make the capital market as a whole more competitive and help enhance the most sound and productive firms.

In recent years, the focus of attention has shifted from the problem of the financial structure of firms to that of their growing interest in owning a stake in banks. The increase in the net profit margins of some large industrial groups has not only created new centres of economic power but also established favourable conditions for investing in various productive sectors, including credit services.

Such investments are not always inspired by the need to equalize marginal expected yields on alternative assets net of risk; sometimes they are motivated by the desire to secure finance at below-market cost and to bring the banks involved into line behind the particular strategy of the industrial group.

These aspects are rightly causing concern among banking supervisory authorities, who are now having to tackle problems that paradoxically appear to be the opposite of the problems that have traditionally been regarded as the result of changes in the ratio of debt to equity capital. It should also be noted that, at a time when the proportion of the economy's value-added produced by the credit sector and financial intermediaries is steadily declining, the injection of capital by other sectors of the economy is viewed by some as a threat to the competitive equilibria of the markets, but by others almost as a necessary consequence of efficient resource allocation among the various sectors. In tackling this problem, account must therefore be taken of the unique characteristics of each case and it must be ensured that the financial sector continues to pursue its specific objectives, which almost always contrast with those of the firms that turn to the credit institutions for finance.

15

The Effects of Financial Subsidies and Tax Concessions on Private Investment

15.1. Firms' financial structure and private investment

The undercapitalization and excessive debt of firms in the 1970s were important contributory factors in the deterioration in firms' profitability. The recent return to profitability and to a better balance between equity capital and borrowing, in parallel with the slowdown in inflation, appears to have favoured the recovery in output and investment.

The cost of capital seems to carry greater weight in corporate decisions when firms are obliged to raise external finance in order to make up for the shortage of internal resources. Faced with a steady deterioration in their financial situation and fluctuations in their profits, firms are forced by the market to seek an optimum solution that satisfies both their productive and their financial needs. This is the issue studied for us by the Bocconi group headed by Mussati.

According to the estimates produced for us by Faini *et al.* (1987), even investment by state-controlled companies, which do not always apply the principles of optimality and rationality, is sensitive to the cost of capital, which in turn is modified by capital grants, interest-rate subsidies, and tax concessions. A *fortiori*, as illustrated by Ratti and Drudi (1988) and Ratti (1988), these incentives stimulate private investment, but capital grants and tax concessions appear to lead to the substitution of capital for labour, while interest-rate subsidies reduce the cost of capital and have positive effects on investment without apparent adverse implications for employment.

Such financial and fiscal incentives therefore have the expected (and estimated) effect on private investment in Italy, and some other unintended and undesirable results as well, such as the substitution of capital for labour. They give rise to additional costs by distorting the structure of firms' liabilities and altering the leverage costs due to debt ratios, and they may depress employment; the

Mussati group estimates that leverage costs exceed the cost of servicing the additional debt. This finding casts doubt on the implications of the Modigliani–Miller theorem, which maintains that the value of firms and the growth in their output are independent of changes in the composition of their financial liabilities.

The liquidity effect of the incentives does not appear, on the contrary, to be particularly large among the sample of medium and large firms examined. It should be noted, however, that these conclusions are based on the hypothesis of perfect technological substitutability of subsidized credit for market credit, and hence also on relative certainty as to the time of receipt of the assistance, a highly relevant point in deciding between interest-rate subsidies and capital grants as instruments of industrial policy.

In more general terms, our analyses seek to illustrate the consequences of subsidies and other economic-policy instruments not only on investment but also on simultaneous decisions affecting the demand for other production factors, the supply of products, the structure of liabilities, and the payment of dividends by Italian firms. A systematic taxonomy, instrument by instrument, carried out for us by Drudi (1988) provides the necessary basis for a more detailed examination of the various instruments. Unfortunately, however, this classification is not easy to summarize; moreover, it shows that the very meaning of liabilities imbalance, which emerges so clearly from empirical studies (Ratti and Drudi, 1988, and Ratti, 1988, for example) is in reality conceptually obscure, as it depends to a large extent on the particular model used.

More specific conclusions can nevertheless be drawn in the case of some policy instruments that, although aimed mainly but not exclusively at other objectives, in fact have significant effects on real and financial investment. A prime example is that of a capital-gains tax on shares, the possible introduction of which has recently been the subject of political debate in Italy.

In particular, the study carried out for us by Faini *et al.* (1988) assumes that priority is accorded to the objectives of equality of treatment and revenue-raising and that capital losses are tax-deductible only if there are capital gains against which they can be offset. Also for reasons of equity, it posits the introduction of some form of indexation of capital gains and the maintenance of the system of tax credits, which is required in any case for reasons of harmonization within the EEC.

In this context, the expected effect of introducing a capital-gains tax would be that the tax yield would increase, as would firms' leverage, but investors would probably switch to securities with a more favourable tax treatment. The presumed fall in investment (with a reduction in the volume of financial instruments offered by firms) would be compounded on the demand side, owing to the obvious reduced attractiveness of shares. The conclusion is that the increase in tax revenue might be too small to compensate for these damaging real and financial consequences.

15.2. Policy conclusions on fiscal and financial subsidies

In conclusion, it appears that Italian firms almost always reach their financial and real decisions simultaneously. For that reason, industrial restructuring and financial restructuring have proceeded in tandem in the last few years. Both have been largely a spontaneous response to changes in relative prices induced by the market, to the structure of interest rates brought about by monetary and budgetary policies and to the cost of capital, which is affected by credit subsidies and tax concessions.

Government interference in the financial structure of firms is perhaps less pronounced than in other fields and does not appear excessive. Nevertheless, it seems appropriate to conclude with two cautionary observations.

The first is a suggestion based on a proposal made in our group by Mussati (1985), namely that, among the government instruments aimed at improving the financial structure of firms, preference should be given to tax concessions and, among credit subsidies, to capital grants, because growing uncertainty as to the outcome of firms' strategies makes it necessary to avoid policies that distort the composition of firms' liabilities.

The second observation originated in the group co-ordinated for us by Modigliani, is a call to avoid the risk of excessive government interference in the stock market, even if it is motivated by the desire to promote the growth of the market and dampen market fluctuations. The analysis carried out by Perotti (1988) on the basis of a study of the Italian stock market between 1961 and 1984 shows the fundamental informative value of speculative prices, which government interference could only reduce. The recognition that speculative prices presage, anticipate, and reveal information about the entire economy implies that they are useful in shaping expectations about future macro-economic trends.

According to our research group, empirical evidence on Italy confirms this thesis by demonstrating that price changes signal the behaviour of various important variables one quarter or more ahead. Interference with financial prices should therefore be kept to a minimum, even within a regulatory framework aimed at ensuring overall solvency and stability, so that they can continue to act as useful indicators for private and public investment. Finally, economic policy should not become the prime source of instability in the economy by increasing uncertainty.

PART VI

Strategic Intervention in Aggregate Demand

The Welfare State

But in June 1920 . . . I was summoned to Rome, where the old statesman . . . asked me to accept the Ministry of Public Education in the Government he was forming, 'to try (those were his words) to salvage our fatherland from ruin, and (he added) I do not know whether we shall succeed'. . . . I felt I could not refuse, given the state of the country at that time. . . . I also ran the Department entrusted to me with the greatest thrift, to such an extent that to those around me I often appeared curiously anachronistic in the very different climate that was beginning to prevail.

(B. Croce, *Contributo alla critica di me stesso* 1934)

16

General Characteristics of the Welfare State

16.1. The size of the welfare state

Hitherto we have discussed strategic public interventions affecting the most important factors of production—labour and capital—and aggregate supply in the Italian economy, with particular reference to the elimination of regional imbalances (especially with regard to the Mezzogiorno) and sectoral disequilibria (speaking of industrial and financial restructuring).

We shall now analyse the main strategic measures affecting Italian aggregate demand. We shall therefore be dealing with the welfare state, income redistribution, direct taxation, and the public debt.

The first of these topics covers public measures in the fields of health, education, and social security aimed at achieving collective welfare. More precisely, in the OECD's three-way subdivision of public expenditure by function performed, expenditure on the welfare state relates to so-called merit goods (education, health care, housing, leisure and cultural services) and income support; the latter class comprises pensions and social-security benefits whose socio-economic purpose is to substitute for other income (for example, old-age pensions replace income from employment), to provide income supplements (as in the case of family allowances), or to complement income that would otherwise be insufficient (social pensions, for example).

As recalled in the analysis by Malizia and Pedullà (1988: 22) and further illustrated in Tables 16.1 and 1.3, 'public spending on merit goods amounted to Lit. 47,213 billion in 1980 and Lit. 125,894 billion in 1987:[1] in the first and last years of the period examined it represented 48.0 and 44.8 per cent of total expenditure on the welfare state, 29.0 and 25.5 per cent of total public-sector spending and 12.1 and 13.8 per cent of GDP.'

---

[1] Tables 16.1 and 1.3, which have been updated to 1988, show that the trends noted in the analysis by Malizia and Pedullà (1988) continued in the last year for which data are available.

TABLE 16.1. Total general government expenditure by purpose (value in 1980 and index numbers since 1981 with base 1980 = 100)

Purposes	1980 (billions of current Lit.)	1981	1982	1983	1984	1985	1986	1987	1988
Traditional area	25,037	124.2	146.0	177.2	202.2	264.1	271.2	301.8	337.6
National defence	6,472	124.4	149.2	193.0	223.3	260.2	274.5	315.6	351.5
General services[a]	18,565	124.1	145.0	171.8	194.9	265.5	270.0	297.0	332.8
Welfare state	98,332	129.2	155.3	187.3	209.0	238.3	261.1	285.5	318.9
Education	18,476	132.5	155.7	178.9	201.2	223.8	245.6	277.4	306.2
Health	21,622	114.3	136.9	161.9	179.0	203.3	219.3	245.8	288.7
Housing	5,404	130.4	167.8	199.5	221.8	278.3	267.9	294.1	307.4
Leisure, cultural and religious services	1,711	135.4	171.1	197.7	227.4	257.2	279.0	326.7	360.6
Pensions and other social benefits	51,119	134.0	161.1	199.3	222.4	253.5	283.1	303.0	336.1
Mixed economy	39,312	142.0	187.6	220.9	268.9	291.3	338.3	351.1	390.3
Economic services	24,668	120.5	158.9	181.3	209.6	227.2	256.9	264.3	287.9
Expenditure not specified elsewhere	14,644	178.1	235.9	287.7	368.8	399.5	475.5	497.3	562.8
TOTAL	162,681	131.5	161.7	193.8	222.4	255.1	281.3	303.9	339.0

[a] Including expenditure for public order and internal security.

Sources: Malizia and Pedullà (1988) for data from 1980 to 1987; own calculations based on ISTAT unpublished data (kindly supplied by Raffaele Malizia of ISTAT) for 1988.

Malizia and Pedullà (1988: 22–5) add that:

Spending on education was equivalent to about 5.0 per cent of GDP in both years. . . . Expenditure on health amounted to 29.0 per cent of total welfare expenditure in 1980 and 19.8 per cent in 1987 and declined from 5.5 to 5.4 per cent of GDP over the period. The Health products and services purchased in the market for use in the national-health system came to Lit. 51,004 billion in 1987. Administrative services accounted for 6.7 per cent of the total, health services (prevention, supervision, hospital assistance, and other services) for 52.3 per cent and social services for 41 per cent. Health care in the narrow sense costs Lit. 47,591 billion in 1987; 55.7 per cent of this represented hospital treatment, 20.7 per cent treatment by general practitioners and specialists, 18.9 per cent the cost of pharmaceuticals, and 4.7 per cent expenditure on prevention and health supervision. Individual items are increasing at different rates, thus changing the composition of health expenditure.

Housing expenditure 'amounted to about 5.6 per cent of total welfare expenditure in the eight years and its share of GDP remained at around 1.5 per cent. Spending on leisure and cultural services represented about 1.8 per cent of welfare expenditure over the period and 0.5 per cent of GDP'.

Expenditure on income support 'totalled Lit. 51,119 billion in 1980 and Lit. 154,868 billion in 1987, equal to respectively 52.0 and 55.2 per cent of total welfare expenditure, 31.4 and 31.3 per cent of total public expenditure, and 13.1 and 15.8 per cent of GDP in the two years considered'.

According to Malizia and Pedullà (1988: 25–6), the model for this expenditure is predominantly redistributive.

Expenditure on social services and social-security benefits to individuals and households to replace, maintain, or complement income in order to overcome cases of hardship involving the total or partial loss of the primary income, an increase in normal needs, or the occurrence of exceptional needs amounted to Lit. 46,204 billion in 1980 and Lit. 137,567 billion in 1987; it represented 90.4 and 88.8 per cent of total income support in the two years. Administrative services accounted for 3 per cent and social-security payments for around 97 per cent. Of the latter, the most important benefits in terms of the volume of resources were old-age pensions and survivors' pensions.

The two latter items, which were equal to respectively 62.8 and 15 per cent of the total in 1987, increased their relative shares by 4.3 and 2.2 percentage points respectively over the eight years starting in 1980. Their share of GDP rose by about two percentage points. It is also significant to note the decline in the relative share of disability pensions over the eight years (from 5.9 per cent in 1980 to 3.2 per cent in 1987) and the gradual reduction in the proportion of expenditure on family allowances from 1981 onwards (from 6.9 per cent in 1980 to 3.7 per cent in 1987).

Spending on services and benefits to supplement inadequate incomes came to Lit. 4,052 billion in 1980 and Lit. 15,770 billion in 1987. In the latter year 2.5 per cent of the total was spent on administrative services, 17.6 per cent on services provided in homes and institutes (for old people, abandoned infants, handicapped persons), crèches, etc., and 82.4 per cent on social-security benefits, primarily in cash, to persons of more than 65 years of age without an income, blind persons, deaf-mutes, civilian invalids, and persons whose income is below the limits set from time to time by legislation or local authority by-laws.

16.2. Why is the welfare state so big?

Although spending on the welfare state declined from 60.4 per cent of total general government expenditure in 1980 to 56.8 per cent in 1988—entirely on account of a slowdown in expenditure on education and health—it still makes up the largest share of public expenditure in absolute terms. This is the main reason why transfer payments (and not spending on collective consumption) are the largest item of current general government expenditure, since for accounting purposes pensions and social security are considered as public transfers, whereas public expenditure on education and on health care is a component of collective consumption.

Given the economic importance of the welfare state and its considerable impact on current budget expenditure, it is appropriate to examine the reasons for its structural size and growth. In Italy perhaps no less than elsewhere in Europe, the welfare safety net is spread wide and is growing still wider in terms of the types of public intervention and the universal and automatic nature of benefits.

It is surprising, however, that public expenditure in Italy should have reached this enormous total without eliminating private spending on the same items. In fact, as indicated in the research carried out for us by Rossi (1986), there is little direct substitutability in Italy between public expenditure and private spending on welfare. According to analyses of Italian data, substitutability was virtually nil over the period 1961–85, while in the 1970s and early 1980s it showed an elasticity of around −0.2.

Several of our studies emphasize that the unwieldiness of the Italian welfare state and its consequent development—positive in some respects but negative in others—are attributable to 'the superimposition of the conflictual model on the particularistic-corporatist model, and to the effects of the political cycle' (Brunetta 1988: 10; see also Brunetta and Tronti, 1991).

At the origin, the welfare state was established to provide to each according to his needs (as long as those needs were of primary importance and worthy of protection), but in the 1960s it spread its cloak more widely, partly because particularly rapid economic and demographic growth made it possible to pursue policies that were no longer confined to specific sections of the population and limited needs. The difficulty of continuing in this course emerged in the following decade as a result of the slowdown in the growth of the Italian economy, rapid inflation (sometimes in double figures) combined with indexation mechanisms for social-security benefits, and the foreseeable but unforeseen change in the age composition of the population, with a relative fall in the proportion of persons of working age to shoulder the contribution burden.

The crisis in the economy as a whole amplified society's demands on the welfare state while at the same time making it more necessary than ever to find a solution that balanced efficiency with equity in order to avoid increasing the already heavy budget deficits, but public action does not appear to have been capable of providing effective and systematic long-term answers. On the contrary, the welfare state proved unable to resist or even co-ordinate the competing demands from different interest groups, none of which was dominant but all of which were driven by a corporatist and conflictual spirit.

In the words of Brunetta (1988: 7), the Italian welfare state has not functioned properly because 'the public finances have been reduced to underwriting the relative positions of individual social groups and their respective income levels, making it impossible to achieve a truly coherent distributive solution, since all demands backed by the power to blackmail were met'.

16.3. Is there a political cycle in Italy?

Another reason put forward by Brunetta (1988: 10) to explain the tremendous expansion of the welfare state is 'linked to the hypothesis of the political cycle, which asserts that economic policy is shaped by the desire to achieve electoral consensus irrespective of economic and social considerations', a view with which we wish neither to concur nor to take issue at present for lack of sufficient quantitative information. Brunetta maintains that

in the Italian situation the validity of this hypothesis can be verified by considering, for example, the priority given to seeking consensus on initial ideological positions; the reduction in class confrontation as the basis for political programmes; and finally the tendency to make politics more pragmatic, which is linked to the process of de-ideologization.

A recent empirical study shows that [in Italy] . . . GDP growth accelerates in the two quarters preceding elections (and then slows down in the post-election period): for the unions, there is greater advantage to be gained by raising the level of demand before or immediately after the elections because of the greater leverage they have during that period in view of the government's limited ability to respond; . . . for the government, it is imperative to be able to enjoy the benefits of settling labour disputes before the elections; finally, the opposition parties can try to encourage the trade-union movement to step up or reduce industrial disputes, depending on their electoral prospects and the possibility of winning a majority.

Although there can be no doubt that the search for an (unattainable) all-embracing consensus among the electorate is a plausible explanation of the long-term trends in the development of the welfare state, we are not persuaded that it is an equally good explanation of its short-term, cyclical dynamics. It seems to us that if the political-cycle hypothesis is to be validated in the case of Italy, more data are needed, not so much on the promises made as on the welfare measures actually adopted before elections. An electoral system such as Italy's, with elections at frequent but uncertain intervals, undoubtedly induces politicians to adopt a short-sighted approach and ignore the long-term consequences. It would also be necessary to show, however, that all the welfare measures promised in the run-up to the elections had been introduced quickly and resolutely before polling day. Would this really be binding, in a country where the state enjoys neither a high reputation nor great credibility?

17

State Pensions, Education, and Health Care

17.1. State pensions

A more precise examination of the main items of welfare expenditure carried out within our research group appears to confirm some of the interpretations indicated above, but also shows that the attempt to win general consensus by means of indiscriminate measures aimed at satisfying everyone ultimately leads to universal (or almost universal) dissatisfaction. In their analysis of pensions policy in Italy over the past forty years, Vitali *et al.* (1988) assert that the primary public objective in the field of social security, namely to ensure that certain sections of the population enjoy a standard of living they would otherwise be unable to attain because of their age or for other reasons, should not inevitably lead to deficits in the social-security accounts and to constant recourse to special funding from the Treasury, as occurred in Italy, especially from the 1970s onwards.

Vitali *et al.* (1988: 11) state that this

reflects instead the inadequate and unprogrammed economic policy pursued in the pensions field, which appears to be concerned more with assuaging conflict between employers and workers than with issuing coherent directives. Analysis of population statistics shows that the low retirement age and lengthening life expectancy mean that social-security institutions in Italy are obliged to pay pensions for an average of twenty years if payment commences at the compulsory retirement age, and that there is a high probability they will be liable to pay reversionary (or survivors') benefits that can also last for two decades.

The state-pension system is therefore extremely vulnerable to policy proposals designed to achieve a short-term social consensus. It is vulnerable in times of economic depression because Parliament will tend to soothe dissent by introducing more generous criteria for defining entitlement to benefits. Vitali *et al.* (1988: 15) assert that

a typical example of such behaviour is to be seen in the use of the pension system to distribute welfare benefits in the decade from 1965 to 1975 (one need only think of the excessive number of disability pensions awarded during that period); however, the legislation on early retirement introduced from 1981 onwards also constitutes an improper use of the pension system.

The pension system is also vulnerable when the economy is performing well, because Parliament can easily be misled by the growth in the resources of the state-pension fund; since contributions are levied as a percentage of wages, substantial increases in incomes generate a larger flow of revenue to the fund. Despite pensions being indexed, their purchasing power appears to be eroded when compared with the increase in effective incomes. Parliament will therefore be persuaded to award significant real increases to pensioners as well. With a ratio of just over unity (in the private sector) between active workers and pensioners, the increase in contribution receipts may not be sufficient to balance the increase in expenditure on all the pensions being paid.

Specific examples of one-off pension increases can be found 'not only on the eve of elections but also in times of satisfactory growth in economic activity and wages (and in employment, although not necessarily to the same degree)', add Vitali *et al.* (1988: 27). 'Moreover, the peculiarity of expenditure on pensions is that once a pension or a pension increase has been decided, it will be payable for decades to come.'

17.2. *Distortions and redistributions of the pension system*

It is clear from the analysis of Italian expenditure on state pensions that Parliament often fails to perform its task properly, providing insufficient protection for the most needy sections of the population and excessive benefits for other groups who are not in need, thereby provoking an escalation in demands. The apparent paradoxes in the Italian pension system are described in Padoa Schioppa (1992*a*, 1990*c*). Despite the high level of employees' and employers' contributions, the benefits provided are much higher still, so that the public-pension system operates at a substantial loss, which we estimate to amount to about 20 per cent of the pensions paid; moreover, despite its great generosity, the system leaves many, if not all, contributors dissatisfied.

This is primarily because average effective pensions are quite modest, with OSD (old-age, survivors' and disability) pensions of private and public employees not even reaching 40 per cent of the current average wage. The reason for this, in the case of old-age and survivors' pensions, is that the effective contribution period at the time of retirement is short, so that many pensions are at the minimum level. In the case of disability pensions, the cause lies in the fact that politicians prefer to extend the coverage to include even individuals who do not display serious disabilities while at the same time restricting the unit benefit, unfortunately also for the genuine needy.

Hence, the needs of those who draw only one pension are poorly covered, although many pensioners receive several pensions (official data do not indicate how many are in this situation). Moreover, since the period between the statutory retirement age and the average age of death is long in Italy (and longer than elsewhere), the burden on society is very heavy despite the inadequacy of effective pension provision. In addition, the benefit formula for old-age pensions is in Italy more generous than elsewhere, particularly and paradoxically for the pensioners at the floor level[1] (less so for those hit by the pension ceiling).

Public policy with regard to pensions has thus lost sight of its true role, namely to cater for a first category of need, in respect of which the promises made by Parliament can be kept at a reasonable cost to the community. Individuals outside that social group, which can be determined on the basis of average incomes from employment, should themselves be responsible for ensuring adequate income in retirement by selecting the products that satisfy their future security requirements from the range of products offered by the private (or public) insurance industry.

These are not the only distortions inherent in the pension system as it operates in Italy. To take only state old-age pensions for private and public employees, the adoption of a pay-as-you-go scheme instead of one funded on a fair actuarial basis entails various kinds of redistribution, not all of which are necessarily desirable.

As highlighted in Padoa Schioppa (1990c), every pay-as-you-go scheme systematically penalizes the sections of the population with a higher fertility rate, a higher rate of increase of wages, a higher

---

[1] According to the general-benefit formula for old-age state pensions (applied for example in the private sector) the pension is calculated as follows. The pension is equal to the average wage of the last five years of the active life, multiplied by a coefficient equal to 2% times the number of years of contribution to social security (for a maximum of 40 years). The multiplicative coefficient in the rest of Europe is not 2% but approximately 1.3%, while in Japan it is 0.75%. This coefficient becomes higher than 2% for those who do not reach a floor pension through the general-benefit formula.

growth rate of employment, not those with higher *levels* of wages, employment and economic prosperity. Some of these aspects have been noted in the literature, but their implications in terms of increased social inequality are overlooked. For example, it is known that pay-as-you-go schemes favour childless and small families over large families (Barro, 1981, Cremer *et al.*, 1987), but to the best of our knowledge no one except Gini (1909) has yet recognized the implications in terms of social inequality arising from the fact that in many countries fertility rates are negatively correlated to family income or welfare. Modern pay-as-you-go social-security systems therefore create a kind of 'spiral of inequality' that penalizes the least developed sections of a dualistic society.

Undesirable intergenerational redistribution effects of this kind are easy to identify in Italy. The Mezzogiorno, which the social-security system aims to protect in various ways (in particular by granting specific contribution relief), ends up transferring resources for old-age pensions to the rest of the country.[2] Indeed, since it has a much higher birth rate than the other areas but the same death rate, the South has a lower old-age dependency ratio (the ratio of the old to the young) than the Centre–North; since its inactivity rate (the ratio of the current rate of retirement among the old to the current rate of employment among the young) is lower, the ratio of pensioners to employed in the Mezzogiorno is half that in the Centre–North. Finally, as the replacement rate (the ratio of the average pension of current pensioners to the average wage of currently employed persons) is approximately the same in all areas of the country, the ratio of contributions to old-age pensions in the Centre–North is only 80 per cent of the Southern ratio, despite the fact that the social-security contribution rate in the Centre–North is 72 per cent higher than in the Mezzogiorno.

Women consititute the second social group to which the Italian pension system aims to provide some degree of assistance by means of limited but specific contribution relief. However, for unintentional demographic reasons, the pay-as-you-go mechanism actually overprotects them. Given women's longer life expentancy and their obligation to retire from private-sector employment five years earlier than men (at age 55), the female old-age dependency ratio is

---

[2] It should be noted, however, that if the same reasoning is applied to all OSD pensions rather than just old-age pensions, the transfer is in the opposite direction, as is clear from Table 7.6.

twice the male ratio. Female inactivity and replacement rates are lower than male rates, but they do not offset the difference in dependency ratios, and the ratio of contributions to old-age pensions is little more than 60 per cent of the corresponding male figure.

Nor are these distorting redistribution effects likely to diminish in the immediate future. Projections of dependency and inactivity rates are enough to show that they will in fact increase unless reforms are carried out to change the pensionable age, the benefit formula for calculating pensionable income, or social-security contribution rates. The observable reduction in fertility rates in Italy will not only cause a decline in population estimated at about 12 per cent of the current resident population over the next forty years but will also lead to a pronounced ageing of the population, distributed unevenly across the variou regions of the country, which will imply a dependency ratio almost twice as high as at present. If social-security policy remains unchanged, in forty years' time the young part of the population will be concentrated mainly in the Mezzogiorno. They will have to finance the pensions paid to the older generations, living mainly in the Centre–North, who will be more numerous than both the old people of today and the young people of tomorrow.

As a result, the ratio of contributions to old-age pensions in the Centre–North will decline even further in relation to that in the South. At the same time and for similar reasons, the ratio for women will fall further behind that for men.

As well as these types of redistribution typical of any pay-as-you-go pension system, two other undesirable redistribution effects are created in Italy by the particular nature of the old-age pension scheme; the first is an intragenerational redistribution due to the link between pensionable income and the income earned in the last five years of working life, whereas pension contributions depend on income over the entire life-cycle, and the second is an intergenerational redistribution caused by the deficit of the pension system. The first favours pensioners whose individual income is particularly high in the closing years of their working life relative to the average life-cycle income; these are high school and university graduates.[3] The second redistribution is the transfer of the pension

[3] According to empirical evidence presented in Padoa Schioppa (1974) and Banca d'Italia (1991), age earnings profiles in Italy used to be in the mid-1970s bell-shaped

burden on to future generations, who will be unable to run a deficit indefinitely and will therefore be obliged to pay our pensions out of their own resources via taxation.

Another potentially important distortion caused by the Italian pension system is in the saving rate; obliging workers and employers to pay contributions into a public-pension fund, thus creating a form of forced saving, may crowd out private saving. The analyses produced for us by Brugiavini (1988) show, however, that in Italy increases in future benefits from the social-security system reduce net non-pension wealth by an amount equal to only about one-tenth of the increase itself, indicating very low substitutability between public and private wealth. This finding is consistent with others discussed above, in which it was observed that present and future public consumption is only a partial direct substitute for current and future private consumption. The resulting high overall saving rate may be explained by the hypothesis that Italian households consider that they receive little or no protection from the present pension system; this point is taken up again in Section 21.2.

17.3. *Efficiency and equity in state education*

We have already seen that the state pension system is misused in Italy, sometimes to provide benefits that are available to all but inadequate for the needy (as in the case of social pensions), or to serve the supplementary purpose of rectifying failures and incompleteness in other markets (such as the use of disability pensions to alleviate endemic unemployment); almost the same can be said of public education.

This is indicated by the way in which various measures have been implemented, such as the extension of compulsory schooling and the liberalization of university entrance; students receive only modest financial and material assistance which is distributed indiscriminately and bears little relation to actual need (free book- and meal-coupons for all at the compulsory level, bursaries and grants of only small amounts for students at the higher levels of educa-

for income-earners at all levels of education except for university graduates. Apparently, in more recent years, maximum earnings are obtained in Italy in the latest working years at all educational levels except for high-school graduates. But even now the differential in earnings between high-school and university graduates on the one hand and less formally educated workers on the other is definitely larger in the last five years of the active life than in the rest of the life-cycle.

tion, because they are not always targeted on the able and deserving youth without resources).

It is also proved by the move away from school selection on the basis of merit over the last twenty years. The fact that merit-based selection is correlated with class-based selection, as indicated by various tables on school survival and drop-out rates according to social origin (see Padoa Schioppa, 1974), does not mean that the adoption of pseudo-egalitarian methods (such as awarding group grades as opposed to individual grades or giving all pupils the maximum grade) attenuates class-based selection;[4] on the contrary, it accentuates it, since the school loses its screening function, thus increasing the importance of family origins for the success of young people. Such a response to the demands of the student movement of 1968 appears to be popularist and to be welcomed by the masses, but in fact it reflects the interests of the happy few because it limits the supply of labour by providing somewhere to 'park' potential unemployed workers rather than increasing the probability of their gaining qualified employment.

The distortions that reduce efficiency without increasing equity are particularly evident in state higher education in Italy. There is some suspicion that education policy has regressive effects in the same way as the old-age pension system described above. The analysis carried out for us by Saba (1988) emphasizes this point, maintaining that at present Italian state-funded universities (i.e. almost all Italian universities) 'succeed in the tremendously difficult task of combining inefficiency and regressivity'.

The way in which the resources available to finance the right to study are allocated sometimes leads to greater assistance being given to those whose need is least, thus exacerbating the existing imbalances. The almost symbolic nature of university fees means that the taxpayer bears almost the entire cost of the higher-education service, which is still supplied, in the **majority** of cases, to youths belonging to the medium–upper social class. Moreover, there does not exist any correlation between the scale of the fees and the social benefits that may derive from the educational

[4] These politically motivated methods, which were adopted in the immediate aftermath of the student unrest in the late 1960s, have now been abandoned, but other practices decided at the same time and for the same reasons are still in use; e.g. almost all Italian public-funded universities continue to allow students to resit examinations every two months, and in some cases monthly.

process. The absence of adequate alternative instruments for financing university studies and the rejection of price as a criterion for allocating and rationing educational resources render freedom of choice meaningless and make the students' evaluation of the quality of the service virtually useless; they reduce the stimuli for competition between the universities and hence for innovation and diversification in educational methods and products.

Public funding of university institutions also increases the bureaucratization of the system by magnifying the effects of a monolithic organizational structure based on the virtual state monopoly over higher education and a predilection for centralized regulation.

Accordingly, as in the case of pension policies, we propose a complete revision of the relationship between the public and private parts of the strategic sector of higher education in order to restore a significant degree of competitiveness, pluralism, and efficiency, compatible with safeguarding extensive and equal educational opportunities.

Four main proposals emerge from the analysis by Saba (1988): the gradual restoration of price (university tuition fees) as a means of demand selection and for determining users' preferences and needs; entry-level testing of students' ability and willingness to study in types of institute of a different standard (such testing is totally lacking at present), combined with the abolition of the legal privilege connected with holding a University degree, regardless of the intrinsic quality of the educational attainment; this is an undesirable form of regulation, just as uniformity in the salaries paid to all university lecturers is also undesirable; the change-over from a policy of subsidizing educational institutions to a system of adequate direct finance for students—but only those who are able, deserving, and lacking in resources—and the trial introduction of different instruments of substantial monetary value (vouchers, tax allowances, loans, bursaries) to be spent at the institution of higher education of the student's choice; finally, the granting of considerable autonomy and competitiveness to the universities, in parallel with greater and more direct responsibility for raising their own financial resources.

17.4. *Universal coverage and primary needs in public-health care*

Finally, the health policy pursued in Italy also lends itself to the interpretation proposed so far with regard to the welfare state as a whole.

Brunetta (1988: 14–15) asserts that

although objective factors have contributed to the expansion in public-health spending (population growth, the increasing proportion of older people, the emergence of new social diseases, etc.), other causes associated with health-policy choices also deserve to be mentioned. They have not only encouraged the consumption of public-health services without any real justification but have also led to the failure of the rationalization that was supposed to result from the 1978 reform.

In fact, the establishment of the national health service gave rise to expenditure flows whose purpose was similar to that of the assistance policies used to ease social conflicts; moreover, the problems of finance emerged at a time when the economic crisis was causing difficulties in the public finances, eroding the accumulated resources that had made it possible to pay for the expansion in public-health care at the beginning of the 1960s.

Furthermore, the compulsory nature of contributions to the national health service and, as with state education, the potential use of the service to provide universal coverage rather than to cater for particular needs or users do not appear to imply, as one might expect, that it could totally replace private-health expenditure. According to the analysis carried out for us by Piergentili and Granaglia (1988), private-health spending amounted in Italy to approximately 15 per cent of total health expenditure in the last five years examined and has shown a more recent tendency to rise, whereas before the reform it had fallen from about 15 per cent in the early 1970s to around 11 per cent in 1978.

It is difficult to interpret the level of this significant piece of information or the change that has occurred over time, but yet again it could indicate that universal public-health care combined with a poor standard of service was both distorting and inequitable in relation to the primary and strategic needs of the citizens to be protected.

A high proportion of private-health spending on general or specialist medical treatment may be an indicator of the poor quality of public services or their unavailability unless patients are prepared for a long and exhausting wait, or of the fact that they are almost totally lacking in certain fields, such as dental care. High private expenditure on pharmaceuticals could reflect a substantial degree of self-prescribing, perhaps on account of the excessive waiting period before many medical consultations, with consequent poor utilization or waste of the drugs in question. Only if private expenditure were used solely to pay for health care that was deliberately not provided by the national health system (cosmetic surgery, homeopathic medicines) could it be claimed that there was not partial substitution but complementarity between private and public expenditure on health.

17.5. *Redistribution effects of health expenditure*

A further concern relates to the suspicion that the Italian health system has perverse redistribution effects, given the private expenditure needed to supplement public-health services of dubious quality and effectiveness. This issue, and the more general question of redistribution in Italy, warrants more detailed examination, part of which is deferred to Chapter 18.

The work carried out for us by Dirindin (1988) who analyses the redistribution connotations of the tax-deductibility of private-health expenditure, represents a step in this direction. Under the Law establishing the national health service (Law 833 of 1978), citizens have a general obligation to contribute to the public-health system but are free to supplement the services available by seeking treatment in the private-health market. Those who intend to seek private treatment have basically three options: to take the risk of incurring expenditure and, if it arises, to pay the cost of the services they purchase themselves; to pay premiums for individual membership of a private health-insurance scheme; to belong to a group insurance scheme arranged by their employer. Dirindin (1988: 19–20) comments:

the three options differ as regards tax treatment, among other things. Recourse to the private market in health services without insurance (the first option) is treated as 'deductible expenditure' under the existing tax regulations: expenditure on health care borne directly by the taxpayer can be deducted from taxable income, provided it is shown on form 740 [the basic income-tax return]. The regulations contemplate two types of expenditure: fully deductible (mainly specialist treatment) and partly deductible (general treatment, with only the part of total expenditure in excess of 5 per cent of declared income being eligible for deduction).

Premiums for individual private health insurance (the second option) are not deductible from taxable income (in contrast to other types of welfare insurance, such as life and accident insurance). . . . Group insurance arranged by the employer for his staff or for certain categories (the third option) is taken into consideration when calculating taxable income from employment. The premiums paid by the employer are not part of the employee's taxable income and, at the same time, they are deductible from the employer's income.

Tax concessions for private-health expenditure therefore have extremely fragmented and varied redistribution effects, sometimes benefiting all taxpayers on medium or high incomes, at other times favouring small groups of taxpayers with diverse socio-economic characteristics but mainly on medium-to-high incomes. The tax saving increases in proportion to taxable income, and it favours expenditure on items that would largely be classified as luxuries, or at any rate not within the reach of the less well-to-do classes.

Hence, in the strategic field of health care too, it seems logical to think that provision for a first category of need on grounds of equity could be achieved at lower overall cost to the public purse but with higher unit benefits, and thus more effectively, by redirecting public-health expenditure towards that specific aim and leaving the market to provide unsubsidized services to cater for patients who do not need the support of the community.

17.6. *The efficient use of public-health resources*

An OECD report on health care (OECD, 1987) reaches similar conclusions about the efficiency and effectiveness of public-health systems in various countries. Whereas in the past the fundamental objective of health policy everywhere was to ensure universal access to health services, today attention is turning more to the issue of efficiency. The main concerns appear to be to control the cost of public-health services and to reduce the intensity of use.

As to the first aspect, Nonis (1988: 62–3), summarizing the OECD report for us, states that it would be possible to move to alternative methods:

towards prospective payment systems (as in the United States), to the setting of price levels that encouraged the efficient use of resources, to the indexation of health expenditure to the general inflation rate (rather than solely to the rise in health costs), or to the introduction of market principles. . . . As to the second aspect, which complements the first, a policy of cost-sharing . . . could be one of the ways of containing costs. However, there is a feeling, particularly in Europe, that the introduction of systems of this kind would produce only an initial saving, followed by a return to the previous level of consumption or only a partial reduction in expenditure.

Another method would be to encourage

alternative low-cost systems in order to reduce congestion in hospitals, the main source of expenditure. The problem is how to ensure identical safety and quality of treatment, especially the latter. In most OECD countries there is in practice no efficient system of quality control (in the United States . . . it has been possible to establish an effective system of control based on peer reviews and Federal inspections of hospitals).

As to the reduction in the volume and range of services that can be provided or in the proportion of the population that can benefit,

the OECD notes that in several countries user choice is restricted, with limitations on access to services. In other cases less flexible criteria of public-health need have been set in order to limit the demand and supply of universally accessible services. In the United Kingdom, Ireland, Spain, and Denmark, the established system is to limit choice on the basis of residential criteria.

Income Redistribution

For that reason I declare openly that I always hate injustice, whenever it occurs, whomever it benefits, whomever it harms; I hate it if it benefits my enemies; I hate it if it benefits my friends; I hate it if it benefits me; I would hate it if it benefited the persons I hold most dear in the world or the attainment of my most ardent desire, which is to see Italy *truly* united. In the light of this, one can appreciate my profound distress at being noble and knowing full well that no force in the world could ever erase that fact; my misfortune therefore knew no remedy. I envied those who did not bear such a stigma, and considered their happiness to be immense. . . . But at that time I believed the nobility was rightly hated for its overbearing behaviour, and that it alone could act in such a way; I believed that those who disparaged the nobility would not want to become knights and counts, even if their life depended on it! What a fool! If I had known then, as I know now, that democracy is an egg from which there hatches a count, I would not have taken it so much to heart.

(M. D'Azeglio, *I miei ricordi*, 1866)

18

'Political' Prices

18.1. Income redistribution via interest on the public debt

Up to this point we have touched upon income redistribution when dealing with social security, education, and health, and have expressed our suspicion that public expenditure in these strategic fields displays regressive tendencies. Income redistribution is obviously also achieved in other ways, in particular via transfer payments for interest on the public debt, interference with relative prices (and inflation[1]), and via direct taxation.

Interest payments on the public debt, which are shown in 'Expenditure not specified elsewhere' in Table 16.1, appear to be by far the fastest growing item of general government expenditure in Italy; we must confess to our ignorance (and that of others) about their redistribution effects, mainly owing to the lack of micro-economic data on the holders (firms or families) of government securities. In the analysis carried out for us, the Central Statistical Office (ISTAT) researchers Malizia and Pedullà (1988: 20–1) state explicitly that 'it is not possible to say whether the observed growth has been favourable or not to households or firms, because we do not yet have information on the sectoral (or socio-demographic) distribution of interest paid by general government, a variable which, as we have seen, is the most dynamic and decisive in the redistribution process'.

Nevertheless, in their opinion, (pp. 20–1)

depending on the distribution of public-debt instruments among different types of economic agent, and hence on the distribution of interest payments by general government, one of the following events may have occurred: a redistribution of income in favour of firms, which comes in

---

[1] Public intervention with regard to inflation has both direct and indirect redistributive implications: direct because it alters the creditor/debtor relationship unless financial assets are index-linked, and indirect through the correlation between inflation and the variability of relative prices. Our research brought no deeper insight into the first aspect, which is more monetary than real; with regard to the second aspect, see the work carried out for us by Casella and Feinstein (1987) and Cuckierman and Padoa Schioppa (1986).

addition to the redistribution to the detriment of households (as a result of the reduction in welfare expenditure as a percentage of GDP in recent years); or a redistribution of income in favour of households, which may offset the adverse redistribution described above.

In the latter case, however, redistribution has occurred within the household sector, favouring holders of public-debt instruments in proportion to the value of their holdings.

Since the welfare state applies to all households without distinction, and should, in theory at least, have greater effects on the welfare of less well-off households, who probably have proportionately smaller holdings of public-debt securities, we can deduce from analysis of the aggregates at macro level that the income redistribution generated by the actions of the public sector in the 1980s has tended to be regressive; in other words, the composition of public expenditure has changed in a way that appears to have benefited high-income households and/or firms.

For the moment this is no more than a suggestion, the researchers conclude, since to draw more definite conclusions

it would be necessary to analyse the income of households and firms at a micro-economic level by attempting to quantify the effects of the various flows initiated by general government and structural changes therein on the incomes of households according to income bracket and type of house-hold. This is an issue that will have to be tackled in the future.

Some empirical evidence gathered in 1987 through a combined representative sample of Italian households analysed by Banca d'Italia and of Italian clients of the commercial Banca Nazionale del Lavoro (see Banca d'Italia, 1989*b* and Cannari *et al.*, 1990: 29) allows us now to utilize relevant micro-economic information on households' financial portfolios, confirming some of the Malizia and Pedullà assumptions described above. Indeed, 38.1 per cent of the households' financial portfolio is now observed to be devoted to government securities, and the percentage is smaller in the Mezzogiorno than in the Centre–North and among the less formally educated families. Moreover, '29.4 per cent of Italian families own government securities . . . The percentage is higher in medium–upper social classes, showing a positive correlation with households' income. At a given income, the effect of other variables on the percentage of families owning government securities is more limited but significant: this percentage depends on the households' geographical residence, being higher in the Centre–North than in the South, and depends on the age of the head of the family as well' (a point to which we will come back in the concluding remarks).

18.2. The redistribution effect of administered prices

Income redistribution can be achieved via relative prices, since in Italy the behaviour of consumers differs significantly according to socio-demographic group and region, as illustrated in several of our analyses (Bollino and Rossi, 1988; Patrizii and Rossi, 1991). For example, at given relative prices, 'households in Southern Italy and the islands need to spend around 20 per cent more than the representative household to achieve a given level of welfare, while the additional cost to agricultural workers (in any capacity) is between 20 and 30 per cent more' (Patrizii and Rossi, 1991: 23).

In fact the representative household is not the same in all areas of the country, and the cost of living, or the weight of the various products in the consumption basket, or the distribution of relative prices are not identical in the Centre–North and the South, as described in detail in Section 8.2 above.[2] A glance at Table 8.5 may be sufficient to convince us of this; if the households' consumption deflator is set at 100 in 1970 for all areas, by 1987 it stands at 808.03 in the South, 803.22 in the Centre (including Latium), and 879.68 in the North. In the light of the variations in relative prices during the 1970s and 1980s, it cannot therefore be argued that the Mezzogiorno has been penalized. On the contrary, as Patrizii and Rossi (1991: 23) also reiterate, 'less well-to-do families of above-average size living in Southern Italy and/or the islands whose head of household works in the agricultural sector (in an employed or self-employed capacity) appear to have recorded large welfare gains'.

[2] The hypotheses on which the analysis by Patrizii and Rossi (1991) was conducted were therefore different from those on which we based our discussion of the Mezzogiorno, for example. In the latter instance, we take explicit account of the fact that the representative Southern household is not the same as the representative Centre–North household, in that we consider the archetypal worker, identical in all the regions of Italy, to be a rhetorical figure. Patrizii and Rossi (1991: 25) are right, however, when they maintain that, in so doing, 'traditional analysis, being unable to distinguish the specific effects of socio-demographic characteristics, produces results that mix up the implication of different levels of expenditure with that due to the characteristics themselves'. For that reason we believe that both approaches can provide useful indications for economic policy.

Moving on to examine the influence of economic policy on relative prices and hence on income redistribution, it can be noted that there are three main ways in which the public sector interferes with relative prices: through administered prices and public-utility charges, through value-added tax, and through excise duties (it being assumed that the last two are both passed on fully to prices).

Let us first consider measures with regard to administered prices and utility charges. The system of administered prices (excluding monitored prices) is the main instrument used by the Interministerial Committee on Prices (CIP), which operates in accordance with instructions from the Interministerial Committee for Economic Planning. As Patrizii and Rossi (1991: 27) point out, one of the objectives of the CIP since its inception has been

to foster the transition from a war economy, in which all prices were frozen . . . to a free-trade economy. This original objective was later reformulated by the Budget Ministry as an indeterminate redistribution objective with the goal of protecting the purchasing power of various categories of consumer and at the same time curbing the rise in the general price index for society as a whole. In more recent years, an additional objective has been to reduce the burden on the public finances. The redistribution effect of administered prices is evaluated in relation to changes in the prices of other goods or services in the category to which they belong.

Taking 1977 as the base year, the year to which the start of the present policy of price controls can be dated, and thus looking only at changes over the period 1977–87, the results suggest that, contrary to general belief, administered prices have had a redistribution effect in favour of higher-spending groups, since on average administered prices (except utility charges) have risen more rapidly than uncontrolled prices of goods and services in the same categories.

18.3. The redistribution effect of VAT and excise duties

Let us now consider the effects of VAT and excise duties on relative prices and hence on income redistribution in Italy. Patrizii and Rossi (1991: 24–5) show that the incidence of VAT on private consumption was progressive over the fifteen-year period under consideration (1973–87); in 1987 it was

equal to 9.0 per cent of expenditure for households with a low level of expenditure (Lit. 500,000 a month), 9.5 per cent for those with expenditure at the national average (around Lit. 2 million a month), and approximately 9.8 per cent for high levels of expenditure (Lit. 5 million a month). Note that these estimates were made without altering the socio-demographic characteristics of households. In other words, the case considered is that of a worker household receiving various levels of pay. . . . A higher level of expenditure is usually a characteristic of large families; nevertheless, it is generally recognized that in this case the level of total expenditure is not a good indicator of individual welfare if it does not take due account of the number of family members. On the other hand, lower levels of expenditure traditionally prevail in Southern Italy, but this does not necessarily mean that a policy of general income redistribution in favour of the Southern regions is appropriate unless geographic location is the discriminating criterion and not the level of expenditure.

On this last point, the analyses by Patrizii and Rossi (1991) show us that the effects of geographic location are minor; for a given total expenditure, the incidence of the taxes in question is around 9.5 per cent in the Centre–North and 9.3 per cent in the Mezzogiorno. The redistribution implications of VAT change over time, however, with the incidence of VAT being almost the same for households in all areas of the country in the mid-1970s.

For a given level of total expenditure, a given size of household, and a given geographic location, the professional status of the head of household is of some importance. Again, there is no evidence of behavioural differences between employees and self-employed, but redistribution effects can be observed between sectors of economic activity, with agriculture the main beneficiary.

We must also consider the implications of changes in excise duties on relative prices, and hence on income redistribution. Whereas VAT applies to goods and services at all stages of production, irrespective of the final user, excise duties are specific taxes, and in the manner in which they are levied in Italy, they appear to be more akin to traditional single-phase taxes on final consumption.[3]

The incidence of excise duties in 1987 was 4.4 per cent for households with a low level of expenditure, 3.7 per cent for those

---

[3] For many years until 1985 the state fiscal monopolies (essentially on tobacco) were a category apart; it was not strictly correct to describe their prices as taxes, since the state's intervention consisted in setting a final price and controlling production. At present the system is based on a two-part consumption tax: a small specific element and a larger *ad valorem* element related (in the case of cigarettes) to the price of the most popular brands.

in the middle range, and 3.3 per cent for higher levels of expenditure, thus showing a significant degree of regressivity. This finding contrasts quite markedly with that obtained by Bollino *et al.* (1988). The discrepancy is due largely to differences in the method of computing the incidence; Bollino *et al.* assume homothetic and separable preferences, whereas Patrizii and Rossi (1991) take account, among other factors, of the possibility of substitution and associated welfare losses.

Excise duties differ from VAT as regards their socio-demographic impact; in the case of excise duties the groups penalized are entrepreneurs and self-employed workers who, for a given total consumption, spend a higher proportion on transport and communications, and hence on complementary products that are subject to excise duty, such as petrol.

18.4. Potential effects of the European tax harmonization

If we therefore adopt the methodology of Patrizii and Rossi (1991) and examine the current overall redistribution effect of value-added tax, excise duties, and controls on administered prices, we find some degree of regressivity, and an increasing one over the last decade.

In the near future, however, relative prices in Italy might undergo a number of changes, primarily as a result of two trends: first, the planned harmonization of indirect-tax rates in the EEC, and secondly the reforms that will make it possible to adjust public-utility charges in line with average production costs in the sector in question.

Patrizii and Rossi (1991: 28) estimate that the second of these changes, which is aimed at raising electricity, railway, postal, telephone, and transport charges, would entail an 'additional cost of only Lit. 2,000 for less well-to-do families (as defined above) and Lit. 35,000 for more wealthier households'. This finding contrasts sharply with the common belief–often accepted even by Parliament –that the adjustment of utility charges in line with changes in average production costs would have an undesirable redistribution effect.

As regards the European proposal to harmonize VAT rates, the hypothesis examined by Patrizii and Rossi (1991: 28) assumes that rates will be close to the maxima defined in the EEC Commission's first draft in order to keep the total tax yield unchanged. 'The cost would therefore be around Lit. 5,000 a month for less well-off households, but more than Lit. 100,000 a month for households with average monthly expenditure in excess of Lit. 5 million. Hence it is clear that the net effect would be to accentuate the progressivity of the system.'

Other papers on the implications of the proposed European harmonization of indirect taxes, written for us by Brugiavini and Weber (1988) and Milana (1988a) complement the work quoted above, as they employ different methods, or adopt different harmonization hypotheses in view of the range of variation in the European proposals, or consider effects other than redistribution.

The analysis by Brugiavini and Weber (1988) is based on the supposition that Italian excise duties would be modified in accordance with the Commission's first proposal (which basically reduces the tax on petrol and tobacco and increases that on alcohol), that VAT on products currently taxed at 2 per cent would be increased to 5 per cent and the highest rate of VAT would rise to 20 per cent.[4]

On these hypotheses, the rise in food prices and the reduction in the price of petrol would cause increases of about 8, 10, and 9 per cent respectively in tax payments by households on low, medium, and high incomes, given differences in their preferences and budgets as reflected in differences in income and substitution effects. The resulting redistribution is not easy to estimate at first sight, but the greater the authorities' aversion to inequality, the less desirable it would be.

Moreover, there would be an increase in tax receipts, equal initially to 8 per cent but declining subsequently to 7 per cent. However welcome such a result would be from the point of view of the budget deficit, it should be treated with great caution, first and foremost because it is highly sensitive to the particular hypotheses associated with each model. In the study by Bollino *et al.* (1988), for example, the budgetary effects of harmonizing VAT and excise duties in accordance with the particular Community proposals on which the study is based would be to increase the general government borrowing requirement by Lit. 2,100 billion in the first year and to reduce it by Lit. 6,500 and 1,500 billion

---

[4] More detailed information on the European tax harmonization proposals is contained in Bollino *et al.* (1988), for example.

respectively in the two following years. Secondly, it should not be forgotten that a reduction in the budget deficit due to an increase in taxation as a result of the harmonization of VAT and excise duties could also have distorting effects on resource allocation, as recalled by Milana (1988a, 1988b).[5]

[5] Milana (1988a: 27) focuses more on the distorting effects of the European harmonization proposals than on their redistributive effects. In an attempt to quantify the deadweight loss of a possible tax reform, he states that the potential efficiency and welfare changes 'should be compared with the current tax system, which is certainly distortive and inefficient. The losses are not easy to quantify, not only because of the non-existence of the basic statistical information, but also because we must represent the consumer preferences and the producer behaviour in a realistic and convenient way. That is a formidable task that involves time-consuming research work and leads at best only to approximating results.'

19

Direct Taxation

19.1. *Vertical equity in direct taxation*

Finally, we wish to touch upon the income redistribution effected by the system of direct taxation. Three criteria have traditionally been suggested as a basis for judging the system: vertical equity, whereby those with a greater capacity to contribute are required to pay higher taxes; horizontal equity, whereby the revenue from incomes of equal amount but different types must be identical; and efficiency, in order to minimize the distorting effect of taxation on optimum resource allocation, which has been partly discussed above with regard to the choice between consumption and saving, between work and leisure.

The first two aspects are closely linked with the problem of income redistribution, and cannot always be separated from the third, for if the tax structure unwittingly discriminates in favour of certain categories of taxpayer or types of income and penalizes others, it is a source of both horizontal (and sometimes vertical) inequity combined with allocative distortions. In fact, our analyses seem to indicate that the Italian income-tax system is in precisely such a situation within the Pareto-optimal frontier, so that improvements could be made simultaneously in terms of efficiency as well as both concepts of equity without altering the revenue yield.

Let us therefore examine the characteristics of the Italian income-tax system in greater detail in order to understand why fiscal changes can have positive implications in terms of one or more of the three criteria mentioned above.

The vertical equity of a tax system depends on the relative importance attached on the one hand to income tax (which is generally progressive) or wealth tax and on the other to consumption taxes (which are generally more neutral), and on the progressivity criteria that can be built into any type of tax. The Italian tax system lays greater importance on direct taxation than those in other countries. On the other hand, indirect tax rates differ markedly in Italy. This would seem to imply that the Italian tax system displays greater vertical equity, even though the small importance attached to wealth taxes could indicate the opposite.

The evidence gathered for us by Quintieri and Rosati (1987) shows, however, that a progressive income tax is not sufficient to generate a stable trend towards vertical equity—the shape of the progressivity curve and its constancy over time in relation to changes in nominal aggregates are also important.

Analysis of the equity characteristics of direct taxation in Italy shows that vertical and horizontal equity have gradually decreased since the tax reform of 1973–4, not so much because of explicit legislation as because of fiscal drag due to the progressivity of tax rates combined with the escalation in nominal incomes caused by inflation in the absence of legal fiscal indexation of tax brackets, allowances, and deductions.

In this situation some types of income managed to maintain their real net purchasing power better than others by means of wage bargaining (cf. Padoa Schioppa, 1990a). Moreover, with all nominal incomes rising rapidly, the fact that the fiscal system was not legally indexed meant that personal income taxes became ever less able to reduce the concentration of post-tax incomes despite a substantial increase in the overall average income-tax rate; this occurred in the decade ending in 1984, despite the fact that average and marginal tax rates estimated for each income bracket remained broadly unchanged and that along the tax functions the average and marginal tax rates increased with the rise in income. In the second half of the 1980s, however, important changes in the number and value of marginal personal income-tax rates have occurred in Italy (cf. Padoa Schioppa, 1992d). Together with the so-called compensation for fiscal drag, discussed in Section 12.4, these changes implied that personal income taxes became *de facto* discretionarily indexed.

19.2. Horizontal equity in direct taxation

We shall examine the effects of the Italian income-tax structure on horizontal equity with particular reference to the taxation of investment income. It is here that the greatest discrepancies appear in the treatment of different kinds of income. Some income (interest on deposits, corporate bonds, government securities) is taxed at a flat rate, while other types of income (such as dividends) are subject to a flat withholding tax, with any higher-rate tax being collected through the tax return. Identical or similar financial assets may be taxed differently depending on the nature of the issuer or holder; this provides scope for arbitrage, which may lead to a substantial loss of revenue, as indicated in the analysis carried out for us by Vagliasindi (1988). Corporation taxes (IRPEG) and local taxes on non-labour income (ILOR) vary significantly over time (and in fact also from region to region), not only in terms of rates but also as regards cumulability (the situation until 1977), deductibility (since 1978 local corporation tax has been deductible from taxable income subject to central corporation tax), and the presence or absence of double taxation (eliminated in 1977 as a result of the introduction of tax credits for dividends). For that reason, as we are reminded by Devereux *et al.* (1990: 1) tax rates 'vary widely across different companies because of the different mix of capital assets they own and the alternative ways they can be financed, because of the different sectors they belong to, and because of the different profitability conditions they find themselves in.'

In this situation, the proposal to standardize the taxation of investment income seems reasonable from the point of view of efficiency as well as that of horizontal equity. However, the question of the appropriate rate remains open: should it be the maximum marginal rate, with the taxpayer receiving a tax credit for any reimbursement due to him, or a lower rate, which would avoid the accumulation of tax rebates and would therefore be more acceptable to middle-income taxpayers?

The problem of horizontal equity also affects the tax treatment of different types of income from employment. In traditional Italian doctrine on public finance, income from self-employment has usually been considered qualitatively different from income from dependent employment owing to the greater risk it entails. According to Einaudi, equal tax treatment for income from dependent employment and from self-employment is a convenient legal falsehood. As the self-employed have greater opportunities for tax avoidance and evasion, their effective rate of tax would be lower than that for employees. Parliament is fully aware of this, and thus taxes income from self-employment more heavily while turning a blind eye to tax evasion, which brings the effective rate back to an appropriate level.

In view of this, it would be fitting to re-examine the question of the equivalence between income from dependent employment and self-employment, partly because it is doubtful whether the current system of deductions can offset the risk differential between the two types of activity. However, it should not be forgotten that in theory a self-employed person could replicate the no-risk income situation of an employee by taking out adequate insurance, although in fact some forms of insurance are not available owing to the market incompleteness we have mentioned above, or are not available at a reasonable price.

19.3. Tax evasion

The problem of the difference in the tax burden on employees and the self-employed and that of tax evasion warrant more detailed examination. First, there are statistical grounds for treating a particular category of citizens as potential tax avoiders or evaders, and thus taxing them more heavily, but there is no moral justification. As we know, the average is only a statistical fiction; all citizens have the right and duty to be taxed individually at a rate that obviously depends on their actual resources, and not on an average basis according to the professional category to which they belong.

Fiscal authorities who are incapable of checking taxable income individually and who work on the assumption of an average discrepancy between the effective and declared income of a particular category of taxpayers are not only incompetent and unjust, because they penalize honest members of the suspect category while allowing the dishonest to escape, but they are also inefficient, because it is likely that the higher the tax rates, the greater the incentive and probability of tax evasion. This is bound to create a vicious circle in which an excessive tax burden leads to evasion, which leads to an amnesty and then to even harsher taxation than before. The only (though costly) way to break the circle is to establish a more competent and credible tax administration adequately equipped to assess the tax position of each taxpayer without prejudging suspect groups.

Secondly, tax evasion on a substantial scale makes it difficult to assess a country's fiscal pressure. This indicator, which is usually expressed in terms of tax revenue (or current general government receipts) as a percentage of GDP is almost meaningless if there is an area of income that escapes taxation and statistical recording. Here too, the reason is that the indicator is an average figure, represented by the average of the tax burden on honest taxpayers and a number of zeros corresponding to tax evaders.

Comparisons over time and between countries can therefore be very misleading if careful consideration is not given to tax evasion. One example is provided by the interpretations that many Italian observers put on Table 19.1, which comes from OECD sources; on the basis of these figures, it has been claimed that the ratio of tax revenue to GDP in Italy is below the EEC average and closer to the levels in Mediterranean countries, so that some upward adjustment of tax rates is advocated.

In the remainder of this section we intend to argue a different case, and to begin by contesting the premisses.

If we compare the OECD data on Italy shown in Table 19.1 with those on Italy from the same source published three years earlier (Table 19.2), we see that the figures diverge considerably from 1980 onwards. Take the year 1983, for example; unlike the latter set of statistics, the old figures show that fiscal pressure in Italy was above the EEC average and higher than in the United Kingdom or Germany but not in France.

The reason for this discrepancy, which could lead to a completely different judgement about the need for an increase in tax rates, is extremely simple. In 1986 the Central Statistical Office (ISTAT) carried out a far-reaching revision of the national accounts that brought previously unrecorded incomes back within the coverage of the statistics. This increased the recorded gross domestic product, and thus reduced the fiscal-pressure index by increasing the denominator of the ratio.

To come back to the example of 1983, the revised data shown in Table 19.1 suggest that Italy's ratio of tax revenue to GDP is below the EEC average (but still higher than that for the seven major countries and for all OECD countries), at 37.7 per cent. This is the average between a (high) tax rate of 45.3 per cent on those whose incomes did not escape public scrutiny (by the statisticians and, it is to be hoped, by the tax authorities as well) and a zero corresponding to the rate paid by the estimated 17 per cent of tax evaders. If this is the true situation, it would probably be wrong to conclude that tax rates should be raised in order to produce a higher ratio of tax revenue to GDP. As the percentage of

TABLE 19.1. Current revenue of general government as a %age of GDP: international comparisons, 1967–1987

Country	1967	1968	1969	1970	1971	1972	1973	1974	1975	1976	1977	1978	1979	1980	1981	1982	1983	1984	1985	1986	1987
United States	27.1	28.7	29.9	28.9	28.2	29.3	29.6	30.3	28.8	29.5	29.7	29.9	30.5	30.8	31.6	31.1	30.7	30.7	31.2	31.3	32.0
Japan	19.3	19.6	19.7	20.6	21.6	21.5	22.5	24.5	24.0	23.6	24.7	24.5	26.3	27.6	29.1	29.5	29.8	30.4	31.2	31.5	33.2
Germany	36.7	37.8	39.3	38.3	39.4	39.8	42.2	42.7	42.7	44.0	45.0	44.7	44.4	44.7	44.8	45.4	45.1	45.3	45.6	44.9	44.4
France	38.2	38.8	39.8	38.3	37.6	37.8	37.8	38.4	39.7	41.8	41.4	41.1	42.7	44.5	45.1	45.9	46.6	47.6	47.6	47.1	47.6
United Kingdom	36.2	37.6	39.5	40.4	38.3	36.6	35.9	39.5	40.2	39.3	38.8	37.4	38.3	40.0	42.3	43.1	42.4	42.4	42.5	41.6	—
Italy	31.0	31.6	30.7	30.4	31.1	30.9	30.4	30.6	31.2	32.9	34.3	36.0	35.7	33.1	34.1	35.9	37.7	37.4	38.0	39.0	39.3
Canada	30.3	31.5	33.5	34.2	34.7	35.2	34.9	37.2	36.1	35.8	36.1	35.7	35.5	36.2	38.5	39.1	38.7	38.7	38.5	39.4	39.5
7 major countries	29.2	30.3	31.3	30.7	30.5	31.0	31.5	32.6	32.1	32.6	32.9	32.8	33.9	34.6	35.0	35.0	34.7	34.5	34.9	35.3	35.9
4 major European countries	36.0	36.9	37.9	37.3	37.2	37.0	37.9	38.9	39.5	40.7	40.7	41.0	41.3	41.5	42.3	43.2	43.4	43.6	43.8	43.5	44.0
EEC	34.9	35.9	36.8	36.5	36.6	36.5	37.3	38.1	38.9	40.1	40.7	40.7	41.0	41.4	42.1	43.0	43.5	43.7	44.0	43.8	45.1
OECD Europe	34.9	35.8	36.7	36.6	36.9	36.8	37.7	38.5	39.4	40.8	41.4	41.3	41.5	41.9	42.6	43.4	43.8	44.1	44.5	44.3	45.4
TOTAL OECD	29.5	30.6	31.5	31.1	31.1	31.5	32.1	33.2	33.0	33.6	34.0	34.0	34.9	35.6	35.9	36.0	35.7	35.6	36.0	36.5	37.2

Source: OECD, Economic Outlook (1988) for 1967 and (1989) for 1968–87.

TABLE 19.2. Current revenue of general government as a %age of GDP: international comparisons, 1964–1983

Country	1964	1965	1966	1967	1968	1969	1970	1971	1972	1973	1974	1975	1976	1977	1978	1979	1980	1981	1982	1983
United States	26.5	26.5	27.3	27.1	29.3	30.6	29.6	28.9	30.0	30.4	31.2	29.7	30.6	30.8	31.1	31.7	32.0	32.7	32.1	31.7
Japan	20.5	19.5	19.1	19.2	19.5	19.5	20.7	21.6	21.5	22.4	24.4	24.0	23.6	24.8	24.6	26.6	28.0	29.4	30.0	30.4
Germany	36.2	35.5	36.1	36.7	37.8	39.3	38.3	39.4	39.8	42.2	42.7	42.6	44.0	45.0	44.6	44.3	44.6	44.7	45.3	45.2
France	38.0	38.4	38.4	38.2	38.8	39.8	39.0	38.3	38.2	38.6	39.4	40.3	42.5	42.4	42.3	43.7	45.5	46.1	47.0	47.0
United Kingdom	31.5	33.1	34.3	36.2	37.6	39.5	40.4	38.4	36.7	36.0	39.7	40.3	39.4	39.0	37.6	38.5	40.0	41.9	43.3	42.5
Italy	30.6	30.1	30.1	31.0	31.6	30.7	30.4	31.1	30.9	30.4	30.6	31.2	32.9	34.3	36.0	35.7	37.5	39.3	41.9	45.3
Canada	27.8	28.1	29.4	31.0	32.4	34.5	35.2	35.3	35.9	35.6	37.8	36.9	36.3	36.5	36.2	36.1	36.7	38.7	39.6	39.0
7 major countries	28.6	28.6	29.1	29.6	30.7	31.7	31.2	31.0	31.4	32.0	33.2	32.7	33.3	33.6	33.5	34.6	35.6	35.9	36.1	35.8
4 major European countries	34.5	34.7	35.2	36.0	36.9	37.9	37.5	37.4	37.2	38.1	39.2	39.6	41.0	41.5	41.3	41.6	42.6	43.5	44.7	45.1
EEC	34.1	34.4	35.1	35.9	36.8	37.8	37.7	37.9	37.7	38.7	39.9	40.5	41.7	42.2	42.2	42.5	43.4	44.1	45.3	45.1
OECD Europe	33.0	33.4	34.0	34.9	35.9	36.8	36.8	37.1	37.1	38.0	38.9	39.7	41.1	41.7	41.7	41.9	42.8	43.6	44.5	44.7
TOTAL OECD	28.6	28.7	29.3	29.9	31.0	31.9	31.6	31.6	32.0	32.6	33.7	33.6	34.4	34.8	34.7	35.7	36.6	36.8	37.0	36.2

Source: OECD, Economic Outlook (1985).

evaders would increase if tax rates were raised, rates should, if anything, be reduced.

19.4. *International comparisons on fiscal pressure*

It must be recognized that international comparisons on fiscal pressure are difficult in any case, for three reasons. First, because the extent of tax evasion is not the same in each country, as the categories of employment with a higher probability of evasion are distributed differently in the various regions of the world; where craft industries are important and growing and where agriculture still employs a significant, albeit declining, number of workers, as in Italy, it is normal that evasion is greater than in countries with a high proportion of employees in manufacturing and services.

Secondly, if one looks carefully at international data and adjusts them for presumed tax evasion it can be seen that the revealed preferences of the fiscal authorities differ widely; Table 19.1 shows that in 1985, for example, there existed a differential of more than 15 percentage points in the ratio of tax revenue to GDP in the seven major countries, that the most successful countries economically are those with the lowest ratio, and that Italy is somewhere in the middle of the range.

Thirdly, there can be marked intercountry differences in the tax structure, by which we mean the distribution between direct and indirect taxes, between taxes on income and taxes on consumption, with greater or lesser encouragement to save, and more or less pronounced divergences in the taxation of financial assets. Given these structural differences, which are partly documented in Table 19.3, the resulting average fiscal pressure is expected to be different. According to Padoa Schioppa (1993*a*), however, intercountry differences, in that proxy for the average fiscal pressure which is the tax wedge, are now much more attenuated than in the past, particularly within the EEC.

Moreover, what logic demands that the tax revenue/GDP ratio be standardized in countries with different patterns of personal and social preferences? And standardized by whom and in accordance with what criteria? Why should Italy's ratio be increased if countries such as the United States and Japan have a lower ratio? And why, if it were decided to do so, would it have to be achieved by raising tax rates rather than widening the tax base? And why should it be done without altering the tax structure?

TABLE 19.3. Tax revenue of general government in six major countries as a %age of GDP

Country	1980	1984	1985	1986	1987	1988	1989[a]
Direct taxes							
United States	15.6	14.2	14.5	14.6	15.6	15.0	15.4
Japan	10.8	11.8	12.1	12.3	12.9	13.0	12.8
EEC	11.3	12.2	12.4	12.2	12.4	12.4	12.4
Germany	12.7	12.1	12.5	12.3	12.2	12.1	12.4
France	8.4	9.1	9.2	9.4	9.5	9.3	9.3
United Kingdom	13.4	14.6	14.6	13.8	13.3	13.3	13.4
Italy	9.6	12.6	13.0	12.9	13.3	13.4	13.7
Indirect taxes							
United States	7.8	8.3	8.3	8.2	8.1	8.0	7.9
Japan	7.4	7.7	7.8	7.6	8.2	8.8	9.4
EEC	12.5	13.1	12.9	13.1	13.1	13.2	13.2
Germany	13.1	12.9	12.6	12.2	12.2	12.2	12.5
France	14.6	15.0	14.9	14.5	14.7	14.7	14.5
United Kingdom	15.8	16.4	16.0	16.6	16.4	16.4	16.0
Italy	8.6	9.2	9.0	9.1	9.6	10.1	10.6
Social-security contributions							
United States	7.9	8.6	8.9	8.9	8.8	9.1	9.2
Japan	7.3	8.1	8.3	8.4	8.6	8.6	8.7
EEC	13.7	14.6	14.6	14.6	14.6	14.5	14.4
Germany	16.8	17.3	17.5	17.5	17.5	17.4	17.2
France	19.6	21.0	21.1	20.8	20.9	20.8	21.0
United Kingdom	6.0	7.0	6.8	6.9	6.9	6.9	6.9
Italy	12.7	13.5	13.5	14.0	13.9	13.9	14.2

[a] Forecast.

Source: Ministero del Bilancio e della Programmazione Economica (1988) for 1980–4 and (1989) for subsequent years.

Without wanting to anticipate our general reply to these questions, we wish to point out that the urgent need to increase the ratio by adjusting tax rates, widening the tax base, or altering the composition of tax revenue is usually justified by pointing to the size of Italy's budget deficit and public debt.

As Table 19.4 shows, Italy is the only large EEC country still to have a general government financial deficit net of interest payments and is unique in having a net public debt approaching 100 per cent of GDP. It therefore seems obvious that increasing resources must be found in the short term to finance current public expenditure and interest payments, which are clearly out of line with those of other major countries, as illustrated in Table 19.5.

However, if our analysis hitherto is convincing and the thread running through it is logical, it is reasonable to propose in Italy a

TABLE 19.4. General government budget deficit and net public debt in six major countries as a %age of GDP

Country	1980	1984	1985	1986	1987	1988	1989[a]
General government deficit (−) or surplus (+)							
United States	−1.3	−2.8	−3.3	−3.4	−2.3	−2.0	−2.0
Japan	−4.4	−2.1	−0.8	−1.0	0.6	1.3	1.8
EEC	−3.8	−5.3	−5.2	−4.8	−4.3	−3.6	−3.0
Germany	−2.9	−1.9	−1.1	−1.3	−1.8	−2.0	−0.3
France	0.0	−2.7	−2.8	−2.9	−2.5	−1.6	−1.7
United Kingdom	−3.4	−3.9	−2.7	−2.4	−1.5	−0.8	1.7
Italy	−8.5	−11.5	−12.6	−11.7	−11.2	−10.6	−10.4
General government financial balances net of interest payments							
United States	0.0	−0.6	−1.0	−1.2	−0.1	0.3	0.6
Japan	−1.3	2.4	3.7	3.5	5.0	5.7	6.3
EEC	−0.4	−0.5	−0.2	−0.2	0.5	1.2	1.8
Germany	−1.0	1.1	1.9	1.7	1.1	0.2	2.4
France	1.2	0.0	0.1	0.0	0.3	1.2	1.2
United Kingdom	1.3	1.0	2.2	2.1	2.8	4.8	5.1
Italy	−3.1	−3.5	−4.6	−3.1	−3.2	−2.4	−1.4
Net public debt							
United States	19.0	25.2	27.2	29.3	30.7	30.6	30.3
Japan	17.0	26.9	26.6	27.1	25.4	22.6	19.4
Germany	14.3	21.5	21.9	21.6	22.6	23.5	22.8
France	14.3	21.1	23.1	25.9	25.8	25.5	25.3
United Kingdom	47.5	47.6	46.6	45.8	43.4	38.4	35.5
Italy	53.6	74.3	81.3	86.2	90.6	92.4	94.6

[a] Forecast.

Sources: For data on general government financial balances both including and net of interest payments, Ministero del Bilancio e della Programmazione Economica, (1988) for 1980–4 and (1989) for subsequent years; for data on the net public debt, OECD, *Economic Outlook*, 1989.

Table 19.5. Current expenditure of general government in six major countries as a %age of GDP

Country	1980	1984	1985	1986	1987	1988	1989[a]
Collective consumption							
United States	17.6	18.1	20.4	20.6	20.4	19.8	19.8
Japan	9.8	9.9	9.7	9.8	9.5	9.2	9.1
EEC	18.1	18.3	18.6	18.5	18.5	18.3	18.0
Germany	20.1	19.9	20.0	19.8	19.8	19.4	18.9
France	18.1	19.6	19.4	19.2	19.0	18.8	18.6
United Kingdom	21.3	21.8	20.9	21.1	20.6	20.0	19.5
Italy	14.6	16.2	16.3	16.2	16.9	17.1	17.2
Transfers to households							
United States	11.7	11.9	12.0	12.0	11.8	11.7	11.7
Japan	10.5	11.0	11.0	11.3	11.7	11.8	12.0
EEC	15.9	18.6	17.7	17.6	17.5	17.2	17.1
Germany	17.1	17.0	16.7	16.4	16.5	16.5	16.3
France	19.2	22.0	22.1	22.0	21.9	21.9	22.0
United Kingdom	11.1	13.4	13.2	13.4	12.7	11.8	11.4
Italy	14.3	17.0	17.1	17.2	17.3	17.2	17.3
Interest payments							
United States	1.3	2.2	2.3	2.2	2.2	2.3	2.6
Japan	3.2	4.5	4.5	4.5	4.4	4.4	4.5
EEC	3.3	4.7	5.0	5.0	4.8	4.8	4.8
Germany	1.9	3.0	3.0	3.0	2.9	2.8	2.7
France	1.5	2.7	2.9	2.9	2.8	2.9	2.9
United Kingdom	4.7	4.9	4.9	4.5	4.3	4.0	3.4
Italy	5.4	8.0	8.0	8.6	8.0	8.2	9.0
Total current expenditure net of interest payments							
United States	29.5	30.3	32.6	32.6	32.6	31.9	31.8
Japan	21.7	22.7	22.3	22.8	22.7	22.4	22.5
EEC	37.4	40.6	40.0	39.7	39.6	38.9	38.4
Germany	41.4	41.0	40.7	40.2	40.3	40.2	39.5
France	40.8	46.0	45.9	45.5	45.5	44.4	43.6
United Kingdom	35.6	38.3	37.1	36.7	35.5	33.8	32.8
Italy	32.2	36.7	37.1	37.4	37.9	37.9	37.8
Total current expenditure							
United States	30.8	32.5	34.9	35.1	34.8	34.2	34.4
Japan	24.9	27.2	26.8	27.2	27.1	26.9	27.0
EEC	40.6	45.3	45.0	44.7	44.4	43.7	43.2
Germany	43.0	44.0	43.7	43.2	43.2	43.0	42.2
France	42.3	48.7	48.8	48.4	48.3	47.2	47.0
United Kingdom	40.3	43.2	42.0	41.2	39.8	37.8	36.2
Italy	37.6	44.7	45.1	46.0	46.0	46.1	46.8

[a] Forecast.

Source: Ministero del Bilancio e della Programmazione Economica, (1988) for 1980–4 and (1989) for subsequent years.

contraction in the public sector and a consequent expansion of the market by means of deregulation, privatization, reductions in public expenditure in sectors of no strategic importance, and adjustments in intervention 'at no cost to the state'; that being the case, it is clear that government receipts need not increase in the medium-to-long term, provided their composition is revised as part of a more general reform of the tax structure.

20

Tax Structure and Proposals for Tax Reform

20.1. The taxation of income from investment and employment

There is no convergence of opinion in Italy on the form a tax reform should take. Some argue it would be sufficient to increase the tax burden on self-employed persons and small firms and to raise indirect taxes, which appear to be relatively low today; others consider the Italian tax system should be radically overhauled in much the same way as elsewhere, since the present tax regulations are highly distorting, and thus cause serious economic inefficiency and conspicuous inequality of treatment.

This is most evident in the taxation of investment income, which is subject to no fewer than twenty different tax regimes in Italy. It should be remembered that from an economic point of view all income derived from savings, and not only 'financial yields' (i.e. interest on loans, deposits, bonds, etc.), is investment income, and should be taxed as such. It typically includes dividends, capital gains, income from property, and so forth. By its nature, the category is therefore homogeneous, and in strictly logical terms there is little sense in distinguishing certain types of investment income from others, or in debating the tax treatment to be given to particular types alone.

In fact, from a theoretical point of view, even the distinction between investment income and income from employment is far from convincing, and the same applies to the assertion that investment income should be taxed more heavily than employment income, which led to the introduction of local as well as national taxes on investment income and to the denial of tax allowances to persons receiving only investment income.

It is not true that investment income is always acquired more easily than employment income, nor that all occupations from which employment income is derived are equally arduous, so that tax discrimination based on the nature of the income does not appear acceptable. Moreover, although tax discrimination against investment income could be justified on theoretical grounds, in fact such income is treated much more favourably in Italy. In any case, to conceive of the possibility of treating investment income separately and differently—whether more favourably or not—means rejecting the idea of a general tax on income and, as far as Italy is concerned, continuing to argue for a tax system of the kind in force before the 1973 reform.

20.2. *Determination of the tax base*

Another very important aspect from the point of view of the rationality of the tax system consists in correctly defining the tax base, for which uniform criteria should be used if one wishes to avoid disparities in tax treatment and economic distortions or inefficiencies. By almost unanimous agreement, the real increase in personal resources in a given period of time is regarded as income, after allowing for the replacement of (human or other) capital used in production.

According to the analysis carried out for us by Vincenzo Visco (1992: 26–9), perhaps the most important problem with income tax is that of legal indexation of the tax base and tax allowances.

The distorting effects caused by the lack of fiscal indexation, even in times of very low inflation, are so well-known, evident, and pronounced that there can be no shadow of a doubt in this regard; the technical difficulties of introducing fiscal indexation are limited and can be overcome, but up to now resistance to the introduction of mechanisms to compensate for the effects of inflation has prevented any action being taken. . . . The parameters for personal income tax have been indexed in almost all Western countries, without any particular adverse consequences.

The lack of fiscal indexation for investment income, Visco continues, is also the reason for several corrective and compensatory measures in Italy,

beginning with the exclusion of interest and capital gains from the tax base for progressive personal income tax, and continuing with the regulations on accelerated depreciation, and many other concessions that have gradually been introduced in many countries, with very serious effects on resource allocation, the efficiency of the economy and the distribution of the tax burden (pp. 26–7).

Nor should it be forgotten that the tax systems of many countries already provide for at least one form of automatic indexation, which is distorting owing to its sectoral nature:

this is the possibility of valuing stocks according to the LIFO method, which is equivalent to indexing an important balance-sheet item to replacement prices. Moreover, all countries have passed laws permitting the revaluation of company assets in order to correct for the effect of inflation on balance sheets (and hence on companies' tax liabilities). Revaluation is obviously only a surrogate for a fiscal indexation mechanism, and in fact is merely another instance of concessions being granted to firms, often without justification, or even of largely arbitrary manipulation (p. 27).

Hence, the income on which the tax liability is calculated should be the real increase in wealth achieved by each individual in a given period, whatever its origin or nature. Two critical comments may arise in this regard; it may be advisable first to consider not only the average income but also its variance to take account of risk when determining tax rates, and second to recognize the fact that increases or reductions in risky incomes are due partly to the actions of the individual himself and partly to external events.

Despite these two critical comments, we endorse the tax-reform proposals set out for us by Vincenzo Visco along the lines of his previous work (Visco, 1986). For the sake of clarity, let us summarize their implications. An income tax should be levied on total income, without regard to the manner in which it is used (saved or consumed, for example) or to the source from which it is derived (employment or capital), or whether it represents an increase in economic resources that is actually realized (monetized) or only accrued. A correct definition of income for tax purposes also implies that taxable income is net income, that is to say calculated after deduction of the costs incurred in producing it and defined in real terms, which necessarily entails indexation of the tax system.

As to capital gains, since the above definition of income coincides with the algebraic sum of consumption by each taxpayer during the tax period and of every capital variation occurring during the same time-span, it is evident that capital gains should be considered as income in every respect, as they represent an effective increase in economic resources. This means that they should be taxed in the same way as income from any other source, even if they are unrealized, and that capital losses should be fully deductible.

In conclusion, if one accepts the logic of an all-encompassing, personal income tax (the only acceptable definition from the point of view of equity, tax rationality, and economic efficiency), it can be argued that there is no theoretical justification for treating investment income differently from employment income, or for differentiating between different types of investment and employment income.

In reality, these criteria have not always been applied in full in Italy since the 1973–4 reform. This may be due to practical reasons related to the need for administrative simplicity (such as the decision to tax only realized capital gains, rather than all accrued gains), the contingent requirements of economic policy (the need to create incentives or disincentives), or conservatism and cultural resistance (which explain the refusal to index the tax system, especially for entrepreneurial income).

Nevertheless, the general principles set out above remain valid, and they should be used as a basis for assessing the existing arrangements and understanding the direction in which policy intends to move or in which proposals for modifying or reforming the tax system would lead.

20.3. *Alternatives to income tax*

Different, but appropriate, results in terms of equity and efficiency would also be achieved if it were decided to abandon the principle of taxation on the basis of income and to adopt an alternative system based on the taxation of personal consumption (an expenditure tax) or corporate cash flow, as analysed for us by Barsella (1988).

Obviously, in an expenditure-tax system the tax base would no longer be income (in other words, the annual increase in wealth) but each taxpayer's consumption of resources during the tax period. This would mean levying tax uniformly not only on expenditure from current income but also on that financed by drawing on past saving (wealth), using realized capital gains, selling shelter goods, and so on. The problems of indexation in times of inflation would become irrelevant in such a system.

It is clear that the philosophy of this approach is completely different from that underlying income taxes. For example, a system based on the taxation of expenditure would entail taxing not the resources firms retain but all those they expend, in other words not only dividends but also interest payments, which in an income-based system would be considered as costs and deducted from taxable income. All provisions set aside within the firm would be exempt, which would make every tax regulation on depreciation, stock valuation, and the treatment of reinvested capital gains irrelevant, as the proceeds would automatically be exempt if they were written to provisions, and taxed at the full rate if distributed.

As to the size of the tax base, it is not a foregone conclusion that an expenditure tax would always be levied on a narrower base than an income tax, for in theory at least the dissaving in a given period could be equal to or greater than total current saving.

Nor is it necessarily true that an expenditure tax would generate less revenue than an income tax; if a tax rate of 50 per cent on income of Lit. 1,000 produced revenue of Lit. 500, and if the taxpayer's propensity to consume were 80 per cent, a tax rate of 62.5 per cent on the consumption of Lit. 800 would be enough to achieve the same result in tax terms. For similar reasons, it is not always true that a tax on expenditure would be less progressive than one on income. The main difference between the two would be that a tax on expenditure might entail widely differing tax burdens on taxpayers with identical incomes but different propensities to consume and would therefore have different properties as regards horizontal equity.

In short, a system based on the taxation of expenditure would be entirely consistent on a theoretical plane, but would be distinct from and incompatible with one based on the principles of the taxation of income.

20.4. A policy-mix of income and expenditure taxes

Since income and expenditure taxes are alternatives and are based on essentially different criteria, it does not seem right to superimpose mechanisms drawn from both systems, as this would cause economic distortions and unacceptable disparities in tax treatment. For example, assuming the present income-based system of taxation is retained, it appears decidedly questionable to invoke Einaudi—an advocate of the taxation of expenditure—to assert the need to grant tax exemption for profits or reinvested capital gains, or to give more favourable tax treatment to investment income. In this instance one would be calling not for tax rationalization but for a tax incentive and an exemption from the general principles that would continue to apply to other forms of income and other taxpayers.

Of course, there is nothing to prohibit the granting of tax concessions or the use of the tax system to achieve various economic policy objectives, some of which we have discussed above, provided there are well-defined, strategic, and hopefully temporary, grounds for doing so.

In fact, it is not impossible to imagine a theoretically consistent tax system with features drawn from the two alternatives based on the taxation of income and expenditure. In such a system investment income could be subject to a single, proportional tax at a rate below the (progressive) average rate for income from employment, or, alternatively it could be absorbed into the tax base for normal income taxes, after deduction of an identical fixed or percentage allowance. This would obviously maintain preferential treatment for all investment income, but would not discriminate between different types and would thus have a neutral impact on the allocation of savings flows.

Such a solution would not be simple to apply in practice, primarily because it would entail dividing entrepreneurial income into the components of employment income and capital income. Moreover, from a theoretical point of view one would have to explain the reason for abandoning the principle of equal tax treatment for all forms of income and even reversing the maxim that investment income should be taxed more heavily than employment income. Finally, the envisaged solution would pose serious problems of equity, as investment income is far more concentrated than income from employment, so that the distribution of the tax burden would be uneven and perhaps even regressive. These problems could be overcome, however, by introducing a wealth tax or increasing inheritance tax.

The system described would obviously be an alternative, albeit an intermediate and non-definitive one, and would have the advantage that it would be easier to implement than other potential proposals for tax reform. Indeed, we must not ignore the fact that it is very difficult at present to envisage taxing investment income at very high and rapidly rising rates such as those currently used for personal income tax, especially as no adjustment is made to offset the effects of inflation on nominal incomes.

These observations do not absolve us from outlining proposals for a more permanent tax reform in Italy. According to Vincenzo Visco, whose opinion we share, this should have the following features: a widening of the tax base for personal income tax, making its coverage increasingly comprehensive; a simultaneous reduction in tax rates, to leave a maximum rate of no more than 30–5 per cent and reduce progressivity, which has a strong disincentive effect on the volume and price of production factors; a rate of corporate income tax equal to the highest rate of personal income tax; the indexation of income brackets and tax allowances for tax purposes, especially investment income and capital gains; the introduction of a withholding tax equal to the highest rate of personal and corporate income tax for all investment income apart from company profits, leaving the taxpayer the option between considering the withholding tax as a payment on account in respect of personal income tax or as the final impost.

For a large proportion of taxpayers receiving investment income, who are usually the more wealthy members of the community, the choice would in practice be immaterial if personal income-tax rates were low and the number of tax brackets were small. In any case, the possibility of remaining anonymous for tax purposes would be a very important factor for many income earners. Choosing this option might entail a tax cost for taxpayers on marginal tax rates below the highest band.

One of the basic ideas underlying these proposals is that of widening the tax base and reducing tax rates, along lines followed in other countries' fiscal reforms (e.g. in the UK by the conservative Thatcher government), and in Italy proposed by Professor Visco (1986: 1096–7), current member of the Parliament elected in the former Communist party list:

widening the tax base and at the same time reducing tax rates have become a compulsory part of every tax-reform proposal. In Italy this means tackling primarily the problem of taxing income from residential property (partly because imputed property income is too low compared with the obvious alternative of calculating taxable income on the basis of rent in accordance with the Fair Rent Law less maintenance costs, and partly because evasion appears to be widespread, which implies the need to improve the basis for making assessments, such as the land register), agricultural income (which is *de facto* almost tax-exempt), and investment income. . . . Another way of widening the tax base would of course be to eliminate or drastically reduce the deductions that can be made from taxable income. The amounts involved appear to be small by comparison with other countries (little more than Lit. 9,000 billion in 1982) but are rising rapidly and steadily, partly as a result of recent legislation. In this regard, it is interesting that the draft tax reform put forward by the US Treasury in 1984 included a proposal to abolish almost every deduction from taxable income for both federal and local income tax. Recent financial literature includes many theoretical studies and proposals showing that income tax should ideally be 'linear', in other words there should be a flat tax rate, with progressivity being ensured solely through deductions and fixed allowances. The advantages in terms of simplicity and reduced administrative costs are obvious, and are in addition to the economic benefits. Numerous reform proposals that provide for a limited number of narrow tax bands have been put forward in the United States and are now under discussion in Congress.

The last three salient points of the tax reform suggested to us by Visco would be as follows: the introduction of a modest wealth tax that would be general and indexed in order to equalize the tax burden and encourage risk taking and the productive use of savings; a marked shift from direct to indirect taxation within the limits laid down by the EEC proposals on tax harmonization; and the abandonment of the massive relief from social-security contributions, which has proved incapable of permanently reducing unit labour costs and hence of promoting employment in the private sector.

Budgetary Measures

Before discussing whether taxes and borrowing have the same or different effects on the present and future generations, we must allay the doubt whether it is legitimate to speak of successive generations having different interests, or whether instead we should adopt the principle of continuity between generations of citizens as the logical and *de facto* premiss of financial reasoning. If we acknowledge that the son succeeds his father without solution of continuity and if we accept that in society as a whole it is impossible to discern the moment when one generation ends and the next begins, we could agree with De Viti de Marco that 'the question of distributing the cost of public services between present and future generations would cease to exist in these terms as a separate question and would become part of a more general question that could be termed a question of the "value of time"'.

(B. Griziotti, *La diversa pressione tributaria del prestito e dell imposta*, 1917)

21

The Budget Deficit and the Public Debt

21.1. The public-debt unsustainability

The tax-reform hypotheses formulated so far may not appear sufficiently draconian to tackle the imbalances in Italy's public finances. This is not in fact true; as explained above, since the sphere of direct and indirect public intervention in the Italian economy has to be reduced, we believe it is inappropriate to think of increasing the overall tax burden in order to achieve the perennial objective laid down in every policy document from the so-called Amato Plan[1] to the latest Finance Bill, namely to eliminate the primary budget deficit (i.e. the budget deficit net of interest payments on the public debt).

As the then Treasury Minister (now Prime Minister) Giuliano Amato affirmed in 1988 (Ministero del Tesoro, 1988: 15),

on the basis of available estimates, it is thought that the economy could tolerate a reduction in the borrowing requirement net of interest payments by 0.7 percentage points (in relation to GDP) in each year of the period under consideration (1988–92); in any case, any adverse effects could, if necessary, be offset by appropriate monetary measures. Such a reduction would make it possible to achieve a small surplus in the overall public-sector accounts net of interest payments in the final year of the period under consideration and would induce a fall in interest rates, so that the debt/GDP ratio would stabilize at the end of the period.

The authorities became even more ambitious in their objectives in the late 1980s, as can be seen from the remarks of the Governor of the Bank of Italy (Banca d'Italia, 1989a: 175):

five years ago we indicated the elimination of the borrowing requirement net of interest payments as a first objective; it would have been a significant achievement had it come early enough to curb the rise in interest

---

[1] Cf. *Ministero del Tesoro (1988)*. Until Sept. 1988, the Amato Plan appeared to be in line with the forecasts for the PSBR for that year and with the corrective action contained in the Government's package of economic measures. At the end of 1988, when the final data on the PSBR for the year were published, it became clear that it would be difficult to achieve the Plan's objectives by the original deadlines and in the ways initially proposed.

payments caused by the growth of the public debt. This goal remains to be fulfilled, but the ultimate objective must be to eliminate the budget deficit on current account. If the attack is not directed at the root causes of the deficit, all progress in curbing its effects will prove inadequate and appear tenuous to those who entrust their savings to the state.

It is therefore now widely acknowledged that, unless effective corrective mechanisms are put in place, there will be a further substantial deterioration in the Italian public finances, which will expose the economy to the risk of financial instability, limit its growth and exacerbate the external constraint, making it even more difficult for Italy to meet the already demanding obligations associated with the single European market of 1993.

Hence for several years many Italian policy-makers have been proclaiming their desire to reduce public intervention on aggregate demand, without obtaining appreciable results, perhaps because of the pressure of corporatist lobbies in the Parliament or because of a neo-Keynesian approach, prevalent within the government.

Our analysis shows why some of the certainties of a Keynesian flavour concerning the benefits of rising budget deficits and public debt are now shaky in Italy too, although the available empirical evidence is open to doubt and differences of interpretation.

The work carried out within our research group by Attanasio and Marini (1988) and Galli and Masera (1988) helps us understand why the Italian public debt is approaching an unsustainable level. 'The problem of the sustainability of the public debt', write Attanasio and Marini (1988: 5), 'is caused in Italy by the fact that real interest rates are positive and often higher than the rate of growth of the economy.' Noting the similarity between a situation where there is an unsustainable stock of public debt and so-called 'speculative bubbles' in financial markets, they deduce from their empirical tests that 'Italy's public debt is growing out of control'.

From their analysis of Italy's debt/GPD ratio over the last twenty years, Galli and Masera (1988) reach similar conclusions, indicating that the change-over to a non-accommodating monetary policy after years of financing budget deficits by monetary means and with high inflation brought to light many contradictions and showed how difficult it was to continue with such a fiscal stance.

In their policy conclusions, they state (1988: 37) that 'the inherited imbalances are so large that they will not disappear spontaneously, even if it were possible to maintain a high rate of growth until the end of the century and to keep the real interest rate on the debt constant at the current level'. In any case, interest rates would tend to rise 'to allow an ever increasing share of government securities to be absorbed into private portfolios. . . . Hence in present conditions the prime objective of economic policy in Italy must be to resolve the budget problem.' In the opinion of Galli and Masera (1988: 37) this means that the deficit net of interest payments or primary deficit 'must be eliminated; in fact, this was the objective laid down by the Government in its three-year fiscal adjustment plan of 1985. The authorities must be careful to prevent the emergence of deflationary forces that could influence the dynamic relationship between growth and interest rates. From this point of view, gradual adjustment is preferable to shock treatment'.

Whether a zero primary deficit is a sufficient condition for debt sustainability remains, however, an open question, the answer to which depends on the way sustainability is defined and on the difference between the real interest rate and the growth rate. According to a commonly used definition, which was recently adopted by Blanchard *et al.* (1990: 11–12),

a sustainable fiscal policy can be defined as a policy such that the ratio of debt to GNP eventually converges back to its initial level. . . . If the difference between the real interest rate and the growth rate[2] is positive, a primary surplus is needed to maintain a constant ratio of debt to GNP. . . . For a fiscal policy to be sustainable, a Government which has debt outstanding must anticipate sooner or later to run primary budget surpluses.

However, if the difference between the real interest rate and the growth rate is negative, Blanchard *et al.* (1990: 15) add,

the Government no longer needs to generate a primary surplus to achieve sustainability. With the primary balance in surplus, the debt to GNP ratio would steadily decline over time. The Government could even run permanent primary deficits of any size, and these would eventually lead to a positive but constant level of debt. . . . Theory suggests that this case, which corresponds to what is known as 'dynamic inefficiency',[3] cannot be excluded, and that in such a case, a Government should, on welfare grounds, probably issue more debt until the pressure on interest rates made them at least equal to the growth rate.

---

[2] Appropriately, Galli and Giavazzi (1992) underline that in conditions of uncertainty the relevant comparison is the one between the yield on capital and the growth rate of the economy, rather than the relationship between the real interest rate and the growth rate.   [3] See also Diamond (1965).

21.2. Sustainability, credibility, and neo-Ricardian theory

The link between the sustainability of the public debt—by which we mean the tendency for it to stabilize relative to GDP and remain under control—and the credibility of economic policy-makers is addressed in part in another piece of research carried out for us by Nicoletti (1987).

The author shows that Italy and Belgium are the only two OECD countries where the so-called neo-Ricardian theory holds true; it is no accident that they are among the countries whose public debt is heading towards unsustainability. According to the theory, it is irrelevant whether a given level of public expenditure is financed by issuing government securities or levying taxes, as individuals do not consider financial assets held as a counterpart to the public debt to be wealth.

This could be due to the borrower's credibility having been undermined, as partly argued in the concluding remarks of the book; however, the usual reasons advanced to support the theory are quite different and are linked to the ultrarationality hypothesis. The latter has its origins in Ricardo but has also been upheld by the Italian school of public finance and most recently and insistently by Barro (1981), for example. According to the hypothesis, economic agents correctly perceive the intertemporal budget constraint and adjust their behaviour appropriately; in general[4] they do not suffer from any liquidity constraint and know that public indebtedness must sooner or later give rise to a tax, which is assumed to be non-distortive. Hence they do not regard as wealth the public financial liabilities that will have to be redeemed by them or their heirs, who are perfect substitutes in their utility function.

The ultrarationality hypothesis has two main theoretical consequences. First, private consumption depends on total private resources rather than on disposable income; for this reason, a change in public saving is exactly offset by a change in private saving with the opposite sign. Secondly, the public debt is not wealth of the private sector, as its value is exactly balanced by the discounted value of future taxes that we or our heirs will have to pay to finance the flow of interest payments.

The importance of the ultrarationality hypothesis for economic

---

[4] As Hayashi (1985) shows, Ricardian equivalence may continue to apply even in the presence of certain forms of liquidity constraint.

policy stems from the insignificant effect that a reduction in taxes financed by the issue of government securities has on real aggregates such as private consumption, national saving, investment, and real interest rates, given that private saving grows when public saving decreases, and vice versa. There would be no indirect crowding-out[5] attributable to increases in interest rates caused by the accumulation of debt, and the rise in public expenditure would have no effect on national saving if there were complete substitutability between private and public consumption. This proposition, which according to Nicoletti (1987) is not invalidated by the Italian data, is therefore called the Ricardian equivalence theorem in view of its implications.

21.3. Is the Ricardian equivalence theorem applicable to Italy?

Various observable facts nevertheless seem to throw doubt on the realism of certain assumptions and implications of the neo-Ricardian stance in an Italian context. These include the evidence collected for us by Attanasio and Marini (1987) on certain characteristic features of the tax system, which shows that non-distorting tax rules consistent with the Ricardian neutrality proposition have not been adopted in Italy. The presence of liquidity constraints also contradicts the hypotheses that are at least partly necessary if the Ricardian equivalence proposition is to hold true; according to empirical evidence brought to us by Jappelli (1987) and Jappelli and Pagano (1987, 1988), which has already been discussed in Section 13.2, liquidity constraints apply to a wide range of income earners in Italy.

Other evidence gathered by our group is not consistent with the implications of the neo-Ricardian approach. The analysis carried out by Modigliani and Jappelli (1988), which builds on previous work by Modigliani and various co-authors,[6] aims to demonstrate a direct correlation between the public debt and interest rates in Italy, contrary to what should happen if Ricardian equivalence theorem applied; they contend that Italian consumers did not, in fact,

[5] Two of our theoretical works make a critical examination of the analysis of the impossibility of indirect crowding-out: those by Marini and Van der Ploeg (1987) and Reichlin (1987); indeed, the latter sets out the reasons for possible crowding-in, induced by the presence of financial wealth among firms' assets.

[6] See Modigliani and Jappelli (1988) and Modigliani *et al. (1985)*. On this and other issues concerning the debate about the validity and applicability of Ricardian equivalence to Italy, see the work carried out in our group by Jappelli (1991).

neutralize the higher budget deficits of the 1970s and 1980s by saving more.

The available evidence on the relationship between saving and interest rates in Italy and on direct crowding-out is contradictory. Italian literature on the subject has long maintained that real interest rates influence consumer spending mainly through the interest component of disposable income, and that the intertemporal substitution effect is more than offset by the income effect. From this flows the rather awkward implication that an increase in real interest rates has an expansionary impact on economic activity, as observed in some Italian macro-econometric models. In keeping with more recent findings (Banca d'Italia, 1986), the empirical evidence gathered by members of our group (Rossi, 1986; Attanasio and Weber, 1987; Nicoletti, 1987) appears, however, to reaffirm, albeit in very modest quantitative terms, the traditional positive link between Italian households' propensity to save and real interest rates.

This relationship appears to have played a not insignificant role in the early 1980s, in conjunction with the reversal of the sign of expected real interest rates in the same period. However, there is no reason to believe that a change in expected real interest rates is followed by a substantial variation in the average propensity to save.

As to the hypothesis of direct substitutability (or complementarity) between public and private expenditure, our analyses described in section 16.2 above indicate a direct substitutability of practically zero in the 1960s and a low one in the subsequent period. Using Barro's model (Barro, 1981), this would imply that the public debt had a negative effect on national saving if, as in Italy, the public debt stemmed from an expansion in public expenditure rather than a contraction in tax revenue.

Similar results could be achieved from life-cycle models that take account of the labour-supply endogeneity (Quintieri and Rosati, 1986a, 1986b), where the characteristics of collective consumption —complementarity or substitutability in relation to private consumption and leisure—might significantly alter the effects of changes in the budget deficit on saving and the labour supply, as recalled in Section 12.3 above.

21.4. *Policy conclusions on budgetary measures*

Hence, although many doubts remain whether Barro's approach is valid in the case of Italy, there is a high degree of agreement within our group that it is not particularly relevant for explaining the dynamics of Italian saving, in that the theory is observationally equivalent to others; indeed, the theories that accept the relevance of the neo-Ricardian proposition to Italy and those that deny it agree that, as the budget deficit is due to an increase in public expenditure rather than a reduction in tax revenue and as in practice public expenditure and private consumption are not substitutes in Italy, the budget deficit is one of the factors that lead to a fall in national saving.

Of course, accepting or denying the applicability of Barro's hypothesis to Italy entails very different expectations as to the effects of possible future action to reduce the deficit, depending on whether it involves a reduction in expenditure or an expansion in government revenue. From what has been stated above, all agree that a reduction in expenditure would lead to an increase in national saving, but opinions differ as to the implications of an expansion in tax revenue; the advocates of Ricardian equivalence maintain that this would not affect national saving, because the decline in private saving would exactly offset the rise in public saving, whereas those who assert that there is no equivalence believe national saving would increase, since private saving would decrease by less than the growth in public saving.

All agree, however, that demographic and economic growth would be the main factors explaining the behaviour of national saving adjusted for inflation in Italy. In this regard, it would have to be demonstrated that economic agents considered only real interest payments as part of their income, and were thus not victims of money illusion. In that event, inflation would have an effect on (unadjusted) private saving via the erosion of the existing stock of public debt, so that an inflationary accounting[7] would be relevant, especially the adjustment of disposable income and public debt.

For a long time, the empirical analyses on this issue (Rossi and Schiantarelli, 1982; Marotta, 1983 and 1984; Lecaldano Sasso La Terza *et al.*, 1984, Modigliani *et al.*, 1985) were inconclusive, as it proved impossible to distinguish between the two extreme situations of total or zero money illusion. However, our research on

---

[7] The problem of inflationary accounting (the adjustment of the national accounts for inflation) was tackled for us by Felli (1984).

this subject (Rossi, 1986; Nicoletti, 1987) makes it possible not to reject the second hypothesis of complete Hicksian 'correction', but at the same time suggests that the adjustment is rendered almost completely irrelevant by full tax discounting by consumers, to the extent that the Ricardian equivalence theorem is in fact confirmed in the case of Italy, as recalled by Nicoletti (1987).

The above findings are laden with implications for the use or non-use of a budgetary policy in Italy, albeit contradictory ones. In this sense, the main points can be summarized as follows.

There appear to be good grounds for believing that macro-economic budgetary policy is of only limited effectiveness if it depends on consumer behaviour. Moreover, its effectiveness appears to be linked to the inefficient operation of certain markets, and in this sense it is plausible that it will decrease further. In addition, the room for manœuvre on the budget deficit is certainly limited by a volume of public debt that tendy to unsustainability.

Obviously, these considerations apply only to the portion of the deficit not invested in publicly owned productive capital, in other words capital able to generate a flow of future profits comparable to those generated by private capital.

Contrary to conventional wisdom and as confirmation of what has been demonstrated above, there are reasons for not rejecting the hypothesis that the public debt in Italy has a negligible wealth effect. Measures to reduce the deficit by increasing tax revenue could have minimal effects on national saving. A reduction in public expenditure, on the other hand, could induce an increase in national saving, at least as long as the substitutability between public and private consumption remained low. Clearly, however, it would be desirable for the contraction in public expenditure to be accompanied by an improvement in the quality of spending so that public consumption could replace part of private consumption. From this point of view too, it would be preferable, *ceteris paribus*, to curb collective consumption rather than increase the tax burden.

Is there an Italian 'Economic Miracle'?
Concluding Remarks

> It is true that men have themselves made this world of
> nations (and we took this as the first incontestable principle
> of our Science, since we despaired of finding it from the
> philosophers and philologists), but this world without doubt
> has issued from a mind often diverse, at times quite contrary,
> and always superior to the particular ends that men had pro-
> posed to themselves; which narrow ends, made means to serve
> wider ends, it has always employed to preserve the human
> race upon this world.
>
> (G. B. Vico, *La Scienza Nuova*, 1744).

Throughout this work I have tried to outline, hopefully in a convincing way, a number of deep-rooted structural problems inherent
in public intervention in Italy. Why then, one might ask, does Italy
continue to rank among the seven most industrialized nations and
to enjoy an enviable rate of growth,[1] notwithstanding obvious mistakes in economic policy?

The answer is certainly far from straightforward, as a number of
issues are still unresolved and legitimate doubts linger as to the
interpretation of the Italian 'economic miracle'.

My tentative answer is based on three main considerations.

First, certain policies that lie outside the scope of this book have
been rewarded with remarkable success. One could mention the
achievements of monetary and exchange-rate policies, particularly
since the end of the 1970s, as recently illustrated by Barca and
Visco (1991) and Banca d'Italia (1992). In all the period under con-

---

[1] Italy's real GDP grew by almost 50 per cent between 1976 and 1990 (at an
annual average rate of 2.8 per cent). This performance is remarkable by comparison
with that of other countries; over this period economic growth in Italy was 6 %age
points above the average of the EEC, and consumption was 13 points higher.

sideration, with few exceptions,[2] such policies have been instrumental in keeping Italy in the EMS and in making the EMS effective in exerting downward pressure on Italian domestic costs and prices.

More generally, all the policies that Italian governments have pursued with the aim of bringing the country closer to Europe seem to have been considered socially necessary and have therefore been easy to enforce. The feeble leadership of national authorities when they have lacked the backing of international bodies may possibly derive from Italy's historical flair for supranational affairs.

It is precisely the analysis of the Italian economy within the European context that leads me to my second consideration. Italy may not be as prosperous as some economic statistics and theories would lead us to believe: some sobering indicators were brought to public attention at the European summit in Maastricht in December 1991, as outlined in a recent book on Italy by Menet-Gentry (1992*a*: 262):

in fact, according to the criteria defined in Maastricht, Italy is not ready for Economic and Monetary Union:

— its inflation rate of 6.9 per cent is exceeded only by those of Greece (17.9 per cent) and Portugal (10.2 per cent), while inflation rates in the other countries range from 1.8 per cent (Denmark) to 5.7 per cent (Spain);

— its budget deficit of 9.9 per cent of GDP is the highest in the Community after that of Greece (17.5 per cent), whereas those of other member countries are between 1.5 per cent (France) and 6.3 per cent (Belgium), and Luxembourg even manages to show a surplus of 2 per cent of GDP;

— its public debt is equivalent to 103 per cent of GDP, exceeded only by that of Belgium (128 per cent);

— long-term interest rates stand at 11.9 per cent, similar to Spanish rates (11.6 per cent) and lower only than those in Portugal (14 per cent) and Greece (19.5 per cent).

These adverse indicators[3] should nevertheless be viewed in perspective, as

---

[2] Like all the other value-judgements expressed here, this is also based on structural—not cyclical—considerations. They cannot be invalidated by short-run movements like those recently hitting the lira, which was devalued by 7% relative to other EEC currencies in September 1992, and after 'black Wednesday' was temporarily pulled out of the ERM. The potential negative implications of these facts on costs, prices, and competitiveness of Italy are in any case to be considered transitory, in my opinion.

in 1991 only three countries out of twelve (Denmark, France, and Luxembourg) satisfied all the criteria.

Many observers would summarize the growing anxiety about the future, induced by a pervasive though possibly obscure malaise in the Italian economy, by pointing out that Italy's public debt, which is high and rising, is approaching the limits of sustainability. Nevertheless, theoretical economists would typically deny that the public debt is technically unsustainable at this level, because (as mentioned in Chapter 21) sustainability is usually defined by some transversality conditions over an infinite horizon.

Over a finite time frame, in other words a period that is a reality for mortal men and women, even the most eminent economists have little to say.[4] As a consequence, explanations of the kind *post hoc ergo propter hoc* become widespread: the debt appears to be sustainable (*ex post*) if it continues to be financed, while it appears to be unsustainable (*ex post*) if the 'animal spirits' of the financial community fail to keep their confidence level high.

It then remains to be understood why the Italian public continues to finance the budget deficit by investing in government securities, while perceiving the tendency for the debt to grow indefinitely. In my view, there are three possible explanations. First, subscribers of government paper may be influenced by the theoretical economists mentioned above, and believe that, although the public debt is high and growing, it cannot be deemed unsustainable as long as there is a chance that drastic budgetary cuts will be implemented in the distant future but before infinity.[5]

Secondly, there is a likelihood that subscribers will engage in 'short-term speculation against the state' until the maturity of the securities, even though default is expected to occur at a later stage. The state is thus viewed as solvent only in the short run, when it is assumed it will honour its paper. In this event, the demand for Treasury bills and other short-term Treasury paper co-exists with a rational belief in the long-run unsustainability of the debt.

[3] Other indicators of the Italian malaise could be added to those listed by Menet-Gentry; e.g. in 1990 unemployment stood in Italy at 10.6 per cent, lower only than in Spain (16.5 per cent) and Ireland (16.2 per cent) (Padoa Schioppa, 1991*a*).

[4] The literature on this topic is so extensive that it cannot be treated fully here. Anglo-American readers may find it useful to refer to Buiter (1985), Giavazzi and Spaventa (1988), and Blanchard *et al.* (1990).

[5] This idea seems true, but it is as irrelevant as the verse about Jacques de La Palice, which stated that 'un quart d'heure avant sa mort, il ètait encore en vie'.

Finally, even the subscription of medium- or long-term Treasury bonds may be compatible with an expectation of long-term unsustainability, to the extent that traders focus on coupons and disregard repayment of the principal. This may happen because the information and transaction costs associated with other less liquid or less easily available securities are too high compared with the differential benefits over the relevant period and/or because bondholders are less concerned about the welfare of those on whom the results of an inefficient portfolio selection will rebound, namely their heirs who will fail to recover the principal.

Such a theory, which runs completely counter to ultrarationality, seems to be supported by recent empirical evidence on Italy (Banca d'Italia, 1991; Cannari *et al.*, 1990), although it deserves further investigation. The frequency of government-securities holding appears to be highest in the second part of the active life-cycle and in the early years of retirement; moreover, as the elderly consume part of their wealth towards the end of their life-cycle, they reduce their holdings of public bonds by much less than those of other higher-yielding but riskier assets.

The possible indifference of the elderly for the welfare of their heirs raises a more general question, namely whether conflicts of interest exist in debt financing as well as in deficit creation, an issue to be dealt with in the future by political economists. Although still at a sketchy stage, my third consideration on the Italian 'economic miracle' takes the role of conflicts partly into account.

Italy is a fairly heterogeneous, fragmented country, much more divided than the conventional concept of economic dualism would imply, though admittedly the regional schism is probably the most painful. The latter is epitomized by the fact that per-capita GDP in certain Northern and Central regions of Italy (Piedmont, Lombardy, and Emilia Romagna) is the same (in terms of purchasing-power) as in the richest areas of Europe (Luxembourg, Île-de-France and the wealthiest German Länder), while the Mezzogiorno has a standard of living similar to that of the weakest areas of the Community (Greece, Portugal, Ireland, and parts of Spain).

One could point to other forms of dualism that have equally far-reaching economic consequences: for example, small- and medium-sized enterprises, and the private sector in general, are strong and have growth potential, but large firms and the public sector in the broad sense (the enlarged public sector plus state-controlled companies) exhibit structural weaknesses and their role may be declining.

In other words, some parts of Italy work well, keep abreast of technical progress and are therefore capable of placing the country in the same league as the richest seven nations of the world. This side of the economy is so strong that it offsets the problems of the rest of the country, including those generated by public intervention, which is often debatable in terms of both quality and quantity, as discussed in this book.

It could be argued that the most effective economic unit in Italy is still the family and the small private firm, which is so similar to a family in its organization; this is true not only in agriculture but also in industry and services, both modern and traditional. In this respect, the nation's Catholic roots certainly prevail over the other fundamental source of the Italian *Weltanschauung*, Communism, which one-third of the population openly stated and inwardly felt to be essential until the 1980s but which has now waned, crumbling with the Berlin wall. Nevertheless, on many issues relevant to the shaping of Italian society and economic policy, the Catholic and Communist ideologies have become intertwined in what has been labelled 'Cathocommunism'. That is why, for example, there is a widespread lack of esteem for entrepreneurial profits and economic success, while more emphasis is placed on intentions than on results, contrary to the Protestant tradition (Weber, 1948). As a consequence, Italy has developed a strong tendency towards egalitarianism, generally interpreted by society as a reason for policymakers to place emphasis on guarantees and protection, to reach general consensus through wheeling and dealing, or to indulge in forms of pseudo-solidarism.

The expected outcome should have been a homogeneous, non-selective, non-competitive country, but a number of factors prevented this and—in the words of the eighteenth-century Italian philosopher Giambattista Vico—induced a sort of 'heterogenesis of ends'. In this context one could mention the continued prevalence of the Judaeo-Christian tradition in Italy, which emphasizes the individual rather than the group, or the historical Italian mistrust of rulers, who are perceived as strangers or even aliens, or the balance in judgement coupled with a good dose of scepticism (ingrained in peoples with a long history, such as the Italians) that prevents them, for good or ill, from following general principles to their extreme conclusion, and finally a certain leaning towards double standards of morality, so detested in Protestant countries.

Italians have always been accustomed to adapt to great ideas or to social constraints by devising personal and innovative rules of conduct, irrespective of the leading opinions. This explains why in the last twenty years Italy has voted to introduce divorce and abortion and has the lowest fertility rate in the world, despite being the country where the Church most assiduously intervenes in social and political life, in the name of the Catholic unity of the society.

The Italian people display an almost unique imagination, as well as an ability to maintain its balance and to play against the rules: Italian prosperity therefore appears to be an 'economic miracle' because it has been achieved in spite of Italy's apparent value-premisses and thus seems totally unexpected. In reality, however, it is the logical result of a collective propensity to ignore general principles and dominant ideas and to circumvent laws, affirmative actions, and economic-policy rules.

To be more precise, Italian society is already doing what in this book I suggest the state should allow it to do, primarily by introducing deregulation and flexibility in matters economic. Italy is achieving these results through the underground economy, by evading taxes and union rules in small private enterprises, but it is largely failing to do so in large companies and in the public sector. In short, the country is developing in spite of, and not as a result of, its policy-making, thanks to what the Italians call 'l'arte di arrangiarsi'—their generalized talent for improvisation, cutting corners, and muddling through—thus providing living proof that deregulation and flexibility work.

Of course, the presumption is that the Italian economy would grow even more strongly and rapidly if it were not hampered by the present policy-induced rigidities. That is why I argue in this book for a slimmer and better-performing state. Here again, one might be wrong, as it is well known that individuals perform best in a difficult situation; a casual empiricism shows that imagination and ingenuity are negatively correlated with economic development, so that in Italy, for example, they appear to be more prevalent in the South than in the Centre–North.

In conclusion, any linear, polished opinion on Italy's economic performance would certainly be inaccurate, as an 'economic miracle' probably is taking place. This has to be acknowledged, among others, by those who, like me, were convinced by their reading of the Old Testament that miracles are very unlikely but rationally possible events.

Postscript

I realize I have weighed down this slim volume with statistical data and sometimes even jargon, but I feel this was necessary to prove the validity of the diagnoses and the plausibility of the suggested remedies, especially to those who might tend to disagree with my stance, whether they be experts or laymen.

However, I think it is also possible to understand the work without reference to the tables and figures; indeed, it may be sufficient simply to read the Introduction and the Concluding Remarks.

Be that as it may, I hope that all readers of this book will have found my assertions and argumentation clear, even if they do not necessarily agree with them. The only criticism that frankly I would hope not to hear is that contained in the *Epigramma* of the Italian poet Giuseppe Giusti:

> Common Sense, once the guiding spirit of the schools,
> is now quite dead in many of them.
> Science, her daughter,
> killed her to see how she was made.

BIBLIOGRAPHY

National Research Council (CNR) working papers and books produced for the Sub-project and quoted in the book

Attanasio, O. P., and Marini, G. (1987), 'Equivalenza ricardiana e tassazione ottimale. Una verifica empirica per l'Italia'.

—— —— (1988), 'Sulla sostenibilità del debito pubblico: alcune verifiche empiriche'; later published in Jappelli (1991).

—— and Weber, G. (1987), 'Crescita del consumo e tassi di interesse'.

Barsella, S. (1988), 'Neutralità dell'imposta societaria sul "cash flow"' rispetto alle decisioni di investimento in acquisizioni'; later published in Visco (1992).

Battagliotti, T., and Revelli, R. (1988), 'Modelli di crescita delle imprese: esperimenti sul caso italiano'.

Bentolila, S., and Bertola, G. (1988), 'Firing Costs and Labour Demand: How Bad Is Eurosclerosis?'; rev. version in *Review of Economic Studies* (1990), 57: 3, 381–402.

Bertola (1993), 'Vincoli istituzionali, mobilità del lavoro e sussidi marginali all' occupazione', in Padoa Schioppa (1993*b*).

Boccaccio, M. (1988), 'Concorrenza e monopolio nel pensiero austriaco'.

Bodo (1993), 'Commento a Bertola (1993)', in Padoa Schioppa (1993*b*).

Bollino, C. A., and Rossi, N. (1988), 'Demographic Variables in Demand Systems and Related Measures of the Cost of Changing Family Size'.

Brugiavini, A. (1988), 'Empirical Evidence on Wealth Accumulation and the Effects of Pension Wealth: An Application to Italian Cross-Section Data'.

—— and Weber, G. (1988), 'Welfare Effects of Indirect Tax Harmonization: The Italian Case'.

Brunetta, R. (1988), 'Spesa pubblica e welfare state'; later published in Brunetta and Tronti (1991).

—— and Tronti, L. (1991) (eds.), *Welfare State e redistribuzione*, (Milan: Franco Angeli).

Camerano, F. (1987), 'Struttura del mercato e dimensione dell'impresa in relazione all'attività innovativa'; later published in Szegö (1993).

Casella, A., and Feinstein, J. (1987), 'Inflation and the Organization of Exchanges: The Panic Economy'; rev. version entitled 'Economic Exchange during Hyperinflation' in *Journal of Political Economy* (Feb. 1990), 98: 1, 1–27.

Colombino, U. (1986*a*) 'Orari di lavoro come strumento di selezione in un modello con informazione asimmetrica'.

—— (1986*b*), 'Female Labour Supply and Quantity Constraints in Italy: Behavioural Estimation, Measurement of Disequilibrium Costs and Simulation of Alternative Programmes'.

—— (1986*c*), 'La valutazione di politiche del lavoro con un modello microeconometrico di offerta di lavoro femminile'.

—— (1987), 'Una nota su disoccupazione, inefficienza allocativa e politiche di second best'.

—— (1988), 'Politiche attive per l'occupazione in un modello con salari di efficienza: Applicazioni al mercato del lavoro femminile piemontese'.

Contini, B., and Revelli, R. (1985*a*), 'Caratteristiche demografiche delle imprese italiane'; i. 'Note metodologiche', ii. 'Appendice statistica'.

—— —— (1985*b*), 'The Process of Job Creation and Job Destruction in the Italian Economy'; rev. version in *Labour* (Autumn 1987), 1: 3, 121–44.

—— —— (1986*a*), 'Birth and Death in Italian Manufacturing: Implications for the Study of Market Forms and Job Creation'.

—— —— (1986*b*), 'Patterns di sviluppo e declino delle piccole imprese italiane'.

—— —— (1987), 'A Theoretical Model of Job Creation and Job Destruction'.

—— —— (1988), 'Job Creation and Labour Mobility: The Vacancy Chain Model and Some Empirical Findings from Longitudinal Data of Italian Business Firms'.

Cox, D., and Jappelli, T. (1988), 'Credit Rationing and Private Transfers'; rev. version entitled 'Credit Rationing and Private Transfers: Evidence From Survey Data' in *Review of Economics and Statistics* (August 1990), 72: 3, 445–54.

Crescenzi, A., and Ravoni, L. (1986), 'Il costo del lavoro in Italia: Avvio ad un'analisi comparativa', *Rassegna di Statistiche del Lavoro*, (July–Dec.), 3–4, 3–24.

Cuckierman, A., and Padoa Schioppa, F. (1986), 'Relative Price Variability, Inflation and the Price of Energy'.

Cugno, F., and Ferrero, M. (1987), 'Uno schema di sussidio proporzionale all'occupazione'.

Dal Bosco, E. (1987), 'Struttura finanziaria e processo d'accumulazione nelle imprese'.

Dal Co, M. (1984), 'La crisi delle relazioni industriali in Italia'.

D'Ecclesia, R., and Camerano, F. (1987), 'Intervento pubblico e processo innovativo delle imprese manifatturiere nel corso degli anni '80'; later published in Szegö (1993).

—— and Szegö, G. (1988), 'Fondi chiusi in Italia—una forma di finanziamento per le piccole e medie imprese. Un'analisi di domanda'; later published in Szegö (1993).

Del Monte, A., and Vittoria, M. P. (1988), 'Gli effetti della politica degli incentivi sull'industrializzazione del Mezzogiorno'; later published in Padoa Schioppa (1993*b*).

Devereux, M., Ratti, M., and Schiantarelli, F. (1990), 'Modelling the Corporate Tax System in Italy'.

Dirindin, N. (1988), 'Redistribuzione dei redditi e sistema sanitario'; later published in Brunetta and Tronti (1991).

Drudi, F. (1988), 'Tassazione, incentivi e decisioni ottimali di spesa'; later published in Visco (1992).

Faini, R., Giannini, S., and Nicodano, G. (1988), 'Tassazione dei guadagni in conto capitale, investimenti e scelte finanziarie'.

—— Nicodano, G., and Schiantarelli, F. (1987), 'Capital Market Imperfections, Government Transfers and Factor Demand Decisions: An Application to Italian Public Enterprises'.

Faustini, G., Crescenzi, A., and Ravoni, L. (1986), 'Esame comparato della struttura del costo del lavoro in Italia e negli altri paesi europei, con particolare riguardo alle forme di prelievo para-fiscale e con un tentativo di valutazione degli oneri non monetari'; later published in Visco (1992).

Felli, L. (1984), 'Il fabbisogno del settore pubblico e la sua correzione per l'inflazione'.

—— and Ichino, A. (1988), 'Testing the Effectiveness of the Marginal Productivity Subsidies in a Duration Model with Time Varying Covariates: The Experiment of the Agenzia del Lavoro di Trento', *Labour* (Autumn), 2:3, 63–90.

—— —— (1993), 'Un contributo per la valutazione del programma di sussidi marginali all'occupazione realizzato dall'Agenzia del Lavoro di Trento', in Padoa Schioppa (1993*b*).

Ferrari, M., and Orsi, R. (1988), 'Investment in a Rationing Model: The Italian Industrial Sector'.

Forlani, L. (1985*a*), 'Rapporti di lavoro, politiche del lavoro, "reti" di sicurezza sociale: Un sistema di vincoli o di opportunità?'.

—— (1985*b*), 'Politiche del lavoro, istituzioni di governo del mercato del lavoro, formazione-lavoro nella Repubblica Federale Tedesca'.

Fornasari, F., La Noce, M., and Scandizzo, P. L. (1984), 'Un modello di equilibrio economico generale per la valutazione degli investimenti pubblici in Italia'.

Gabriele, A., and La Camera, F. (1986), 'La valutazione dei progetti di ricerca e sviluppo'.

Galli, G., and Masera, R. S. (1988), 'Il debito pubblico—necessità e costi dell'aggiustamento: Il caso dell'Italia'; later published in Jappelli (1991).

Giordano, S., and Rubino, P. (1991), 'Tariffe e domanda di energia elettrica: Il caso italiano', in Pera (1991).

Guiso, L., and Visco, I. (1987), 'Shocks reali e nominali, tariffe pubbliche e politica monetaria'; rev. version in *Politica Economica* (April 1988), 4: 1, 99–120.

Heimler, A. (1984), 'Price Behaviour in the Italian Manufacturing Industry'.

—— (1987a), 'Factor Demand in the Industrial Countries: A Decomposition Analysis'.

—— (1987b), 'Productive Restructuring, Costs and Profit Margins in the Industrial Countries'.

—— and Milana, C. (1985), 'Ricostruzione di serie storiche settoriali nell'economia italiana'.

—— —— (1986), 'Factor Demand and Productivity Growth in the Italian Economy'.

Jappelli, T. (1987), 'Consumption and Liquidity Constraints: A Direct Estimation Approach'.

—— (1991) (ed.), *Bilancio pubblico e risparmio privato* (Milan: Franco Angeli).

—— and Pagano, M. (1987), 'Liquidity Constraints and Capital Market Imperfections: An International Comparison'; rev. version entitled 'Aggregate Consumption and Capital Market Imperfections: An International Comparison' in *American Economic Review* (Dec. 1989), 79: 5, 1088–105.

—— —— (1988), *Liquidity Constrained Households in an Italian Cross-Section* (Discussion Paper, 257; London: CEPR).

Malizia, R., and Pedullà, G. (1988), 'L'attività delle amministrazioni pubbliche nel sistema economico con particolare riguardo al welfare state'; later published in Brunetta and Tronti (1991).

Marini, G., and Van der Ploeg, F. (1987), *Monetary and Fiscal Policy in an Optimizing Model with Capital Accumulation and Finite Lives* (Discussion Paper, 277; London: LSE).

Marzano, A. (1992) (ed.), *Crisi e ristrutturazione delle imprese a partecipazione statale* (Milan: Franco Angeli).

—— and Marzovilla, O. (1988), 'Gli obiettivi delle partecipazioni statali: Evoluzione e compatibilità'.

Milana, C. (1985), 'Direct and Indirect Requirements for Gross Output in Input-Output Analysis'.

—— (1986), 'Le importazioni di beni intermedi nel moltiplicatore del reddito in un'economia aperta'.

—— (1988a), 'Production and Welfare Effects of Indirect Tax Reform in Italy', in *Dynamic Modelling and Control of National Economies* (Institute of Measurement and Control: London, 1989), 607–13.

—— (1988b), 'Equity vs. Efficiency of Indirect Tax Reform in Italy: An Applied General Equilibrium Analysis'.

—— (1992a) (ed.), *Processi di accumulazione e politica industriale in Italia* (Milan: Franco Angeli).

—— (1992b), 'Introduzione', in Milana (1992a).

Modigliani, F., and Jappelli, T. (1988), 'The Determinants of Interest Rates in the Italian Economy', *Review of Economic Conditions in Italy*, (Jan.–Apr.), 1, 9–34.

—— Padoa Schioppa, F., and Rossi, N. (1986), 'Aggregate Unemployment in Italy: 1960–1983', *Economica* suppl. (1986), 53: 210, 246–73.

Mussati, G. (1985), 'Ruolo degli incentivi nella funzione degli investimenti: Esame critico delle politiche basate sugli incentivi finalizzati alla formazione di capitale'.

Nahmijas, A. (1988), 'Confronti di efficienza tra imprese pubbliche e private: Una rassegna e un'applicazione al caso italiano'; later published in Marzano (1992).

Nicoletti, G. (1987), 'Private Consumption, Inflation and the Debt Neutrality Hypothesis: The Case of Eight OECD Countries'; rev. version entitled 'A Cross-Country Analysis of Private Consumption and the Debt Neutrality Hypothesis' in *OECD Economic Studies*, (Autumn 1988), 11, 43–87.

Nonis, M. (1988), 'Finanziamento e spesa nei sistemi sanitari'; later published in Brunetta and Tronti (1991).

Norton, R. D. (1986), 'Technical Change in Models of Economic Equilibrium'.

Orsi, R. (1988), 'Estimation of Macroeconomic Rationing Model for Italy using Business Survey Data'.

Padoa Schioppa, F. (1988a), 'Underemployment Benefits Effects on Employment and Income Distribution: What We Should Learn from the System of the Cassa Integrazioni Guadagni', *Labour* (Autumn), 2: 2, 101–24.

—— (1990a), 'Union Wage Setting and Taxation', *Oxford Bulletin of Economics and Statistics* (May), 52: 2, 143–67.

—— (1990b), 'A Discussion of Italian Employment in the Private Sector, 1960–1984: Combining Traditional Concepts and Disequilibrium Macroeconomics', in J. H. Drèze, and C. R. Bean (1990) (eds.), *Europe's Unemployment Problem* (Cambridge, Mass.: MIT Press), 288–328.

—— (1992b), Fissazione dei salari e traslazione delle imposte', in Visco (1992).

—— (1992c), 'Effetti marginali ma non transitori sull'occupazione di una tecnologia putty-clay', in Milana (1992a).

—— (1993b) (ed.), *Squilibri e rigidità nel mercato del lavoro italiano: Rilevanzo quantitativa e proposte correttive* (Milan: Franco Angeli).

—— (1993c), 'Disoccupazione strutturale e non, disoccupazione classica e keynesiana, Italia, 1960–1984', in Padoa Schioppa (1993b).

Pandolfelli, M. (1986), 'Sviluppo e crisi della regolamentazione economica negli Stati Uniti 1970–1975'.

—— (1987a), 'La critica delle economic regulations negli USA'.

—— (1987b), 'Economic regulations e monopolio naturale negli USA: Rassegna critica'.

—— (1988a), 'Regolamentazione e deregolamentazione con riferimento al caso italiano: Appunti per una ricerca'.

240   Bibliography

—— (1988*b*), 'Regolamentazione e deregolamentazione con riferimento alla esperienza italiana: Le limitazioni alla concorrenza'.

—— (1991), 'Regolamentazione e deregolamentazione del trasporto aereo: Alcuni elementi di valutazione per la situazione italiana', in Pera (1991).

Patrizii, V., and Rossi, N. (1986), 'L'allocazione della spesa pubblica'.

—— —— (1991), *Preferenze eterogenee, prezzi relativi e redistribuzione* (Bologna: Il Mulino).

Pera, A. (1988*a*), 'Privatizzazioni e risanamento finanziario: Il caso dell'Italia'; later published in Marzano (1992).

—— (1988*b*), 'Deregulation and Privatization in an Economy-Wide Context'; rev. version in *OECD Economic Studies*, (Spring 1989), 12, 159–204.

—— (1991) (ed.), *Regolamentazione, efficienza, mercato* (Milan: Franco Angeli).

Perotti, E. (1988), 'A General Approach to Tests of Efficiency of Stock Prices, with an Application to the Italian Stock Market 1961–1984'.

Piergentili, P., and Granaglia, E. (1988), 'Dinamica e ripartizione della spesa sanitaria dal 1982 al 1986'.

Pochini, S. (1988), 'La tassazione in materia ambientale'; later published in Pera (1991).

Pupillo, L. (1988*a*), 'Politica tariffaria in teoria e in pratica: Il caso delle telecomunicazioni'.

—— (1988*b*), 'Il servizio telefonico in Italia: Modello organizzativo, caratteristiche economiche e demografiche della domanda e politica tariffaria'.

—— (1991), 'Domanda di accesso al telefono e mutualità delle tariffe: Il caso Italiano', in Pera (1991).

Quintieri, B., and Rosati, F. C. (1986*a*), 'Struttura fiscale e comportamento individuale'.

—— —— (1986*b*), 'Fiscal Policy and Labour Supply'.

—— —— (1987), 'La progressività dell'imposta sul reddito in Italia: 1976–1982'.

—— —— (1988), 'Politica fiscale ed offerta di lavoro in Italia: Un'analisi su serie temporali'; later to be published in Padoa Schioppa (1993*b*).

—— —— (1990), *Politica fiscale ed incentivi al lavoro ed al risparmio* (Milan: Franco Angeli).

Ratti, M. (1988), 'La Teoria Q dell'investimento: Una rassegna critica'.

—— and Drudi, F. (1988), 'Un modello econometrico di domanda dei fattori basato sui dati di bilancio: Risultati preliminari'.

Ravazzi, P. (1987), 'Trasferimenti pubblici e partecipazioni statali: Erogazioni settoriali e struttura economico-finanziaria delle imprese pubbliche in Italia'.

Reichlin, P. (1987), 'Domanda precauzionale di titoli finanziari da parte delle imprese'.

Revelli, R., and Tenga, S. (1987), 'Demografia delle imprese: Ulteriori approfondimenti sulla misurazione della natalità e sulla stima della mortalità'.

—— —— (1988), 'I determinanti della formazione di nuove imprese: Stime per l'industria manifatturiera in Piemonte'.

—— and Vitelli, M. (1988), 'Rappresentatività settoriale e territoriale dei dati sull'occupazione'.

Romani, F. (1987), 'Teoria economica delle partecipazioni statali'.

—— (1988a), 'Deve una legislazione italiana sulla concorrenza occuparsi della concentrazione?'

—— (1988b), 'Problemi di una legislazione a tutela della concorrenza in Italia'.

Rosati, F. C. (1987), 'Traslazione delle imposte dirette e politica fiscale'.

Rossi, N. (1986), 'Spesa pubblica, tasso di interesse reale e risparmio delle famiglie'; later published in Jappelli (1992).

Rubino, P., and Visco, I. (1987), 'Politica tariffaria e prezzi al consumo: Un'analisi applicata'; later published in Pera (1991).

Saba, P. (1988), 'Aspetti di efficienza e di equità nel finanziamento dell'istruzione'.

Salvemini, M. T., and Salvemini, G. (1989), *Il credito automatico del Tesoro presso la banca centrale* (Milan: Franco Angeli).

Scandizzo, P. L. (1985), 'Modelli di equilibrio economico generale per la valutazione degli investimenti'.

—— (1987a), 'L'analisi di equilibrio economico generale dei progetti di investimento'; later published in Milana (1992a).

—— (1987b), 'Un'analisi costi-benefici dei processi di pubblicizzazione e privatizzazione'; later published in Marzano (1992).

—— (1988), 'I trasferimenti pubblici e la loro distribuzione sul territorio: Significato economico, problemi metodologici e prime stime'.

—— and D'Angiolini, V. (1988), 'La stima dei coefficienti di conversione per la valutazione dei progetti di investimento pubblico'; later published in Milana (1992a).

—— and Tuccimei, A. (1988), 'Una valutazione costi-benefici degli investimenti previsti dall'intervento straordinario per il Mezzogiorno'; later published in Padoa Schioppa (1993b).

Schiantarelli, F., and Ratti, M. (1988), 'Testing Q Models of Investment on Micro Data: Evidence from a Panel of Italian Companies'.

Stazi, G. (1988), 'Stato e mercato nella politica ambientale: Regolamentazione e diritti di inquinamento'.

Stillitano, A., and Virno, C. (1987), 'Fondi pubblici, ricorso al mercato e politiche industriali delle partecipazioni statali'.

Szegö, G. (1993) (ed.), *Rinnovamenti e ristrutturazione industriale: Il ruolo dello stato e del mercato* (Milan: Franco Angeli).

Tronti, L. (1987), ' "Slowdown" e aggiustamento: La produttività del sistema economico italiano a confronto con quella dei maggiori concorrenti 1960–1984', *Rivista di Politica Economica*, (Mar.), 77: 3, 3–87.

Vagliasindi, P. A. (1988), 'Considerazioni in tema di tassazione dei titoli pubblici nel contesto della tassazione dei redditi da capitale'.

Visco, V. (1992) (ed.), *Imposte e prezzi relativi* (Milan: Franco Angeli).

Vitali, L., Grasso, F., and Focarelli, D. (1988), 'Sistema pensionistico e sviluppo economico'.

Other National Research Council (CNR) working papers and books produced by the Subproject

Atella, V. (1986), 'Matrici "input-output" e matrici di contabilità sociale (SAM): Un esercizio di ricostruzione delle serie storiche in Italia nel periodo 1970–1983 e analisi di dominanza e dipendenza'.

—— (1988), 'La matrice di contabilità sociale nel contesto regionale italiano: Lo sviluppo delle stime di base'.

Baechler, J. (1987), 'Marché et autocratie'.

Casella, A. (1988), 'Instability of Steady State Equilibrium in Aggregate S,S Pricing Models: A Note'.

Corneo, G. (1990), 'La politica dei trasferimenti statali all'industria negli anni '80: Un'interpretazione in chiave di lungo periodo'.

Cortesi, M. (1988), 'Introduzione alle statistiche sulla finanza pubblica'.

Cugno, F., and Ferrero, M. (1987), 'Free Access vs. Revenue Sharing as Alternative Systems for Managing Employment Externalities'.

Ferrari, A. (1987), 'Intermediari finanziari e sviluppo: Una rassegna teorica'.

Fornasari, F. (1985), 'Stime preliminari degli effetti di modifiche negli oneri sociali sul livello di attività economica'.

—— (1986), 'Estensione della matrice di contabilità sociale italiana ai flussi monetari'.

Galeotti, M., and Schiantarelli, F. (1988), 'Generalized Q Models for Investment and Employment'.

Granaglia, E., and Arcangeli, L. (1988), 'La spesa sanitaria programmata'.

Jappelli, T. (1990), 'Who is Credit-Constrained in the U.S. Economy?', *Quarterly Journal of Economics*, (Feb.), 105: 1, 219–34.

Lupi, R. (1988), 'Principi civilistici e norme fiscali nella determinazione del reddito e del patrimonio delle società di capitali'.

Maffioletti, A. (1990), 'Aspetti economico-istituzionali degli interventi di politica industriale negli anni '80'.

Manera, M. (1990), 'Domande di fattori e sostituibilità nel settore manifatturiero italiano: Un modello di dualità dinamica'.

Manfroni, S. (1984), 'Serie storiche degli investimenti delle attività extra industriali e dei beni durevoli di consumo'.

Mocarelli, M., and Rigotti, L. (1990), 'La struttura finanziaria delle imprese in Italia 1968–1987: Un'indagine empirica'.

Mussati, G. (1990), 'Strumenti ed incentivi di politica industriale in Italia: Differenze fra gli anni '80 e gli anni '70'.

Padoa Schioppa, F. (1986*a*), 'Price Stickiness and Relative Price Variability'.

Pietrobelli, C. (1986), 'Commercio orizzontale, penetrazione delle importazioni e cambiamento tecnologico: Una rassegna della teoria e delle analisi empiriche'.

Quirino, P. (1988), 'I problemi connessi con una più equilibrata ripartizione del fondo sanitario nazionale'; later published in Brunetta and Tronti (1991).

Ratti, M. (1987), 'Real and Financial Decisions of Firms: An Empirical Investigation'.

Sabattini, G. (1985), 'Sviluppo delle piccole e medie imprese e assetti istituzionali con riferimento alla politica dei servizi ed alle condizioni operative rispetto alla grande impresa'.

Tronti, L. and Cucchiarelli, A. (1988), 'Gli effetti redistributivi della spesa sociale: Un'analisi orizzontale'; later published in Brunetta and Tronti (1991).

Vaglio, A. (1987), 'Le interpretazioni dello sviluppo economico postbellico in Italia: Una rassegna critica ed alcune osservazioni sugli anni '70'.

Other works quoted

Ackley, G., and Spaventa, L. (1962), 'Emigration and Industrialization in Southern Italy: A Comment', *Banca Nazionale del Lavoro Quarterly Review* (June), 61, 192–204.

Ajmone Marsan, M., and Padoa Schioppa, F. (1992), 'Competition through fares and fare accesses on the air transport market', paper prepared for the 37th meeting of the Applied Econometrics Association, Brussels, 3–5 Dec.

Attanasio, O. P., and Padoa Schioppa, F. (1991), 'Regional Inequalities, Migration and Mismatch in Italy, 1960–1986', in F. Padoa Schioppa (1991*b*), 237–320.

Banca d'Italia (1986), *Relazione annuale* (Rome: Banca d'Italia).

—— (1989*a*), *Ordinary General Meeting of Shareholders: Abridged Report for the Year 1988* (Rome: Banca d'Italia).

—— (1989*b*), 'I bilanci delle famiglie italiane nell'anno 1987', *Supplemento al Bollettino Statistico* (Jan.), 42: 5.

—— (1991), 'I bilanci delle famiglie italiane nell'anno 1989', *Supplemento al Bollettino Statistico* (Oct.), 1: 26.

—— (1992), *Relazione annuale* (Rome: Banca d'Italia).

Barca, F., and Magnani, M. (1989), *L'industria fra capitale e lavoro: Piccole e grandi imprese fra 'autunno caldo' e risanamento* (Bologna: Il Mulino).

—— and Visco, I. (1991), 'L'economia italiana nella prospettiva europea', report presented at the study meeting in memory of Stefano Vona: 'La posizione estera dell'Italia' (Rome, 6–7 Dec.).

Barro, R. (1981), *Money, Expectations and Business Cycles: Essays in Macroeconomics* (New York: Academic Press).

Baumol, W. J., and Oates, W. E. (1988), *The Theory of Environmental Policy* (Cambridge: Cambridge University Press).

Battaglia, A. (1987), *Audizione davanti alla commissione per le attività produttive alla Camera dei Deputati* (Rome, Camera dei Deputati, 13 Oct.).

Biehl, D. (1986) (ed.), *The Contribution of Infrastructures to Regional Development: Final Report* (Brussels: Commission of the European Communities).

Biondi, G. (1989), 'Servizi alla produzione e territorio nello sviluppo industriale del Mezzogiorno', in FORMEZ (1989), 77–117.

Blanchard, O., Chouraqui, J. C., Hagemann, R. P., and Sartor, N. (1990), 'The Sustainability of Fiscal Policy: New Answers to an Old Question', *OECD Economic Studies*, (Autumn) 15, 7–36.

Bodo, G., and Sestito, P. (1989), *Disoccupazione e dualismo territoriale* (Temi di Discussione, 123, Rome: Banca d'Italia).

Bollino, C. A., Ceriani, V., and Violi, R. (1988), *Il mercato unico europeo e l'armonizzazione dell'IVA e delle accise* (Temi di Discussione, 109, Rome: Banca d'Italia).

Buiter, W. (1985), 'A Guide to Public Sector Debt and Deficits', *Economic Policy* (Nov.), 1, 13–79.

Cananzi, G. (1988), 'Produttività e qualità nei principali servizi pubblici vendibili in ENEL, Alitalia, SIP, ASST, ITALCABLE' (mimeo).

—— and Fiorito, R. (1986), 'Estensione a tre aree territoriali della banca dati per il modello territoriale dell'ISEL' (National Research Council Working Paper, Sub-project 1).

Cannari, L., D'Alessio, G., Raimondi, G., and Rinaldi, A. I. (1990), 'Le attività finanziarie delle famiglie italiane' (Temi di Discussione, 136; Rome: Banca d'Italia).

Centorrino, M. (1984), 'Mafia e nuova economia del Mezzogiorno', *Nord e Sud* (July–Sept.), 31: 3, 41–53.

—— (1985), 'Economia della mafia: Una nuova antologia', *Politica ed Economia* (Sept.), 9, 12–13.

Ciciotti, E. (1989), 'Il terziario per il sistema produttivo come fattore di sviluppo economico', in FORMEZ (1989), 19–37.

Coase, R. H. (1960), 'The Problem of Social Cost', *Law and Economics*, (Oct.), 3, 1–44.

Cremer, H., Kessler, D., and Pestieau, P. (1987), 'Fertility Differentials and the Regressive Effect of Public Debt', *Economica*, 54, 79–87.

De Caprariis, G., and Heimler, A. (1988), *Struttura produttiva del Mezzogiorno e commercio con l'estero*, (CSC Ricerche, 3, Rome: Confindustria).

De Rita, G. (1984), 'Il dualismo tra Mezzogiorno e società', in Ente per gli Studi Monetari, Bancari e Finanziari 'Luigi Einaudi' (1984), 483–90.

Diamond, P. A. (1965), 'National Debt in a Neoclassical Growth Model', *American Economic Review*, 55: 12, 1126–50.

Di Palma, M. (1986), 'Summary of the Italian Report', in Biehl (1986), 379–408.

Direzione Centrale dei Servizi Postali (1988), 'Indagine sui tempi di recapito delle corrispondenze' (mimeo, May).

Direzione Generale SIP (1992), *Bollettino qualita'* (Rome: SIP).

Ente per gli Studi Monetari, Bancari e Finanziari 'Luigi Einaudi' (1984) (ed.), *Moneta, dualismo e pianificazione nel pensiero di Vera C. Lutz* (Bologna: Il Mulino).

—— (1986) (ed.), *Oltre la crisi: Le prospettive di sviluppo dell'economia italiana e il contributo del sistema finanziario* (Bologna: Il Mulino).

—— (1992*a*) (ed.), *Il disavanzo pubblico in Italia: Natura strutturale e politiche di rientro* (Bologna: Il Mulino).

Faini, R. (1982), *Investment Functions for Southern Italy* (Essex Economic Papers, 193; Essex University).

Feldstein, M. (1973), 'The Economics of the New Unemployment', *Public Interest* (Spring), 33, 3–42.

FORMEZ (1987), *La produttività nella pubblica amministrazione*, Report to the National Economic and Employment Council (Milan: Il Sole 24 Ore).

—— (1989), *Aree attrezzate e servizi alla produzione nello sviluppo del Mezzogiorno* (Naples: FORMEZ).

Galli, G., and Onado, M. (1990), 'Dualismo territoriale e sistema finanziario', in Banca d'Italia, *Il sistema finanziario nel Mezzogiorno* (Rome: Banca d'Italia), 1–63.

—— and Giavazzi, F. (1992), 'Tassi d'interesse reali e debito pubblico negli anni ottanta: Interpretazioni, prospettive, implicazioni per la politica di bilancio', in Ente per gli Studi Monetari, Bancari e Finanziari 'Luigi Einaudi' (1992*a*), 227–354.

Giannola, A. (1986), 'Problemi e prospettive di sviluppo nel Mezzogiorno d'Italia', in Ente per gli Studi Monetari, Bancari e Finanziari 'Luigi Einaudi' (1986), 209–43.

—— and Imbriani, C. (1988), 'Le politiche di lungo termine per il superamento del dualismo Nord–Sud: Problemi e prospettive', Paper presented to the 29th annual scientific meeting of the Società degli Economisti, Rome, 27–8 Oct.

Giavazzi, F., and Spaventa, L. (1988) (eds.), *High Public Debt: The Italian Experience* (Cambridge: Cambridge University Press).

—— —— (1989), 'Italy: The Real Effect of Inflation and Disinflation', *Economic Policy* (Apr.), 4, 133–72.

Gini, C. (1909), 'Il diverso accrescimento delle classi sociali e la concentrazione della ricchezza', *Giornale degli Economisti* (Jan.), 20: 38, 27–83.

Graziani, A. (1979), 'Il Mezzogiorno nel quadro dell'economia italiana', in Graziani and Pugliese (1979), 7–66.

—— and Pugliese, E. (1979), *Investimenti e disoccupazione nel Mezzogiorno* (Bologna: Il Mulino).

Guiso, L., and Jappelli, T. (1991), 'Intergenerational Transfers and Capital Market Imperfections: Evidence from a Cross-Section of Italian Households', *European Economic Review*, 35: 1, 103–20.

Hayashi, F. (1985), *Tests for Liquidity Constraints: A Critical Survey* (NBER Working Paper, 1720; New York: NBER).

Heimler, A., and Milana, C. (1984), *Prezzi relativi, ristrutturazione e produttività* (Bologna: Il Mulino).

IRER (1986) (ed.), *La distribuzione regionale della spesa dello stato* (Milan: IRER).

ISTAT, *Annuario di contabilità nazionale*, various years (Rome: ISTAT).

—— *Annuario statistico italiano*, various years (Rome: ISTAT).

—— *Conti economici nazionali*, various years (Rome: ISTAT).

—— *Dati regionali di nuova contabilità* (mimeo) (Rome: ISTAT).

—— 'Rilevazione delle forze di lavoro. Media annua: Nord–Centro Mezzogiorno', *Supplemento al Bollettino mensile di statistica*, various years.

—— *Statistiche demografiche*, various years (Rome: ISTAT).

—— (1985*a*) 'Popolazione e bilanci demografici per sesso, età e regione. Ricostruzione per gli anni 1972–1981', *Supplemento al Bollettino mensile di statistica*, 14.

—— (1985*b*), 'Popolazione residente per sesso, età, regione: Anni 1982–1985', *Supplemento al Bollettino mensile di statistica*, 21.

—— (1989), *Statistiche sulla amministrazione pubblica: Anni 1985–1987* (Rome: ISTAT).

Kahn, A. E. (1971), *The Economics of Regulation*, ii (New York: Wiley).

Lange, P. and Regini, M. (1989), *State, Market, and Social Regulation: New Perspective on Italy* (Cambridge: Cambridge University Press).

Lecaldano Sasso La Terza, E., Marotta, G., and Masera, R. S. (1984), 'Consumo, risparmio e tasso d'interesse', *Moneta ed Economia Nazionale* (Turin: Cassa di Risparmio di Torino), 75–99.

Leccisotti, M. (1979), 'Imprese private a partecipazione statale e imprese pubbliche a partecipazione privata', *Rassegna Economica*, 43: 1, 1–18.

Lutz, V. C. (1954), 'Development Problems in Southern Italy: The Second Conference of the Cassa per il Mezzogiorno', *Banca Nazionale del Lavoro Quarterly Review* (Jan.–June), 28–9, 45–51.

—— (1961), 'Some Structural Aspects of the Southern Problem: The Complementarity of Emigration and Industrialization', *Banca Nazionale del Lavoro Quarterly Review* (Dec.), 59, 367–402.

—— (1962), 'Reply' (to Ackley and Spaventa (1962)), *Banca Nazionale del Lavoro Quarterly Review* (June), 61, 205–19.

Malinvaud, E. (1978), *The Theory of Unemployment Reconsidered* (Oxford: Basil Blackwell).

Marotta, G. (1983), 'Un'indagine econometrica sui consumi privati in Italia: 7102–8004', in Banca d'Italia, *Ricerche sui modelli per la politica economica* (Rome: Banca d'Italia), i, 127–58.

—— (1984), 'Un'indagine econometrica sui consumi nazionali: 7201–8104', in Banca d'Italia, *Ricerche quantitative per la politica economica* (Rome: Banca d'Italia), ii. 1–44.

Menet-Gentry, J. (1992a), 'Forces et faiblesses de l'Italie à l'échéance de 1993', in Menet-Gentry (1992b), 261–8.

—— (1992b) (ed.), *L'Économie italienne. Les Paradoxes d'une réussite* (Paris: La Documentation Française).

Ministero dei Trasporti (1988) (ed.), *Radiografia delle Ferrovie dello Stato*, Anno 1987 (Rome: Istituto Poligrafico dello Stato).

Ministero delle Partecipazioni Statali, *Relazione programmatica delle partecipazioni statali*, various years. (Rome: Istituto Poligrafico dello Stato.)

Ministero delle Poste e Telecomunicazioni (1985) (ed.), *Parametri standard e metodologia per la revisione delle tariffe telefoniche* (Rome: Istituto Poligrafico dello Stato).

Ministero del Bilancio e della Programmazione Economica, *Relazione previsionale e programmatica*, various years (Rome: Istituto Poligrafico dello Stato).

Ministero del Tesoro (1988) (ed.), *Documento di programmazione economico-finanziaria di cui all'articolo 3 della legge 11 marzo 1988, n. 67*. Legge Finanziaria (Finance Bill) 1988 (the Amato Plan) (Rome: Istituto Poligrafico dello Stato).

—— (1992), *Libro verde sulle partecipazioni dello Stato*, (Rome: Istituto Poligrafico dello Stato).

Modigliani, F., Jappelli, T., and Pagano, M. (1985), 'The Impact of Fiscal Policy and Inflation on National Saving: The Italian Case', *Banca Nazionale del Lavoro Quarterly Review* (June), 153, 91–126.

NOMISMA (1987), *La produttività dell'economia italiana* (Milan: Il Sole 24 Ore).

OECD, *Economic Outlook*, various years.

—— (1987), *Financing and Delivering Health Care* (Paris: OECD).

Onofri, R., Patrizii, V., and Zangheri, P. (1987) (eds.), *Analisi della gestione e del funzionamento dei servizi della amministrazione delle poste e delle telecomunicazioni* (Rome: Commissione Tecnica per la Spesa Pubblica).

Padoa Schioppa, F. (1974), *Scuola e classi sociali in Italia* (Bologna: Il Mulino).

—— (1977), *La forza lavoro femminile* (Bologna: Il Mulino).

—— (1979*a*), 'Assenteismo e turnover nell'occupazione femminile. Un confronto fra l'Italia e gli Stati Uniti', *Queste Istituzioni*, (Jan.–June), 29, 23–44.

—— (1979*b*), 'I diversi effetti del finanziamento del deficit pubblico', *Giornale degli Economisti e Annali di Economia* (Jan.–Feb.), 1–2, 67–93.

—— (1983), 'Crowding Out in an Inflationary Open Economy: The Italian Case', *European Economic Review* (Sept.), 23: 1, 117–39.

—— (1986*b*), 'La politica dei redditi e il tasso di disoccupazione in Italia', in Ente per gli Studi Monetari, Bancari e Finanziari 'Luigi Einaudi' (1986), 683–745.

—— (1988*b*), 'Note in margine al dibattito su flessibilità e occupazione', *Politica Economica* (Apr.), 4: 1, 69–76.

—— (1989*a*), 'Etica ed economia: Un commento al libro "Etica ed economia" (Rome: Il Sole 24 Ore, 1988)', *Technology Review* (Jan.), 5, 70–1.

—— (1989*b*), 'Il sistema retributivo verso gli anni '90: Strumenti ed obiettivi della politica dei redditi', in Regione Emilia Romagna and CNR (eds.), *Il sistema retributivo verso gli anni '90* (Bologna: Jovene), 69–74.

—— (1990*c*), *Redistributions in the Retirement Public Pension Scheme and Population Trends: The Italian Case*, (Discussion Paper, 463; London: CEPR).

—— (1990*d*), 'Classical, Keynesian and Mismatch Unemployment in Italy', *European Economic Review* (May), 34: 2–3, 434–42.

—— (1990*e*), 'L'energia e l'armonizzazione fiscale nel mercato unico europeo', *CEEP Economia*, 2, 30–7.

—— (1991*a*), 'Sectoral Mismatch in the 1980s', in Padoa Schioppa (1991*b*), 1–43.

—— (1991*b*) (ed.), *Mismatch and Labour Mobility* (Cambridge: Cambridge University Press).

—— (1992*a*), 'Evoluzione demografica, crisi e redistribuzione del sistema pensionistico', in Ente per gli Studi Finanziari, Bancari e Monetari 'Luigi Einaudi' (1992*a*), 357–427.

—— (1992*d*), *A Cross-Country Analysis of the Tax-Push Hypothesis*, (Working Paper, 11; Washington, DC: IMF).

—— (1993*a*), 'Tax Rates, Progressivity and de facto Fiscal Indexation in Ten European Countries', in A. Heimler and D. Meulders (eds.), *Empirical Approaches to Fiscal Policy Modelling* (London: Chapman and Hall).

—— and Padoa Schioppa, T. (1984), *Agenda e non agenda: Limiti e crisi della politica economica* (Milan: Comunità).

Parmentola, N. (1983), *La spesa pubblica consolidata nelle regioni centro-meridionali: Anno 1978, Rapporto Generale* (Naples: FORMEZ).

Parravicini, G. (1971), *Lineamenti dell'ordinamento tributario* (Milan: Giuffrè).

Patrizii, V., and Zollo, R. (1985) (eds.), *Analisi delle condizioni di efficienza del trasporto ferroviario in Italia ed in alcuni paesi europei* (Rome: Commissione Tecnica per la Spesa Pubblica).

Ricossa, S. (1988), 'Etica ed economia: Alla ricerca del bene comune in via indiretta', in *Etica ed economia* (Rome: Il Sole 24 Ore), 141–8.

Romiti, C. (1988), *Quegli anni alla Fiat*, Interview by G. Pansa (Milan: Rizzoli).

Rossi, N., and Schiantarelli, F. (1982), 'Modelling Consumers' Expenditure: Italy 1965–1977', *European Economic Review*, 17, 371–91.

Samuelson, P. A. (1966), 'The Pure Theory of Public Expenditure', in J. E. Stiglitz (1966) (ed.), *The Collected Scientific Papers of Paul A. Samuelson* (Cambridge, Mass.: MIT Press), ii. 1223–5.

Saraceno, P. (1959), *Iniziativa privata e azione pubblica nei piani di sviluppo economico* (Rome: Giuffrè).

—— (1976), 'Imprese private e imprese a partecipazione statale', in *L'impresa nell'economia italiana* (Milan: Franco Angeli), 115–20.

—— (1983), 'Il Mezzogiorno nella crisi delle economie occidentali', *Studi Svimez*, (Mar.), 1–2, 3–11.

Sarcinelli, M. (1989), 'The Mezzogiorno and the Single European Market: Complementary or Conflicting Aims?', *Banca Nazionale del Lavoro Quarterly Review*, (June), 169, 129–64.

Savona, P. (1988), 'Idee per una politica economica più incisiva dell'Europa unita' (mimeo, Università di Roma).

Senato della Repubblica, *Relazione generale sulla situazione economica del Paese*, presented to Parliament by the Minister for the Budget and Economic Planning and the Minister for the Treasury, various years (Rome: Istituto Polografico dello Stato).

Siracusano, F., Tresoldi, C., and Zen, G. (1986), *Domanda di lavoro e trasformazione dell'economia del Mezzogiorno* (Temi di Discussione, 83; Rome: Banca d'Italia).

STET (1988), 'Tempi medi di evasione della domanda telefonica in Italia e nei principali paesi europei' (mimeo, Mar.).

Stiglitz, J. E. (1986), *Economics of the Public Sector* (New York: Norton).

Sylos Labini, P. (1985), *L'evoluzione economica del Mezzogiorno negli ultimi trent'anni* (Temi di Discussione, 46; Rome: Banca d'Italia).

SVIMEZ (1986), *La questione meridionale nel quarantennale della SVIMEZ* (Rome: SVIMEZ).

—— *Rapporto sull'economia del Mezzogiorno* (Bologna: Il Mulino), various years.

Tanzi, V. (1980), *Inflation and Personal Income Tax: An International Perspective* (Cambridge: Cambridge University Press).

Topel, R. (1983), 'On Layoffs and Unemployment Insurance', *American Economic Review* (Sept.), 73: 4, 541–59.

Vickers, J., and Wright, V. (1989*a*), 'The Politics of Privatisation in

Western Europe: An Overview', in Vickers and Wright (1989*b*), 1–30.

—— —— (1989*b*) (eds.), *The Politics of Privatisation* (London: Frank Cass).

—— and Yarrow, G. (1988), *Privatization: An Economic Analysis* (Cambridge, Mass.: MIT Press).

Visco, V. (1986), 'Prospettive di riforma del sistema tributario italiano', *Rivista di Diritto e Pratica Tributaria*, 57: 4, 1089–113.

Weber, M. (1948), *Il lavoro intellettuale come professione* (Turin: Einaudi).

Weitzman, M. (1983), 'Some Macroeconomic Implications of Alternative Compensation Systems', *Economic Journal*, 4: 93, 763–83.

—— (1984), *The Share Economy* (Cambridge, Mass.: Harvard University Press).

AUTHOR INDEX

SUBJECT INDEX